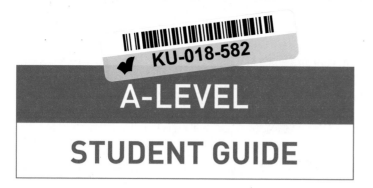

A-LEVEL

STUDENT GUIDE

OCR

Media Studies

Component 1:

Media Messages

Louisa Cunningham

HODDER
EDUCATION
AN HACHETTE UK COMPANY

Hachette UK's policy is to use papers that are natural, renewable and recyclable products and made from wood grown in sustainable forests. The logging and manufacturing processes are expected to conform to the environmental regulations of the country of origin.

Orders: please contact Bookpoint Ltd, 130 Park Drive, Milton Park, Abingdon, Oxon OX14 4SE. Telephone: +44 (0)1235 827827. Fax: +44 (0)1235 400401. Email education@bookpoint.co.uk Lines are open from 9 a.m. to 5 p.m., Monday to Saturday, with a 24-hour message answering service. You can also order through our website: www.hoddereducation.co.uk

ISBN: 9781510429499

© Louisa Cunningham 2019

First published in 2019 by

Hodder Education,

An Hachette UK Company

Carmelite House

50 Victoria Embankment

London EC4Y 0DZ

www.hoddereducation.co.uk

Impression number   10 9 8 7 6 5 4 3 2 1

Year   2023 2022 2021 2020 2019

Cover photo © Vasya Kobelev/Shutterstock

Illustrations by Integra Software Services Pvt. Ltd., Pondicherry, India

Typeset by Integra Software Services Pvt. Ltd., Pondicherry, India

Printed by Bell & Bain Ltd, Glasgow

A catalogue record for this title is available from the British Library.

MIX
Paper from
responsible sources
FSC™ C104740

Contents

■ Getting the most from this book

Study tips

Advice on key points in the text to help you learn and recall content, avoid pitfalls, and polish your exam technique in order to boost your grade.

Knowledge check

Rapid-fire questions throughout the Content Guidance section to check your understanding.

Knowledge check answers

These can be found online at www.hoddereducation.co.uk/ OCRMediaStudiesSG1

Summaries

■ Each core topic is rounded off by a bullet-list summary for quick-check reference of what you need to know. These can be found online at www.hoddereducation.co.uk/ OCRMediaStudiesSG1

Sample student answer

Practise the questions, then look at the student answers that follow.

Practice question

Commentary on the question

Tips on what you need to do to gain full marks, indicated by the icon 🄴

Commentary on sample student answer

Read the comments (preceded by the icon 🄴) following each student answer and then find out what level it would likely be placed at.

Content Guidance

audience who appreciate the retro feel of the video. Younger audiences may also make connections between 'Titanium' and more recent media products such as *Stranger Things* that reference the same location, era and themes.

The poster of *Superargo and the Faceless Giants* in the boy's living room relates to the science fiction genre and superheroes, communicating the boy's interest in science fiction and as the hero in the video. The song title 'Titanium', along with the boy's superhuman ability, can also be understood as a reference to *Terminator 2*. The character T-1000 is made of liquid metal, like titanium, that is resistant to physical injury and damage, and possesses superhuman strength, just like the boy at the end of the video who is able to shield himself from the authorities' bullets.

The use of intertextual references in 'Titanium' marks a departure from Guetta's brand identity, with his previous videos favouring the performance genre and his identity as a D.J. Intertextual references to these cultural products, and the social issues and groups they invoke, positions Guetta as culturally sophisticated. His representation in the video is implicit but can be seen through intertextual references made to him through the mise-en-scene. For example, the poster of Guetta's face on the wall in the high school corridor points to him as the video's author. The juxtaposition of the boy and Guetta's faces in the same shot creates a connection between the two, inviting the audience to understand the boy and his actions as Guetta's, thus creating value transference. This will appeal to the audience who will enjoy spotting the reference to Guetta and will help them connect with the video, indicating that intertextual references are also used to create satisfaction and promote the artist for the audience.

To conclude, intertextual references are used by music videos as a technique to allow directors to create additional meaning, to amplify the lyrics and engage the audience. Intertextual references also enable the director to play with the format conventions of music videos using interesting ways of presenting a brand identity for the artist so the purpose of a music video, to sell the song and artist, can be achieved.

🄴

■ The answer clearly defines intertextuality and is structured with a relevant argument to explain why music videos use intertextuality.
■ The answer clearly refers to a chosen video from List B to respond to the question.
■ Most of the intertextual examples used in the video are discussed.
■ A range of media terms and appropriate terminology is used.

A top-level answer.

2   Explain why magazines outside the commercial mainstream construct alternative representations. Refer to *The Big Issue* magazine in your answer.   [10]

🄴 This question is asking you to demonstrate your knowledge and understanding of *The Big Issue* magazine as a publication that is outside the mainstream magazine industry. In this answer you could discuss:

■ how *The Big Issue* is a business that is focused not on profit for the owner but on providing opportunities for the vendors who sell it, so must appeal to a particular niche audience
■ the media language conventions used by *The Big Issue* and how they are different from mainstream magazines

174   OCR Media Studies

Content guidance

■ Section A: News

Introduction to news

This part of the guide looks at newspaper coverage in the UK. The course requires you to explore how and why print newspapers and their online websites are evolving as media products, and the relationship between both online and offline news. This means you must cover newspapers and online, social and participatory media together.

This section is **in-depth study**. This requires you to look at case study set products in relation to the four theoretical frameworks. The OCR specification refers to these frameworks as:

- media language: how the media through their forms, codes, conventions and techniques communicate meanings
- media representations: how the media portray events, issues, individuals and social groups
- media industries: how the media industries' processes of production, distribution and circulation affect media forms and platforms
- media audiences: how media forms target, reach and address audiences, how audiences interpret and respond to them, and how members of audiences become producers themselves.

In-depth study This requires you to study the unit across all areas of the theoretical framework, contexts and academic ideas.

You will also need to study the news in relation to media contexts, academic ideas and arguments. Here is a summary of the OCR specification coverage for Media Messages, Section A.

Table 1.1 Summary of the OCR specification coverage for Section A Media Messages

Media forms	News	Online, social and participatory media
Set media products	TWO front covers from the *Daily Mail* TWO front covers from *The Guardian* ONE complete edition of the *Daily Mail* and ONE complete edition of *The Guardian*	The *MailOnline* website *theguardian.com* website Two articles from the *MailOnline* website Two articles from *theguardian.com* website Facebook, Twitter and Instagram feeds from the *MailOnline* and *theguardian.com*
Media industries	✓	✓
Media audiences	✓	✓
Media language	✓	✓
Media representations	✓	✓
Media contexts	Historical, political, economic, social and cultural	Historical, political, economic, social and cultural
Academic ideas	✓	✓

The exam paper for Component 1: Media Messages is worth 70 marks in total. Section A: News is worth 45 marks. This is 65 per cent of the exam paper.

There will be four questions for this section in the exam. Three questions will be worth 10 marks. One question will be worth 15 marks. They will be made up of both AO1- and AO2- style questions.

There will be two **unseen sources** for this section in the exam. These might be UK national daily newspaper front covers or examples of social, online and participatory media. These sources will be linked by theme or topic. One or more of the exam questions will directly refer to these unseen sources. You will need to refer to these sources, and your own case study set product examples that you will study in class, in your answers.

Introduction to theoretical frameworks, contexts, academic ideas and set products

Theoretical frameworks

There are four theoretical frameworks in relation to which you must study this unit. To help with your own revision of these frameworks for the News unit, it is useful to have an overview of what you need to learn for each framework:

Media language

- Genre conventions of camera, editing, sound, mise-en-scene and intertextuality. How are these elements used together to construct the media form so that it looks the way it does? How are these elements organised in a certain way to communicate meaning in each newspaper/website/social media site?
- How the content incorporates the viewpoints and ideology of the producer.
- How multiple meanings can be communicated across different but connected platforms.

Representation

- Which different groups, individuals and/or events are presented or shown in each newspaper?
- What positive or negative stereotypes are evident and why?
- What messages and values are communicated about different groups of people, individuals and/or events and what conclusions can we make about these?
- How are representations constructed as real?

Industries

- What are the issues of ownership on the way producers report events, individuals and social groups?
- What is the impact of technological change on the ways in which news is produced and distributed to audiences by owners?
- What is the impact of digital convergence on offline/online content?
- How is the news regulated?

Unseen sources This refers to stimulus visual material that will be included in the exam paper that you will be expected to refer to in at least one of your answers but will not have seen before the exam.

Study tip

The exam questions will focus on any of the four theoretical frameworks, media contexts, and academic ideas and arguments.

Knowledge check 1

How many exam questions will there be for Section A: News? How many marks are they worth in total?

Study tip

The exam question might name a specific theoretical framework for you to discuss. When revising the unit, organise the case study examples into each of the four frameworks. This will help you remember which case study examples to use in the exam.

Audience

- Who is the audience for each news product? How are they similar/different?
- Do different news **platforms** for each product have different audiences?
- How are audiences targeted and addressed by newspapers?
- How are audiences reached by news owners and how do they respond to news?
- How is news content made to appeal to audiences across different platforms?
- How do audiences use and interpret news?
- How is audience interaction and production encouraged?

The four frameworks all connect in some way. For example, the ownership (industries) of a newspaper will affect the type of newspaper it is. Different newspapers will have different house styles and use different conventions (media language) to appeal to their readers (audience) and offer different viewpoints about groups of people, individuals and events in the news they report (representation).

Contexts

There are five **contexts** that you must study in relation to the News unit. These are historical, political, economic, social and cultural.

You will need to consider these contexts when studying your set products and be able to demonstrate how the set products have been influenced by or developed in response to each of the five contexts. For example, it would be helpful to know how the current economic context of the way in which news is funded has impacted on the decrease in print newspaper sales. Or, for example, how the cultural context of the trend in participatory behaviour among contemporary audiences means the readers of news prefer to share online news stories rather than read print news.

Below is a brief overview of what each context means:

Historical context: The specific era or time period in which a product is made. For example, how is the product influenced by the time in which it is made?

Political context: The government, policy and public affairs of a country; the way in which power is used or is achieved in a country or society. For example, is the product influenced by any political bias?

Economic context: Ownership, income, production and distribution of media products, wealth, profit and developments in technology. For example, how have developments in technology influenced the production of news?

Social context: Where people live together and interact with one another on a day-to-day basis; the social structures by which we live our daily lives, such as religion, education, family, media communications, law and government; the impact these social structures have on our behaviour, values and thinking; social issues and movements. For example, is the product influenced by consumerism and changes within our social structures?

Cultural context: The attitudes, values, beliefs, practices, customs and shared behaviour of people, including all aspects of 'life': language, the products we make, the things we do and how we do them. It also includes cultural products such as art, music, literature and media. For example, how does globalisation influence the cultural identities found in the product?

Academic ideas and arguments

As the News unit is a combined in-depth study, you are required to know the 19 set **academic ideas** for this unit.

Each of the academic ideas can be related to at least one of the four theoretical frameworks. It is helpful to organise, learn and revise the theorists' ideas in each of the relevant frameworks.

Table 1.2 Academic ideas related to the four theoretical frameworks

Media language	Representation
Lévi-Strauss	Gauntlett
Barthes	Van Zoonen
Todorov	Hall
Neale	Butler
Baudrillard	hooks
	Gilroy
Industries	**Audience**
Hesmondhalgh	Bandura
Curran & Seaton	Gerbner
Livingstone & Lunt	Jenkins
	Shirky
	Hall

For summaries and examples of applications of these theorists' ideas see pages 107–117 of this section.

An overview of the key ideas that you need to know for each theorist is set out on pages 54–59 of the OCR specification (http://ocr.org.uk/Images/316672-specification-accredited-a-level-gce-media-studies-h409.pdf).

You will be asked one or two questions that require you to apply or discuss an academic idea. There are two different types of theory question. It is useful to understand their differences, as each one requires a different type of answer.

Question type 1: applying a specified theory to the unseen sources in relation to a theoretical framework

This is an application question. This means you will be asked to apply your understanding of an idea to the unseen sources in relation to one of the four theoretical frameworks. For example: 'Analyse the representations in Source A and Source B. Use Butler's concept of gender performance in your answer.' In your response to this, you will need to discuss the theorist's ideas about representation and find examples from both unseen sources to help support your comments. Or, the question may not state the theorist's name but a concept associated with a theory, such as patriarchy.

Question type 2: evaluating the usefulness and limitations of a theory to News, Online, Social and Participatory Media

This type of question will ask you to evaluate how useful, or limited, an academic idea is in helping you understand news and social, online and participatory media and a theoretical framework. For example, you might be asked to evaluate the usefulness of Hall's ideas to News when thinking about audiences. Your response

Study tip

To prepare for an academic ideas question, read through the bullet points provided on the OCR Academic Ideas and Arguments factsheet. Then write down the bullet points for usefulness on one side of a flash-card and for limitations on the other. Ensure you have at least one example from each set product for each bullet point.

Knowledge check 4

How many different academic ideas do you need to learn? Which theorist is named twice?

will need to show your understanding of the theory by providing some ideas from the theory to explain how it is useful and how it is limited in helping you understand features of the news. Then support these ideas with examples from your own case study set products.

The OCR Academic Ideas and Arguments factsheet [http://ocr.org.uk/Images/421658-academic-ideas-and-arguments-factsheet.pdf] is a helpful resource for this type of exam question. For each theory, it lists what can be seen as useful and what can be seen as limiting in relation to news and social, online and participatory media.

An introduction to the set products

The **set products** for news and social, online and participatory media are the *Daily Mail* and *The Guardian*.

These offer contrasting types of **journalism** that have a different ownership model, different readership and a visibly different house style. They often provide different messages and values so they are easy to compare and contrast.

The *Daily Mail* is a tabloid newspaper, which is identifiable by its size and the arguably sensationalised journalism it features. This is sometimes referred to as **soft news**.

The Guardian was, traditionally, a broadsheet newspaper, which is identifiable by its larger size and also for quality, serious news. Today, *The Guardian* is a tabloid-size newspaper, but it is still known for quality journalism and the reporting of **hard news**.

The unseen sources and/or exam questions may not be from the set products of the *Daily Mail* and *The Guardian*. Therefore, it is advisable to study a range of different newspaper outlets that you can categorise into either sensational (soft) or quality (hard) news, as this will help you to recognise, compare and contrast different news outlets in the exam questions.

Table 1.3 Soft and hard news newspaper outlets

Sensational/Soft news outlets	Quality/Hard news outlets
Daily Mail	The Guardian
The Sun	The Times
Daily Express	The Independent (online)
Daily Mirror	i
Metro	Financial Times
	The Daily Telegraph

Study tip

The unseen sources may be two front covers that share the same theme or topic and may offer some comparison or difference. In your revision of front covers, for the set products and other news outlets, look for differences and similarities between them so that you will have had practice at doing this prior to facing the unseen sources in the exam.

Set products The name given to the media products the exam board have stipulated must be studied for the unit.

Journalism The profession of writing for a newspaper, news website, news broadcast or magazine.

Soft news The term used to refer to journalism that is sensational, emotional and personal. It uses conversational language and is expressive.

Hard news The term used to refer to journalism that is very serious, well written and balanced. It uses complex language.

Knowledge check 5

What are the set products for the News unit? What should the front cover case studies have in common?

Print news

The purpose of newspapers

As a **digitally convergent**, information-saturated society, both the way in which we come across 'news', and its appeal to different audiences, varies tremendously.

However, most people agree that the purpose of the news is to inform in some way. News can be defined as:

- the reporting of recent events in the country or world or in a particular area of activity
- information about a recently changed situation or event.

Newspapers are an established media form and the British press can be traced back over 300 years.

Historically, the purpose of a newspaper was to serve local communities. The role of the newspaper was to inform what was happening in the community and ensure that people within this community behaved appropriately.

The reporting of community information is still seen in local newspapers. National daily UK newspapers, however, like the *Daily Mail* and *The Guardian*, will communicate information that could be of interest to anyone in Britain, regardless of where they live. This means they will often report on the same events or situations.

Newspapers help readers become informed about events by providing them with:

- facts
- statistics
- opinion columns
- images.

In addition to reporting about national and global current affairs, most newspapers also have an entertainment function that features all or some of the following in order to engage the reader:

- popular culture/celebrity stories
- lifestyle and travel features
- sports
- television listings and reviews
- comics
- puzzles, quizzes or horoscopes
- readers' letters.

Newspapers also feature adverts. Advertisers pay the newspaper for space in the paper in return for access to the newspaper's audience.

In addition to informing the community, newspapers today still aim to influence behaviour and thinking. The news stories found in a newspaper will reflect the opinion of the owner and the **editor** of the paper. This means that although most **newspaper outlets** share the same purpose, the meanings behind the information they provide will be different. This helps the owners of the paper persuade the reader to think about the news using the same values as the owner.

Digitally convergent
This term refers to the combining of more than one product into one device or platform as a result of technological developments. It means that a range of media content and services can be accessed on one device, such as being able to watch a film, view a tweet and read an email on the same smartphone.

Study tip

You will need to demonstrate your understanding of the purpose of newspapers. Look at a full edition of the *Daily Mail* and *The Guardian*. Find four different articles or features that demonstrate what the main purpose of each paper is: is it to inform or to entertain?

Knowledge check 6

Historically, how did newspapers serve their communities?

Editor The person who is in charge of and decides the final content of the newspaper.

Newspaper outlets Also known as media outlets, these media organisations provide news stories and features for the public through various distribution channels.

Print news: industries

Industries can be defined as the organisations, people and activities involved in making a particular product or providing a particular service. The OCR specification indicates that you must focus on 'how the media industries' processes of production, distribution and circulation affect **media forms** and platforms.'

The news industry is concerned particularly with the production, distribution and circulation of news information and entertainment.

Production, distribution and circulation of printed press

Production

Newspapers are very expensive to produce because:
- they require a large amount of material
- they employ many highly trained staff.

News production is deadline driven, which means that stories must be completed by a certain time in order for the press to be set and the papers printed, ready for distribution in the morning. Journalists must ensure that their stories reach the newsroom and are ready to be printed regardless of where they may be writing the story.

All daily national newspapers in the UK are printed in colour and use offset printing. This enables newspapers to be inked onto rubber presses and printed quickly. Portable satellite technology and **Web 2.0** also enable journalists to report and complete stories more quickly than ever before.

Distribution

Once produced, the newspaper has to be physically distributed across the British Isles. This is another expensive process. Print news outlets are traditionally local or national due to the costs of distribution. However, online media and Web 2.0 mean that there are no global boundaries, so newspaper outlets have become **global** through their online platform.

Alternative distribution methods, such as free newspapers, are becoming increasingly successful. City-based national newspapers such as *Metro* are distributed free near public transport outlets. This enables a huge readership, which is attractive to advertisers, who subsidise the cost of the paper for the owner.

Marketing

News owners need to promote and sell their brands to their target audience, encouraging circulation and readership. Marketing a newspaper will usually involve the following marketing tools:
- advertising – on television, in sister newspapers, on social media
- exclusives cited in other media
- **synergy** deals with other companies and/or offering other products or services.

Media forms
Newspapers, television, websites and radio are all different media forms that can communicate and broadcast news. Each media form is unique in the way it looks and how it communicates to its audience.

Web 2.0 The second phase of the internet that enables dynamic web pages, sharing of files and social media.

Global Worldwide.

Synergy When two companies work together for the combined good of their products.

Circulation

Circulation, when discussing newspapers, refers to the number of newspapers that have been distributed, not those sold. Circulation figures are important because they are used to set advertising rates.

OCR specifies that in your study of the news industry, you must learn about:

- ownership
- economic factors
- technological change and the impact of digital convergence
- the content and appeal of newspapers and how they target, reach and address different audiences
- the impact of the regulatory framework on the newspaper industry.

Ownership

Newspaper titles are owned like any other product or commodity that is produced to be sold to a market.

Ownership refers to who financially supports and produces the paper. Newspaper owners may acquire more than one **brand**, which helps the owner target different audiences, so gaining a bigger share in the market.

In the UK, there are different media ownership models:

1 'Media barons' – wealthy individuals or **proprietors** who own the paper or a 'group' of similar papers or related media.

2 Trusts – a legal arrangement whereby finances from the owner are transferred to a 'trustee' to manage and control the running of the newspaper under certain conditions agreed outside the control of the owner.

3 Cross media converged conglomerates – huge, global institutions that own numerous media outlets and subsidiaries, working alongside each other to profit the owners of the conglomerate. These may be owned by media barons.

Since the 1980s, fewer organisations own the British press. The ownership of news has become very concentrated, with less competition and diversity of opinion as a result.

In the UK, the print news industry is run by just seven companies. Importantly, almost 60 per cent of the market share is owned by just two of these companies: News UK and DMG Media.

Table 1.4 Weekly (Daily plus Sunday) market share of UK national newspaper circulation, by publishing company

Publisher	Newsbrands	Weekly circulation	Market share	Cumulative share
News UK	*Sun; Sun on Sunday, Times; Sunday Times*	12, 831, 063	36.35%	36.35%
DMG Media	*Daily Mail; Mail on Sunday*	8,364,402	23.69%	60.04%
Reach PLC	*Daily Mirror; Sunday Mirror; Sunday People; Daily Express; Sunday Express; Daily Star; Star on Sunday*	8,186,260	23.19%	83.23%

Brand A product made by a particular owner with a specific name.

Proprietor An individual who is the sole legal owner of a business.

Knowledge check 7

Explain why newspapers are expensive to produce and distribute.

Publisher	Newsbrands	Weekly circulation	Market share	Cumulative share
Telegraph Media Group	*Daily Telegraph; Sunday Telegraph*	2,438,411	6.91%	90.13%
JPIMedia Ltd.	*i*	1,432,626	4.06%	94.19%
Financial Times	*Financial Times* (inc *FT Weekend*)	1,063,176	3.01%	97.2%
Guardian News & Media	*Guardian; Observer*	986,872	2.8%	100%
TOTAL		35,302,810	100%	

Source: Figures from Audit Bureau of Circulation figures, November 2018

Economic models and funding

The British press is a business which, in order to survive, must attract audiences to make money.

In 2015, the UK newspaper industry contributed £5.3 billion to Britain's **gross value added** (GVA) and supports 87,500 jobs in the UK. The news industry therefore contributes hugely to the UK economy.

Print newspaper production is financed in a number of different ways. The two main forms of funding are through sales and advertising **revenue**.

Circulation sales

- 14.3 million people read a paper every day.
- 81 per cent of a newspaper's revenue comes from print circulation sales.
- The cost of a daily national newspaper ranges from 30p (the *Daily Star*) to £2.70 (the *Financial Times*).
- The cost of a weekend national newspaper ranges from 80p (the *Daily Express*) to £3.80 (the *Financial Times*).

Advertising

- Advertisers pay for space in the paper.
- Advertising in national newspapers is expensive and dependent on the paper's circulation figures and audience.
- The cost of a full-page colour advert in the *Daily Mail* is over £30,000.
- Newspapers make money from adverts that are placed in both the offline (print) and online (digital) newspaper editions.
- Readers of print newspapers are 75 per cent more likely to read an advert than online readers.

There are also alternative methods of funding print news. These can include:

Subscriptions and donations

- Online subscription feeds known as paywalls, which pay for online services and also fund the print papers.
- Reader donations or memberships.

Study tip

Understanding ownership is vital in answering questions on economic, political, social and cultural contexts, news values and funding, as well as ownership. Ensure you know who owns each of the UK daily news titles and can identify their ownership type and other brands they may own.

Knowledge check 8

Which two companies own 60 per cent of the British press?

Gross value added The economic term given to the measurement of the value of products or services produced by a company.

Revenue Money received from the sale of a product or advertising.

The owner

- 'Media barons', such as Rupert Murdoch, who owns News UK, have money to invest.
- Owners' portfolios will include other news titles and/or media products or platforms. The profit made from these is invested across the portfolio.

However, the British news industry is facing a crisis and many national newspapers have seen a sharp decline in print circulation as more people access news online rather than buying newspapers. Newspapers such as *The Daily Telegraph* saw their circulation figures drop by over 23% between June 2017 – 2018. This represents a loss of almost a quarter of their circulation from 2017.

Figures such as these indicate that the traditional finance model for newspapers through circulation sales and advertising revenue must be revised if print news is to survive.

In February 2018, Prime Minister Theresa May announced a review of the news industry to ensure that quality news and journalism will still have a future in the UK.

Possible funding strategies that the review is expected to suggest may include:

- government or public funding subsidies
- philanthropy
- greater focus on payment from online access
- pooled reporting to reduce the cost of journalists for newspapers
- greater use of freelance agencies for news stories.

Technological developments

Ever since the invention of the printing press in the mid-fifteenth century, technological advancement has shaped the newspaper industry.

Many developments, such as the introduction of colour and offset printing, have benefited owners, making newspapers more appealing for readers and quicker to print.

Since the 1980s rapid development in digital technology, in terms of hardware, software and converged devices, has significantly changed the relationship between news owners and their audiences.

Table 1.5 Effects of technology on news owners and audiences

Technology introduced	Effect on owners and audience
1980s Computers, printers and desktop publishing (DTP) programs	• Audiences have power to create their own print media but little opportunity to distribute it. • Owners still control production and distribution on a mass scale. Use of computers and DTP programs makes writing copy and art direction quicker.
1990s The internet	• Audiences have more control over the information they receive from a greater range of sources at little or no cost. • Growing availability of information through the internet leads to greater competition for owners.

Study tip

In response to an exam question on ownership, economic context, technological developments and regulation, it is helpful to discuss how newspapers are funded. Use circulation figures as evidence to illustrate the funding issues faced by print newspapers.

Philanthropy Generous donations of money to a good cause in order to promote the welfare of others.

Knowledge check 9

What percentage of a newspaper's revenue traditionally comes from circulation sales?

Technology introduced	Effect on owners and audience
2000s Broadband Web 2.0 Smartphones and tablets HD digital cameras Apps	• Audiences can upload their own media to create their own websites and to share news. • Audiences access information through online services and smartphones. • Audiences can produce their own news as citizen journalists. • Owners are no longer in control of the production and distribution of news. • Owners are no longer in control of the information that is circulated among audiences.

Over the past 20 years, and since the introduction of Web 2.0 in 2004, the print industry has undergone significant change in the production, distribution and circulation of newspapers.

In order to remain relevant for audiences and to tackle falling sales of print copies, newspaper owners have expanded their titles online, to become known as news outlets. This has a number of advantages for owners:

- **Production** via websites reduces the environmental costs of producing newspapers with paper and ink, and makes energy savings.
- **Distribution** via the internet reduces the cost of physical distribution and has the added advantage that news outlets can reach readers globally.
- **Circulation** via websites and mobile devices allows audiences to access news and advertising online through apps and social media. This increases overall circulation numbers for the outlet, allows audiences to share and interact with the news and enables owners to monitor which news stories are most popular with their audiences.

However, while there are some economic benefits of digital technology for news owners, the proliferation of technology has led to a reduction in printed newspaper sales, raising the question of whether there is a future for print news.

- *The Guardian* has lost over 200,000 print readers in ten years.
- *The Independent* is now only available online.
- Established news owners are looking to sell their titles. For instance, Richard Desmond sold his print portfolio of the *Express* and *Star* titles to Reach PLC after their circulation dropped by almost 50 per cent between June 2017 and June 2018.

How news owners have adapted to these developments in technology with their online outlets is further discussed in the Social, Online and Participatory Media section in this guide.

News gathering, gatekeeping and news values

The processes of news gathering, gatekeeping and applying news values enable newspaper owners to fulfil the main purposes of a newspaper: to inform and influence behaviour, while appealing to the target audience.

News gathering

Newspapers have teams of reporters who gather news locally or through press agencies such as Reuters and the Press Association (PA). These agencies operate globally to identify key facts when major events happen.

Study tip

To help you understand the impact of digital technology on the print news industry, create a timeline from the 1980s to the present. Above the timeline, mark when new digital technologies were introduced. Below the timeline, note the impact the technology had on the news industry at the time.

Proliferation The rapid increase and development in something, such as digital technology.

Knowledge check 10

In which decade did developments in digital technology gather pace?

Press agencies report facts without judgement so the information they provide to all news outlets is objective. This information is then sold on to different news outlets, such as *The Guardian*, which quickly reshape the story to reflect their newspaper's values.

DMG Media and News UK are shareholders in PA, meaning that, while the information they receive is still free of **bias**, it can be accessed free or at a reduced cost. This is of benefit to news owners, as these two companies control nearly 60 per cent of the UK's national daily news circulation with *The Sun* (News UK) and the *Daily Mail* (DMG Media) being the UK's top-selling newspapers.

Bias Preference or prejudice for or against someone or something

Gatekeeping

Information is brought into the newsroom daily by press agencies, as well as in-house and freelance reporters. Not all of this information can feature in a daily edition, so the editor must decide which information will be printed.

The editor acts as a **gatekeeper**, selecting some news stories over others based upon which are deemed most important and appealing to their audience. These stories must be seen to be in the public interest and must be checked for accuracy.

As part of the gatekeeping process, editors not only carefully select but also omit news. Editors, in their role as gatekeepers, can practise **protective coverage**. This allows them to prevent certain information from reaching a mass audience, such as material that could be harmful to figures in positions of power or to the public.

Gatekeeping and protective coverage suggests that newspapers wield power and can directly influence the information readers can access and what they think.

The process of gatekeeping therefore helps a paper's owner, through the role of the editor, to:

- identify which events or stories are considered the most important, newsworthy and relevant
- persuade the reader to think about the news from the ideological perspective of the owner.

Gatekeeper A person responsible for filtering or selecting stories based on assumptions of their importance or appeal.

Protective coverage The withholding of information or not reporting a story on the grounds that it would be harmful to powerful people or the public, or impede a criminal or legal investigation from taking place.

> **Study tip**
>
> It's important to discuss gatekeeping in exam questions about ownership, bias, media language, representation and the appeal of a paper to the audience. Look at the full editions of three different newspapers. Are the stories selected the same in each paper? How do they differ?

Knowledge check 11

What is the role of the editor as gatekeeper?

News values

News values set the criteria by which different news stories are selected.

The use of news values indicates that news is a **socially constructed** product.

Galtung and Ruge (1973) identified a list of news values. These are different elements seen to have importance, regardless of the paper's identity, when editors are deciding which events are newsworthy and will appeal to audiences.

News values Guidelines used to identify which news is considered to be most valuable, newsworthy and appealing for audiences.

The more values that apply to a story, the more likely it is that it will find itself in a newspaper.

Twelve of the most significant news values they identified are:

1 frequency
2 threshold
3 unambiguity
4 meaningfulness
5 consonance
6 unexpectedness
7 continuity
8 composition
9 reference to elite nations
10 reference to elite persons
11 personalisation
12 negativity.

Once the editor has applied news values and selected which stories will feature in their daily edition, they shape the stories to reflect:

- the ideological viewpoint of the owner or paper
- the interests of the audience
- the type of newspaper it is.

The appeal of news content to the audience is fundamental when selecting stories, and while the editor is in control of the gatekeeping process, the tastes and preferences of the audience are highly influential. A paper needs to appeal in order to sell.

For example, an audience preference for sensationalised stories in tabloid newspapers such as *The Sun* or the *Daily Mail* may make personalisation an important news value, as their mass audience enjoys emotive stories. In contrast, composition may be a significant news value for readers of hard news, such as *The Guardian*, who desire a sense of balance in what they read, have liberal attitudes and appreciate debate.

This leads us to question how much power editors actually have over audiences if news values are, subliminally, affected by audience preferences.

Study tip

You may need to show your understanding of news values by identifying the values in the unseen sources in the exam. To practise, select a range of front covers from different newspapers and identify which of Galtung and Ruge's news values have been applied to the cover story.

Political bias

The British news industry is considered a **free press**.

Since the early 1800s, newspapers have been referred to as the **Fourth Estate**, acting as a watchdog to ensure democracy can exist.

For example, the role of newspapers as the Fourth Estate has been instrumental in bringing to the public's attention issues such as the MP expenses scandal of 2009 and, more recently, the Facebook and Cambridge Analytica scandal of 2016 and 2017. Both cases involved the abuse of political power and social privilege, and were in the public interest.

Socially constructed
When a social process creates and shapes a product, idea or service as a result of human interaction. It involves people and social agencies who help to shape, reinforce or accept the product as reflecting reality.

Study tip
Research the meaning of each news value.

Knowledge check 12
What are news values?

Free press A news industry that isn't restricted or censored by government in its political views or wider values and beliefs.

Fourth Estate A term meaning that newspapers and journalists play a role in safeguarding the public from decisions made by the wealthy or politicians which could influence political and/or national policy and outcomes.

However newspapers, politics and bias have a complicated relationship in the UK. The notion of political bias should be considered in relation to the ownership and regulation of the press. It can also be seen to influence public thinking and political outcomes, and therefore affect democracy.

In the UK, newspaper titles are thought of in terms of being right wing or left wing. This has become a way to describe the political and ideological values of the paper and how they shape and tell their news stories. The more right wing the paper is, the more conservative and traditional its views and **political agenda** will be.

A YouGov survey in February 2017 asked the public how left or right wing they thought each national daily newspaper was.

- 81 per cent of respondents said that the *Daily Mail* was a right-wing paper; 44 per cent identified it as the most right-wing paper in Britain.
- 71 per cent of respondents said that *The Guardian* was a left-wing paper; 30 per cent identified it as 'fairly left wing'.

This YouGov survey indicates that audiences recognise political bias in newspapers and will select and read the newspaper they feel best reflects their own political values.

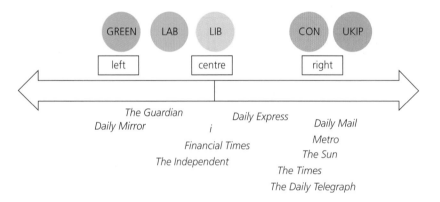

Figure 1.1 The position of UK national papers on the political spectrum. Some papers' positions on the spectrum vary over time and with changes in editors.

From this diagram it can be inferred that half of the UK national daily newspaper titles support right-wing values. This provides a **homogenous** view of our news. DMG group (*Daily Mail*) and News UK (*The Sun*) control over 60 per cent of newspaper circulation in the UK. Both newspapers:

- are right wing
- broadly support and reflect the values of the Conservative Party
- are owned by wealthy, white, male media 'barons'/proprietors who control global media outlets.

Newspaper owners and editors are aware of the power they have in influencing their readers to make national and political decisions that support the paper's political agenda.

The Sun's famous headline in 1992 'It was the Sun wot won it' referred to the Conservative victory in the 1992 general election where *The Sun* encouraged its

Political agenda The topics or issues that reflect the policy of, or are supported by, a particular political group.

Knowledge check 13

What is the Fourth Estate?

Knowledge check 14

Which political bias does the majority of UK national daily newspapers reflect?

Homogenous Singular, similar and undistinguishable. In the news industry this means that most newspapers offer a similar view of the news they report which reinforces a singular view about our culture and the world.

readers to back the Conservatives. Similarly, *The Sun*'s headline 'BeLEAVE in Britain' illustrates its power to influence readers to vote to leave the EU in the 2016 referendum. You can search for these headlines on the internet to find the relevant front covers.

> **Study tip**
>
> Find examples of newspaper front covers that claim to, or have been considered to, influence public voting and opinion. Screenshot the relevant front covers and identify any similarities and differences in the covers that help show their political bias. What outcomes are they trying to influence through each front page? How do they achieve this? What does this tell you about their political bias?

The political influence that can be wielded by newspapers over mass audiences leads critics to question some of the democratic assumptions we have about the press.

Regulation

Regulation may be directed by government legislation or an independent authority to control how an industry is run or how people behave.

Arguments for and against the regulation of the printed press revolve around two opposing views:

- *For:* The news industry has too much political power and influence over the British public, which has reduced freedom of speech, compromises democracy and is not in the public interest.
- *Against:* The printed press should not be regulated or controlled, especially by government legislation. This would affect freedom of speech, democracy and would not be in the public interest.

Regulation of the UK news industry is concerned with maintaining the need for a free press and the function of the Fourth Estate. But the political influence that news owners have over the general public and the need for **plurality** within the industry is also a regulatory concern.

Events in recent history regarding political bias and how journalists access news stories have placed regulation at the top of the political agenda, with the need for a free press called into question.

The World Press Freedom Index ranks Britain as 40th out of 120 countries in the press freedom ratings. The Investigatory Powers Act 2016 is an example of recent legislation that restricts freedom. The act allows for journalists to be under surveillance when reporting on **whistle blowers**.

In light of these debates, regulation of the news industry in the UK focuses on:

- news content and information printed by the press
- ownership and competition laws.

Regulation of news content and information

The British press is self-regulated. This means that, through an independent organisation made up of editors, it regulates itself to ensure adherence to an accepted code of conduct in the production of news content.

> **Study tip**
>
> The unseen sources may be two front covers that share the same topic but have different political bias. When revising front covers, become familiar with identifying examples that reveal the political bias of each paper.

Plurality More than one. In the news industry plurality refers either to the number of companies that own and produce media or to the range of ideas and viewpoints expressed in news reporting. It is the opposite of homogeneity.

Whistle blower A person who informs on immoral or illegal activity conducted by an organisation or individual.

> **Study tip**
>
> When responding to an exam question that assesses your understanding of regulation, you must refer to the regulation of the news industry generally, as well as the set products. Revise the arguments for and against regulation, how content and ownership is regulated, and which body regulates them.

Press regulation adopts a punitive rather than preventative regulation model with regard to content, meaning that editors are punished if they breach regulations. They could face a fine or be required to print an apology.

The Leveson Inquiry was a public-led inquiry set up by former Prime Minister David Cameron in 2011. The purpose of the inquiry was to examine the culture, practice and ethics of the press.

The inquiry looked into the relationship between the press and the public, including phone hacking and illegal behaviour in investigating news stories. It also examined the relationship between the press, the police and politicians.

The Leveson report recommended that future press regulation should take the following approach:

1 to continue to be self-regulated outside the power of the Government
2 to create a new press standards body, created by the industry and with a new, rigorous code of conduct
3 to back up the regulation with legislation to ensure the press remains independent and effective
4 to provide the public with confidence that their complaints will be dealt with effectively
5 to protect the press from government interference.

Knowledge check 15

What is regulation?

Independent Press Standards Organisation (IPSO)

IPSO is an independent regulator for the newspaper and magazine industry in the UK. IPSO is not seen to fulfil Leveson's recommendations so isn't a Leveson compliant regulator with official regulatory status.

In its regulatory role, IPSO:

- holds newspapers to account
- protects the rights of the individual
- upholds standards of journalism
- maintains freedom of expression for the press.

IPSO is funded by the national daily newspaper titles that are members of the body. The public can submit complaints against member newspapers without having to go through the courts and IPSO investigates the complaint. However some newspapers, such as *The Guardian*, have opted out of the scheme and self-regulate outside of IPSO.

IPSO member newspapers include *The Daily Telegraph*, *The Sunday Telegraph*, *The Daily Mail*, *The Mail on Sunday*, *Metro*, *The Times*, *The Sunday Times*, *The Sun*, the *Daily Express*, the *Sunday Express*, the *Daily Star*, the *Daily Mirror*, the *Sunday Mirror* and the *Sunday People*.

Independent Monitor for the Press (IMPRESS)

In 2016, IMPRESS became a Leveson compliant regulator with recognition from the Press Recognition Panel (PRP). It is funded by the Independent Press Regulation Trust (IPRT) meaning that, unlike IPSO, it is commercially independent from the news industry and therefore is not compromised by its funding system. IMPRESS is considered the first of its kind in the UK but hasn't been received positively by newspaper editors, who consider it an attempt by the Government to control the freedom of the press.

Study tip

To support your understanding of news industry regulation, find two examples where regulation has been an issue. These could be breaches in the regulation of content, the ways journalists acquire information or ownership issues. You can refer to these examples in relevant exam answers.

Regulation of ownership and competition laws

Ownership of the media in the UK is regulated by the Communications Act 2003, which takes a liberal approach to the regulation of news ownership. The Enterprise Act 2002 enables discretional intervention by the Government if the Secretary of State considers a cross-media merger could raise plurality concerns.

Plurality refers to diversity in viewpoints, and it is important that the public are exposed to a range of ideas across and within media industries. Plurality within democracy also prevents any one media type or voice from having too much influence over public opinion and political agendas.

The Leveson Inquiry identified there was no regulatory system for addressing plurality concerns which arise as a result of changes in the media. In 2012, **Ofcom** reviewed existing media ownership rules in the UK and recommended that reviews of mergers between cross-media companies or news owners should take place every four to five years.

Currently, plurality and competition within the UK news industry is regulated by the 20/20 rule. This rule prevents a person who runs a newspaper group with a national market share of 20 per cent or more from controlling licences to provide ITV or Channel 5 television news.

Industries and the set products – the *Daily Mail*

The *Daily Mail* was founded in 1896 as a new kind of newspaper for busy, working people. Today, DMG Media describes itself as

> 'delivering brilliant content to millions of loyal customers around the globe 24 hours a day, 7 days a week'
>
> Source: www.dmgt.com

Ownership

The Daily Mail and General Trust (DMGT) is a British media company that manages a multinational **portfolio** and operates in over 40 countries through a number of **subsidiaries**.

DMG Media (formerly Associated News) is a national newspaper and website publisher. As the UK news subsidiary of DMGT it owns:

- the *Daily Mail*
- the *Mail on Sunday*
- *Metro*
- *MailOnline*
- *Metro.co.uk*.

DMGT also owns a 24.9 per cent share in the *Evening Standard* newspaper.

Ownership of DMGT, DMG Media and, consequently, the *Daily Mail* newspaper has stayed within the Rothermere family, who founded and have owned the paper for over 100 years. This proprietor model sees Jonathan Harmsworth (Viscount Rothermere) as the current owner of DMGT and its subsidiaries. He is the Chairman and controlling shareholder.

Ofcom Ofcom is the regulator for the communications services that we use and rely on each day. This covers regulation of broadband, Wifi, home phone and mobile services, as well as TV, On Demand and radio. www.ofcom.org.uk

Knowledge check 16

What does plurality mean and why is it important?

Context

Social context:
The Daily Mail is an established, social institution that is highly visible and influential in our day-to-day lives.

Portfolio The name given to a range of investments owned by a person or organisation.

Subsidiary A small company owned and controlled by a larger, parent company.

Academic ideas

Curran & Seaton 2: For more on applying this theory to news industries and the *Daily Mail*, see the grid on page 111.

Economic models and funding

The traditional newspaper model of acquiring revenue from circulation sales and advertising is still the main source of funding for the *Daily Mail*.

Circulation

- The *Daily Mail*'s circulation figures reach 1,264,810 (June 2018).
- While the *Daily Mail* enjoys almost 25 per cent of the market share in print news, circulation figures have dropped by 12.9 per cent since 2016.
- This indicates that the paper is making less revenue from circulation than it has done in the past.

Advertising

- MailMetroMedia is responsible for developing advertising revenue for the paper.
- A colour display advert in the *Daily Mail* costs £181 per single column centimetre.
- A classified advert usually costs in the region of £300 to £3,000,000, depending on the client.
- A banner advert along the bottom of a page in the *Daily Mail* costs a minimum of approximately £4,000 before tax.

However, if circulation of print news is dropping, advertisers will be less inclined to pay large sums to advertise in the paper, as advertising rates are set in relation to circulation figures.

Alternative revenue options and solutions

DMGT as a multinational, multimedia company published total revenues of £2 billion in 2017, which indicates that while circulation figures of the DMG Media print news titles have dropped, as a parent company it is thriving.

- Revenue for DMG Media in 2017 was £683 million (£23 million less than in 2016).
- DMG Media still made a profit of £77 million in 2017, the same as 2016.

This suggests that while the *Daily Mail* has had less money to spend on the production and distribution of the paper, the owner has offset losses in a number of different ways:

1 with increased profit from advertising across the *MailOnline* brand
2 by an increase in the cover price of the *Daily Mail* from 60p to 65p in February 2018. It is now the most expensive traditional tabloid on the market.
3 Closure of the Didcot printing facilities to reduce production costs of the paper.

Technological developments

The ability to recognise and adopt new technology within the production, distribution and circulation of news is part of the *Daily Mail*'s heritage. For example, it was the first British paper to use the telegraph to break stories quicker than its competitors.

More recently, the *Daily Mail* has successfully adapted to technological change and the proliferation of converged digital technologies, as illustrated by the growth of the *MailOnline*. In July 2017, it was estimated that the *MailOnline* attracted per month:

- 7.7 million online readers
- 22.7 million mobile readers.

Academic ideas

Hesmondhalgh 2: For more on applying this theory to news industries and the *Daily Mail*, see the grid on page 111.

Knowledge check 17

Who owns the *Daily Mail*? What ownership model does it have?

This compares to 8.5 million readers per month of the *Daily Mail* print edition.

DMG Media state that they reach 70 per cent of the UK population with the *Daily Mail* and *MailOnline*. This has placed them at the top of the UK news market with a combined share of 20.1 per cent for print and online circulation.

The ability to develop the *Daily Mail* brand to adapt to new technologies has allowed the paper to offset loss from print sales. The group's strategic plan of 2016 identifies that the digital businesses are enabling DMG Media's growth.

News gathering, gatekeeping and news values

When founded, the *Daily Mail* set a new style of journalism, favouring short articles and persuasive prose. In the 1980s it was rebranded as a tabloid and still places importance on popular, rather than serious, journalism in its coverage of news today.

DMGT state that

> 'the *Daily Mail* has been true to the editorial values that have made the *Daily Mail* the most successful news media brand over the past century'
>
> Source: www.dmgt.com

Its approach to gatekeeping, and its news values, are set by the paper's political agenda. If we use Galtung and Ruge's 12 values, the *Daily Mail* is likely to prioritise:

- negativity
- threshold
- personalisation
- reference to elite people
- reference to elite nations
- meaningfulness
- consonance.

These will be placed above values such as composition.

Paul Dacre, editor of the *Daily Mail* between 1992 and 2018, adopted an editorial approach that favoured sensationalised, personalised news that combined hard and soft news stories. The paper is known for a particular style of reporting on social issues such as immigration, the welfare system and political policy.

The *Daily Mail*'s new editor, Geordie Greig, may adopt a new approach but his application of news values and the way he shapes the *Daily Mail*'s news coverage will need to continue to appeal to the paper's audience.

Political bias

Historically the *Daily Mail* is sympathetic to the right wing, a political bias that was fully established by the 1930s.

Different owners and editors have reinforced this right-wing bias:

- Harold Harmsworth, the owner of the *Daily Mail* in the inter-war years, encouraged positive depictions of right-wing movements.
- David English, editor of the *Daily Mail* in the 1980s, fully supported Prime Minister Margaret Thatcher and the Conservative Party, ensuring the paper's news values and coverage reinforced Thatcher's policies.

Academic ideas

Curran & Seaton 3: For more on applying this theory to news industries and the *Daily Mail*, see the grid on page 111.

Context

Social context: The *Daily Mail* editorial news values are influenced by and reinforce conservative values of law, government, family, religion and education within our society.

Knowledge check 18

Which editorial values or approach did Paul Dacre adopt in the *Daily Mail*'s reporting of news?

Context

Social context: The *Daily Mail* reflects a trend in populism occurring in developed societies such as Europe and America in the twenty-first century.

- Paul Dacre supported the Conservative Party and more recently Conservative politicians who were pro-leave in the EU referendum. This has been reflected in his reporting of the European Union and Brexit.

The political power and reach of the *Daily Mail* is immense. 74% of its readers voted Conservative in the 2017 General Election (YouGov 2017). With its dominant market share in the UK news industry, the paper can reach and influence the political decisions of a large percentage of the British public.

Regulation

The *Daily Mail* is a member of IPSO. DMG Media are required to pay a membership fee to IPSO and are subject to investigations if a complaint is made against them.

As part of its style of reporting, the *Daily Mail* can be seen to be using **hyperbole**, sensationalism and personalisation to report, which can lead to complaints.

Between 2016 and 2018, IPSO investigated 17 cases brought by individuals against the *Daily Mail* newspaper. Most of these were due to breeches in accuracy, privacy and intrusion in the reporting of news stories. Of these 17 complaints, only two were upheld by IPSO.

Apologies and complaints are usually printed in a box on page 2 of the paper but there are sometimes exceptions.

For example, on 15 December 2017, the paper ran a front page story regarding compensation granted to an Iraqi man who was wrongly imprisoned and mistreated by British soldiers. In the case of *Khan v Daily Mail*, IPSO found that the *Daily Mail* was in breach of guidelines by:

1 publishing inaccurate, misleading or distorted information, including headlines not supported by text
2 a significant inaccuracy or misleading statement
3 not distinguishing clearly between comment and fact.

IPSO ordered the *Daily Mail* to print a front page headline directing readers to a full page article regarding the inaccuracies of the news report on page 4 of the paper. This was seen on the 27 July 2018 edition of the *Daily Mail*. You can read more about it here: www.pressgazette.co.uk/daily-mail-runs-front-page-ipso-adjudication-on-iraq-compensation-claims-as-staff-told-making-similar-error-again-would-put-careers-at-risk/

Industries and the set products – *The Guardian*

Initially known as the *Manchester Guardian*, the paper was founded in 1821 at a time when the general public were becoming more educated and politicised. Today, Guardian News and Media Ltd are one of the UK's leading News Media organisations. They state that their journalism does not have any commercial or political interference. You can find more information about the Guardian Media group at www.theguardian.com/gmg/2018/jul/24/aboutguardian-media-group.

Ownership

The parent company of *Guardian* is the Guardian Media Group (GMG). Their main business is Guardian News and Media Ltd, which publishes *The Guardian* newspaper, *theguardian.com* and *The Observer*.

Academic ideas

Livingstone & Lunt 1: For more on applying this theory to news industries and the *Daily Mail*, see the grid on page 112.

Hyperbole Exaggerated statements and claims that are over the top in their expression.

Knowledge check 19

What statistic can be used to indicate that the *Daily Mail* influences its readers politically?

Study tip

To ensure you have examples to support a question on regulation, visit the IPSO website. Pick three of the 17 *Daily Mail* cases investigated by IPSO. Note what they were, what breach was made, the outcome of the case and the reason for the outcome. Draw some conclusions about how effective IPSO is as a regulator.

The Scott Trust, which owns GMG, is a private company that was founded in 1936 to secure the paper's independence and ensure that no single owner could buy and control the paper. The intention of the Trust was to:

- safeguard *The Guardian* from commercial or political interference
- protect *The Guardian*'s news values of honest, fair, liberal investigative journalism.

A board of directors runs and reports to the Trust, and the shareholders make no profit from the organisation. The Trust, rather than GMG as the commercial side of the company, also appoints the Editor in Chief of the paper. This means that the paper's journalism is independent from the commercial aspect of its ownership.

Economic models and funding

Historically, *The Guardian* first received financial backing from middle-class radicals. Until recently, the traditional newspaper model of acquiring revenue from circulation sales and advertising has been the paper's main source of funding.

Circulation

- *The Guardian* has a share of just 2.8 per cent in the UK print news market.
- The paper had a weekly circulation of 986,872 in Nov 2018.
- This indicates that sales of *The Guardian* are declining and the paper will make less revenue from print sales than it has in the past.

Advertising

- A colour display advert rate in *The Guardian* costs £90 per single column centimetre.
- The cheapest advert measures 8 cm x 7 cm and costs £5,000.
- A double page spread advert costs £32,400.

However, *The Guardian* will be less attractive to advertisers if circulation figures keep falling.

Alternative revenue options and solutions

In 2016, GMG set out a three-year business plan to address the potential economic crisis faced by falling print circulation figures and loss of advertising revenue. They aimed to:

- enhance operating efficiency
- reduce costs by 20 per cent
- secure new growth opportunities for GMG as a global news organisation
- adapt to changes in the advertising market.

In response to loss in revenue from print circulation and advertising, *The Guardian* has been successful in developing alternative funding and revenue streams:

1 Donations

More than 800,000 readers fund *The Guardian*:

- 570,000 regular supporters
- 375,000 one-off contributions.

2 The Scott Trust

- The Scott Trust endowment fund focuses on socially responsible investment and all profit from these investments supports GMG.

Academic ideas

Curran & Seaton 1: For more on applying this theory to news industries and *The Guardian*, see the grid on page 112.

Academic ideas

Hesmondhalgh 1: For more on applying this theory to news industries and *The Guardian*, see the grid on page 113.

Knowledge check 20

What is important about the Scott Trust's ownership of *The Guardian*?

- The Trust set up *theguardian.org*, a non-profit organisation that raises funds from groups and private donors.
- The Trust's shareholders take no dividends from the Trust. Any profit made goes straight back into the GMG and running the paper.

3 Philanthropic contributions

These come from wealthy individuals, such as Microsoft owner Bill Gates, who share *The Guardian*'s values.

4 Reducing production costs

- In 2018 the paper transitioned from a Berliner (European) format to a tabloid, which reduced operating costs by £19.1 million, contributing to the 20 per cent reduction in costs aimed for in 2016.
- In 2016 the cover price was raised to £2.00.

5 Off-setting losses with the digital version of the brand

- Digital revenues have increased by 15 per cent since 2016.
- The digital arm of *The Guardian* comprises 50 per cent of GMG's revenue.

The 2017–18 financial report states that GMG has £217 million revenue compared to £214.5 million in 2016–17. Although fewer people are reading *The Guardian*, their parent company is not losing money as a result of these alternative revenue streams.

Technological developments

Recent technological developments have had a detrimental impact on *The Guardian* with print circulation figures indicating that it has the lowest circulation figures of the UK national daily newspapers.

However, *The Guardian* has responded to this and the impact of digitally convergent technology by developing its online brand of the paper through:

- *theguardian.com*
- *The Guardian* app
- a daily tablet edition.

In 2015 GMG had a 15 per cent share in the market for combined print and online circulation, the third largest share of the UK national daily news outlets.

Between April 2017 and March 2018, the paper's combined print and online platforms reached over 24 million readers per month. Across different digital platforms the readership looks approximately like this:

- desktop – 7.8 million
- tablet – 3.1 million
- mobile – 15.8 million.

This suggests that *The Guardian*'s adaptations to changes in digital technology and convergence within the industry is helping the paper to survive and, potentially, flourish.

News gathering, gatekeeping and news values

CP Scott was the editor of the *Manchester Guardian* from 1872 to 1929 and outlined *The Guardian*'s principles and values in his 'Hundred Year Essay' where he stated that:

Academic ideas

Hesmondhalgh 2: For more on applying this theory to news industries and *The Guardian*, see the grid on page 113.

Knowledge check 21

How has GMG reduced production costs of *The Guardian* newspaper?

Context

Cultural context: *The Guardian* supports serious, quality journalism while acknowledging the importance of arts and culture for the public good.

Cultural context: *The Guardian*'s news values reflect the lives of the public from all cultures and walks of life.

- comment is free
- facts are sacred
- newspapers have a moral and material existence
- fairness and a sense of duty are essential ethics in journalism.

Source: www.theguardian.com/sustainability/cp-scott-centenary-essay

The Guardian's current editor, Katharine Viner, has described the paper's values as agenda-setting. Stories are prioritised if they are in the public's interest, are for the common good, and if they reflect equality and freedom. Viner says that journalists need to report on all forms of public life including different cultures, diverse perspectives and community services such as schools and hospitals.

Source: Adapted from Viner, 'A mission for journalism in a time of crisis' (theguardian.com, 16 November 2017)

If applying Galtung and Ruge's 12 news values, it is likely that *The Guardian* will prioritise composition above negativity, threshold or personalisation to reflect their liberal, progressive and balanced approach to news.

Political bias

The Guardian was founded to promote liberal interests, which suggests a traditional bias to the left of centre on the political spectrum.

Twenty-five per cent of the British public think *The Guardian* is slightly left of centre, with 30 per cent believing it is fairly left wing. The majority of the British public see *The Guardian* as Britain's most left-wing paper (YouGov 2017).

The paper's centre-left bias is illustrated as follows:
- In 2004 its editor stated it was a centre-left newspaper.
- Opinion columns and letter pages reflect the centre-left bias with writers such as Owen Jones, a political commentator and left-wing activist.

The political influence of the paper, and the political views of its readers, is demonstrated by 73 per cent of *The Guardian* readers voting Labour in the 2017 General Election (YouGov 2017).

Regulation

The Guardian has opted out of membership of IPSO and IMPRESS. The paper states that it will not join the current regulatory bodies for these reasons:

1. Industry-funded IPSO is unethical and there are governance issues with the Royal Charter that impacts the freedom of the press.
2. Punitive legal costs for news titles that don't sign up to IMPRESS will damage press freedom and investigative journalism.

Since September 2014, *The Guardian* has regulated itself in the following ways:
- *The Guardian* Readers' Editor, appointed by the Scott Trust, hears and reviews all complaints against the paper using criteria such as: how serious the complaint is; the likelihood that harm could occur; the potential the content has to mislead; the risk to *The Guardian* newspaper group.

Context

Cultural context: *The Guardian* supports a plural, diverse view of British culture.

Knowledge check 22

What are the four values of *The Guardian* that Scott outlined in his Hundred Year Essay that still endure in the paper's selection of stories today?

Context

Political context: The paper's content is influenced by its political values, with its electoral coverage in 2017 supporting the Labour Party and Jeremy Corbyn.

Academic ideas

Livingstone & Lunt 1: For more on applying this theory to news industries and *The Guardian*, see the grid on page 115.

- The Scott Trust also appoints two independent figures to work with an **ombudsman** in addition to the Readers' Editor to ensure impartiality.
- *The Guardian* supports the code of practice, adheres to anti-bribery laws and the corruption code of conduct and can self-regulate.

In the past, *The Guardian* has faced potential government action to regulate the paper's role as investigative journalists and their aim to report fairly on information that is in the public interest.

- In 2013, *The Guardian* reported the case of whistle blower Edward Snowden who leaked the United States National Security Agency (NSA) and CIA surveillance disclosures, which affected ordinary American citizens.
- The British Government threatened *The Guardian* with legal action and closure if they didn't hand over Snowden's files. *The Guardian* refused and destroyed them.

Print news: audiences

An audience can be defined as a group of people or the **market** that a product or message is aimed at.

The OCR specification identifies that for print news and media audiences, learners should study:

- the content and appeal of products
- how content is used to target, reach and address different audiences
- how audiences may use and interpret the same media in different ways.

Before studying these issues, it is necessary to develop your understanding of the audience for print news.

Audiences for print news

Media organisations spend much time and money identifying their audience. They need to be certain that the content of their newspaper will appeal to the audience so they will buy it. This helps the owner:

1 earn money through increased sales of the paper
2 attract advertising revenue by selling space in the paper to advertisers wishing to target the same audiences with their products.

It is important to think about news audiences in terms of different market segments and audience types:

Market segments

Audiences can be divided up by **statistical data** such as age and gender or by behaviour and experiences such as attitudes to social issues, where they shop or what car they drive. Segmenting audiences in this way helps newspapers understand their readers better and enables them to market their paper to the reader and attract appropriate advertisers.

Audiences can be segmented and understood in two ways:

- demographically
- psychometrically.

Ombudsman An official appointed to investigate public complaints against a company, organisation or public authority.

Knowledge check 23

Why has *The Guardian* refused to join IPSO and IMPRESS?

Market (In media) A group of consumers who are interested in a product.

Statistical data Information that is collected, analysed and presented in number form.

Demographics

Owners can find and target their audiences by using demographics. This groups the population into very specific categories that include:

- age
- gender
- social class
- ethnicity
- religion
- sexual orientation
- education level
- income level
- occupation
- geographic location.

Demographic profiling tends to focus mostly on age, gender, income level and occupation.

In the early 1900s, the Registrar General's classification system developed the NS-SEC scale, which connected social class to occupation. In the 1960s, the NRS (National Readership Survey) developed this with a social economic grade classification system that correlated the social class and occupation of readers using graded letter codes.

Table 2.1 Social demographic grades correlated with social class and occupation of readers

Social demographic grade	Social class	Household chief income earner's occupation
A	Upper middle class	Elite, higher managerial, professional, e.g. banker, director of public company, judge, hospital consultant
B	Middle class	Intermediate managerial, professional, e.g. GP, journalist, architect
C1	Lower middle class	Supervisory, clerical and junior managerial, or professional, e.g. office worker, IT professional, secretary
C2	Skilled working class	Skilled manual workers, e.g. electrician, plumber, builder
D	Working class	Semi-skilled and unskilled manual workers, e.g. shop assistant, factory worker, labourer, telesales
E	Non-working	Casual or lowest grade workers, pensioners and others who depend on the welfare state for their income

News companies focus on ABC grades:

- These groups are likely to have the greatest disposable income.
- They are more attractive for advertisers.

There are some weaknesses in classifying audiences by their job and social status:

- These social grades are old and don't reflect contemporary occupations and incomes.
- Demographics can't identify values or what might appeal to a specific audience member.

Psychometrics

Psychometrics is another method of categorising audiences. One way is to use 'VALs' typology, which considers:

- values
- attitudes
- lifestyle or behaviour.

Knowledge check 24

What four factors are the focus of demographic profiling? What are the weaknesses of this approach?

There are seven psychometric audience 'types' according to the VALs approach.

Table 2.2 Psychometric types and their VAL characteristics

Psychometric type	VAL characteristics
Aspirer	• Seeks status
Explorer	• Discovers new things
Mainstreamer	• Likes to be part of a larger group of like-minded people • Seeks security
Reformer	• Not impressed by status or materialism • Socially aware
Resigned	• Has built up attitudes over time • Believes in institutions and traditions they trust
Struggler	• Has a 'live for the day' attitude • Sees themselves as a victim • Seeks escape
Succeeder	• High social status • Deserves the best

VALs can lead to stereotyping different audience groups but they do help to explain:

- how audiences in the same demographic can be broken down further
- how audiences may respond differently to the same product due to their personal values.

Different news outlets appeal to different VALs groups. For example, *The Sun* is likely to attract Mainstreamer, Resigned and Struggler audiences. *The Times*, in contrast, is likely to appeal to Succeeders.

Audience types

In addition to an audience's demographic and psychographic profile, audiences can be discussed in terms of their relevance to the product and/or their size:

- **Target audience:** a specific group of people targeted by the newspaper, usually identified by demographics and psychometrics.
- **Mass audience:** a very large audience including a wide range of people made up of different demographics and psychometrics. Print news traditionally attracts a mass audience.
- **Niche audience:** a small, select group of people who have a unique interest so are identified by psychometrics and often by lifestyle preferences.

Print news audiences

Fewer people are reading newspapers than ever before. But 29.1 million people a month still read British newspapers, which is greater than the population of Australia! (PAMCo 2018)

So, newspapers have a mass audience. But who makes up print news audiences?

Demographics

- Men are more likely to read newspapers than women, but by a small margin – 51 per cent are male and 49 per cent female.
- Those aged 55+ are most likely to read a newspaper.
- 57 per cent of millennials are also likely to read a newspaper. That's two in five people every week.
- Both the middle (28 per cent) and working classes (27 per cent) read daily newspapers.

Knowledge check 25

What do psychometrics help us understand about audiences?

Study tip

To develop your understanding of newspaper audiences, find the press kit on the websites of two national daily print newspapers that differ in some way. Summarise in a table the demographic and psychometric breakdown each provides of its audience. Then compare this with the set products.

Millennials Anyone who turned 18 in the early twenty-first century, so they now fall into the 18–35 age group.

Psychometrics

The majority of print news audiences are made up of Aspirers, Mainstreamers, Reformers, the Resigned and Succeeders.

The content and appeal of products

Newspapers must appeal to audiences and advertisers to stay profitable in an increasingly competitive market. They do this through the *content* they offer their audiences.

There are a number of methods used to ensure content attracts a target audience.

1 News stories selected

While the stories featured in a paper reflect the viewpoint of the owner and editor of the paper, they must also reinforce the values and interests of the target audience.

The theory of gatekeeping along with Galtung and Ruge's news values have been discussed (see page 16). When considering how print news content appeals to target audiences, we can also refer to Harcup's news values (2001). These values address the importance and appeal of celebrity and sensationalism in attracting audiences.

Table 2.3 Harcup's news values

Knowledge check 26

Whose news values help address the importance of celebrity and entertainment in contemporary journalism?

	News value	Applies to stories concerning:
1	**The power elite**	Powerful individuals, organisations and institutions
2	**Celebrity**	People who are already famous
3	**Entertainment**	Sex, show business, human interest, animals, unfolding dramas, humorous treatment, entertaining photographs, witty headlines
4	**Surprise**	An element of surprise or contrast, the unexpected
5	**Bad news**	Conflict, tragedy, death, negative topics
6	**Good news**	Rescues, cures, miracles
7	**Magnitude**	Large numbers of people, or the size of the potential impact of a story on people
8	**Relevance**	Issues, groups and nations relevant for the target audience
9	**Follow up**	Subjects already or recently in the news
10	**News agenda**	The newspapers' own agenda regarding the political and social issues they choose to report on and the ideological values they express

Consider how these news values can be applied for the front page of *The Sun*.

Good news
Cheap holidays;
Prince Louis

Bad news
Johnson resigning
from post

Surprise
Johnson resigning
from post

The power elite
Conservative Party
politicians

Follow-up
Ongoing factions in
Conservative Party
over Brexit

News agenda
Political agenda with focus on
Conservative Party; sport is given
priority alongside current affairs

Celebrity
Kate, Duchess of
Cambridge

Relevance
Disputes within the
Conservative Party;
England's success in
World Cup

Entertainment
Football, World Cup,
holidays, witty
headlines

Magnitude
Impact of Brexit,
World Cup and global
reach of royal family

Study tip

Practise applying Harcup's news values to the front covers of two newspapers. For each news value you identify, explain how it attracts the paper's audience. You could create a table to record the news values and how they might appeal to the audience.

Figure 2.1 *The Sun* front page example

2 Technical codes

This refers to the elements used to construct a media product so it looks the way it does. We will look at the **technical codes** of newspapers in detail in the Media Language section but it is useful to identify some of the key technical codes and formatting conventions when thinking how content is made to appeal to audiences:

- **Layout, sell lines and cover lines**
  - The layout of the newspaper front page in particular is designed to attract the audience.
  - Layouts help guide the reader's eye down the paper and to the main points of coverage on the page.
  - Headlines, bylines and copy will be in different sizes to break up information and enable readers to quickly 'skim' the news or digest it at length.
  - The ratio of image to words is dependent on:
    - the genre of the newspaper
    - the educational level of the reader.
- **Colour and fonts**
  - Newspapers rely on colour to appear eye-catching.
    - Popular tabloids use brighter or contrasting colours for impact.
    - Broadsheets or serious newspapers use subdued colour palettes as the style of reporting is the focus for the reader.
  - The masthead, which holds the newspaper's name, will be large and use a familiar font so that audiences clearly recognise the paper as a brand.
  - Newspapers use different font styles to appeal to their audience.

3 Language

Use of language and mode of address often depends on the genre, ideological values and educational level of the target audience for the paper.

- **Mode of address**
  - This refers to the way the paper addresses and talks to its audience.
  - It can be informal and conversational, or formal and serious.
- **Lexis**
  - This refers to the compilation of words and language.
  - It is the vocabulary used by journalists to make the content appeal to the audience; in other words, what they say.
  - The choice of words can be emotive and hyperbolic or objective and balanced.

How content is used to target, reach and address different audiences

Newspapers address the values and interests of their audiences in the content they include in the paper. But in order to reach their target audience, newspapers have to market their news brand to create awareness of the paper and:

1 encourage reader loyalty

2 attract new readers

3 increase sales and advertising revenue.

Technical codes Camera work, editing and mise-en-scene that require technical equipment and skill to produce, such as the use of a camera or editing software.

Knowledge check 27

Which technical codes and media language elements help newspaper content appeal to an audience?

How do newspapers target and reach their audiences?

1 Price
- The cover price is set to appeal to the audience's socio-demographic profile, in particular their income.
- A red top tabloid costs 40–75p whereas a broadsheet or 'quality' newspaper ranges from £1.60 to £2.70.

2 Cross-platform advertising
- Newspapers will market their print news version across a range of converged media.
- This can include adverts for their print paper in their online and social media platforms.

3 Promotional offers
- Offers such as free giveaways, posters, discounts on holidays, book clubs and shopping vouchers are all used to appeal to and reach the target audience.

4 Subscriptions
- Audiences are invited to express their loyalty to the paper by committing to monthly and annual subscriptions where they pay for copies in advance and receive a discount on the cover price.

5 Sponsorship
- Newspapers will sponsor events that reflect the values of the paper and appeal to the interests of the reader. For example, *The Guardian* sponsoring Glastonbury Festival helps market the paper as a good brand for millennials interested in culture and music.

6 Partnership marketing
- These are synergy deals with other companies that help to promote both products to similar audiences with the aim of widening the market share both products can access.
- *The Sun* has a partnership marketing deal with GoCompare, which will appeal to their target audience of largely working-class mainstreamers.
- Yahoo has content partnerships with *The Telegraph*, *The Guardian* and *The Independent*. This means these news outlets can distribute their content on Yahoo websites and mobile apps across the UK, US, Canada, India and Singapore. This helps to widen the global reach for these news outlets.

How audiences use and interpret media

Understanding how audiences use and interpret content in newspapers is less precise than targeting and reaching audiences. Today, audiences are assumed to be active in the way they select, consume and interpret media to the extent that they have different uses and needs of media products.

Blumler, McQuail and Katz identified the Uses and Gratifications theory (1974). Whilst the OCR specification doesn't require you to study this theory, it is helpful to consider when identifying audiences' uses of print news.

Study tip

To develop your understanding of the ways in which newspapers target audiences, pick a news outlet and find out as much as you can about the different ways it markets its newspaper. Use the six methods noted here to help you with your research. You could note down your findings in a table or a mind map.

Some of the uses they identified are explained in Table 2.4.

Table 2.4 Audiences' uses of print news, according to Blumler, McQuail and Katz (1974)

Need or use of the media product	Explanation of the need	Examples from print news to illustrate how the need could be satisfied
Entertainment and diversion	The reader will look to be entertained by the content of the newspaper, which they will see as amusing or a diversion from their everyday life or serious events.	• The stories in popular tabloid newspapers feature celebrities or entertainment news value. • Arts and culture reviews in broadsheet or serious newspapers divert audiences from serious news, current affairs or social issues. • Entertaining language in headlines.
Information and education	The reader will look to be informed and educated by the content. They may also rely on the newspaper to help them develop a viewpoint or opinion of different news stories.	• The stories in quality tabloids or broadsheets provide composition and balance to help educate the reader through objective journalism. • The use of hyperbole, **rhetoric** and political bias in popular tabloid news stories may influence the reader in how to think about social or political issues.
Social interaction	The reader will look for opportunities to either be informed on issues that can enhance their social understanding or lead to social interaction with other people in some way.	• The reporting of social issues allows readers to develop their social understanding. • Celebrity stories and gossip columns emulate chatting to friends socially and/or can reinforce current popular culture discussions that the readers might be having socially.
Personal identity	The reader will look to personally identify with the content through the language used, the images selected and the stories featured.	• The use of technical codes and language appeals to the audience so the story feels familiar and accessible to the reader. • The selection of news stories and application of values reinforces the ideology of the reader so they can personally identify with the content.

Audience and the *Daily Mail*

Audience

As the second best-selling UK national daily newspaper after *The Sun*, the *Daily Mail* has a mass audience and loyal readership. The demographics of the *Daily Mail* readership are summed up by the data sheet that MailMetroMedia produces to attract advertisers:

- 59 per cent are women.
- The average age is 59.
- 62 per cent fall into the ABC1 socio-economic groups (with the largest group falling into C1)
- The majority of readers live in the South East.

- They have average savings of £39,000.
- They spend 52 minutes reading the paper.

Using VALs psychometric types, the typical *Daily Mail* audience can be seen to be made up of Mainstreamers, the Resigned and Succeeders (see page 30 for explanations).

Study tip

To develop your understanding of *Daily Mail* audiences, go to mailmetromedia.co.uk and find out as much as you can about the *Daily Mail* audience. You could organise your information under the headings Demographics and Psychometrics.

How content is used to target, reach and address their audience

The *Daily Mail* has a loyal readership but it still needs to market the paper to ensure it maintains strong circulation figures and advertising revenue.

Table 2.5 Marketing tools used by the *Daily Mail*

Marketing tools used by the *Daily Mail* to target and reach its audience	
Price	65p: The *Daily Mail*'s readers are predominantly ABC and can afford this cover price.
Promotional offers	The newspaper offers a range of promotional offers with companies such as Weight Watchers.
Subscriptions	Readers can subscribe to the *Mail* brand with subscription offers ranging from £9.99 per month for a 12-month contract to £25.75 per month for a premium package.
Partnership marketing	In collaboration with Global Savings Group, the *Daily Mail* offers a range of discounts on groceries, clothing, holidays, technology and services from popular brands such as The Gap. In 2016, the *Daily Mail* and Lego were in a partnership deal where Lego offered free giveaways through the paper. Lego ended the deal following the Stop Funding Hate campaign, stating that the *Mail*'s headlines created a distrust of foreigners.

Content and appeal of the paper

The stories featured in the *Daily Mail* reinforce the values and interests of their conservative, middle-aged, predominantly female target audience, through the use of news values and selected stories, technical codes and language.

News values and selected stories

The example of a *Daily Mail* front page in Figure 2.2 can be seen to use Harcup's news values in the stories that have been selected to attract the target audience.

Study tip

To practise analysis of Harcup's news values in unseen sources in the exam, analyse an unseen *Daily Mail* front cover. Identify as many news values as you can, noting which content on the front cover illustrates the value. You could also identify how each one might appeal to the paper's target audience.

Academic ideas

Shirky 2: For more on applying this theory to audiences of the *Daily Mail*, see the grid on page 112.

Context

Economic context: The *Daily Mail* content, along with the advertisers they attract, is influenced by the economic context of their wealthy readers.

Knowledge check 30

Why must the news values and content of the paper appeal to the target audience?

Table 2.6 News values demonstrated on the *Daily Mail* front cover (Figure 2.2)

	News value	Description of example from the *Daily Mail* front page	Appeals to the target audience interest in:
1	The power elite	Reference to the prime minister	• their trust of the prime minister – they are likely to have voted for her
2	Celebrity	Ant McPartlin	• their consumption of popular culture and mainstream TV
3	Entertainment	An affair, unfolding drama, the World cup	• their consumption of mainstream TV
4	Surprise	England's success in the World Cup	• their nationalistic values
5	Bad news	The NHS costing middle-class tax payers	• their possible distrust of the NHS • their preference to invest money wisely
6	Good news	Going to war on waste Mouth-watering summer recipes	• their liking value for money • print news readers' interest in good food
7	Magnitude	The NHS and paying taxes affects most of the British population	• their nationalistic values • possible distrust of NHS wastage • their preference to invest money wisely
8	Relevance	Reference to the prime minister and British politics. Reference to the NHS alludes to the British welfare state as a social issue	• their nationalistic values • their possible distrust of the NHS
9	Follow-up	Ant McPartlin's rehabilitation recently in the news	• their consumption of popular, mainstream culture • also reinforces stereotypes that women like to gossip about relationships
10	News agenda	Brexit and middle-class tax payers supporting the welfare state corroborates the *Daily Mail*'s conservative agenda	• political and nationalistic values.

1. Sell line using Sans Serif font

2. Masthead using Serif font

3. Sell-line using Serif font

4. Mode of address

Figure 2.2 A *Daily Mail* front page

Use of technical codes and language

The use of technical codes and language used on the front cover also aims to ensure the paper, and the stories featured, appeal to the audience.

Technical code 1: Layout

- The focal point divides the page in two.
- The top half features the masthead, strapline, sell-line, and sub-heading.
- The bottom half features some copy and a second story.
- This layout allows the content to appeal to a cross-section of the audience while communicating the main message about the NHS.

Technical code 2: Sell-lines

Look at annotation 1 on Figure 2.2 pointing to the sell-lines in Sans Serif font. Sell-lines 'sell' the content in terms of gender stereotypes, football for men and dieting for women. They help the reader identify that the content will be relevant to them.

Technical code 3: Colours

Use of black, white and red but also yellow and green. Black, white and red are the traditional colours of a tabloid but the yellow and green make the sell-line stand out, appealing to the female audience.

Technical code 4: Font

- The masthead in Figure 2.2 (annotation 2) uses the traditional font for the title of the newspaper, clearly branding the paper as recognisable to the audience.
- Serif font is used for the headlines (see annotation 3 on Figure 2.2) and copy to reflect the traditional attitudes of the paper.
- Sans serif font is used for the sell-lines to emphasise the range of content in this edition.

Language 1: Mode of address

The mode of address is conspiratorial and united. The paper talks to the audience in a familiar way, with the phrases 'Come on' and 'Let's go' (see annotation 4 on Figure 2.2 and Figure 2.3) appealing to the Mainstreamer's need to feel part of a bigger group of likeminded people.

Language 2: Lexis

- The use of vocabulary helps the content appeal to the audience in two contrasting ways (see annotation 5 on Figure 2.2):
  1 It is conversational, informative and emotive: 'Agony', 'HER friend', 'Come on'.
  2 It is formal in its references to the PM, dividends and middle classes.
- This helps the content appeal to the audience and directly addresses them, so the audience recognise themselves as middle-class Conservatives with savings because the story is directed at them.

Academic ideas

Hall 2: For more on applying this theory to audiences of the *Daily Mail*, see the grid on page 111.

Context

Cultural context: The *Daily Mail*'s news content is influenced by the cultural tastes and experiences of their audiences.

Academic ideas

Gerbner 2: For more on applying this theory to audiences of the *Daily Mail*, see the grid on page 111.

Agony

Let's

Come on!

Mouthwatering

PM

Middle class

Dividend

Comment

Figure 2.3 These words are taken from Figure 2.2 on page 36 and illustrate the modes of address in the paper.

How audiences use and interpret media

If we accept that audiences are active, the *Daily Mail*'s audience will use and interpret the content of the paper to fulfil certain uses or needs they have for reading news. If we apply the Uses and Gratification theory to the front cover in Figure 2.2, we can see how the *Daily Mail* reader may use and interpret the paper's content.

Table 2.7 How the *Daily Mail* satisfies audience uses and gratification

Gratification or use of the media product	Examples from print news to illustrate how audience uses and gratification could be satisfied
Entertainment and diversion	• Use of celebrity culture with Ant McPartlin is entertaining and diverts us from other current affairs. • Weight Watchers summer recipes provide diversion with cooking.
Information and education	• The main story regarding the NHS informs the reader and educates them about the potential changes that may be made to the NHS and might directly affect them. • This also informs the reader with a specific viewpoint that they are encouraged to take or may reflect their personal values (identity).
Social interaction	• The words 'Come on' and 'Let's go to war' speak to the reader as if the audience and the *Mail* are all part of the same group; they encourage social interaction and the idea that the reader is with likeminded people. • The reporting of the NHS and Ant McPartlin stories can be described as 'water-cooler moments' which might provide points of discussion with friends or social groups.
Personal identity	• The news values reflected in the selection of stories and the reporting of them can reflect the reader's own interests and/or their ideological values.

Audience and *The Guardian*

Audience

Although *The Guardian*'s print circulation sales have greatly decreased, it has a mass audience and a loyal readership. The demographics of *The Guardian* print newspaper are:

- 44.2 per cent aged 55+
- 50 per cent male and female
- approximately 75 per cent ABC social demographic.

GMG states that *The Guardian* newspaper 'attracts a unique group of people … [who are] curious about the world around them, who travel, who embrace change and new technology. [They are] Progressive people, valuable people.'

Adapted from: https://advertising.theguardian.com/audience

The Guardian reader is interested in culture, lifestyle and sport, as its circulation for these supplements in the newspaper indicates:

- *Culture*: 6.9 million
- *Life and Style*: 5 million
- *Guardian Sport*: 4.2 million
- *Business*: 2.4 million
- *Technology*: 1.9 million
- *Travel*: 1.5 million

The Guardian defines its audiences as **progressives**. If we consider the Psychometric VALs audience groups the newspaper's target audience can be seen to be: Explorers, Reformers and Succeeders (see page 30 for explanations).

How content is used to target, reach and address their audience

The Guardian has a loyal readership but it still needs to market the paper to ensure it maintains circulation figures for advertising revenue.

Table 2.8 Marketing tools used by *The Guardian*

Marketing tools used by *The Guardian* to target and reach its audience	
Price	£2.00: 75% of *The Guardian*'s audience is ABC and can afford this cover price.
Promotional offers	*The Guardian* provides offers for its readers that support some of the content in its supplement papers such as *Review*, *Culture* and *Travel*. *The Guardian* bookshop provides 30% off the cost of books and also links to *The Guardian* book club.
Subscriptions	*The Guardian* offers a range of subscriptions to reach and attract its audience and encourage loyalty to the paper. Subscriptions range from just the Saturday edition (£10.36 per month) to every day (£47.62 per month). Reader loyalty can also be demonstrated through donations. Readers can commit to a regular monthly donation of £2–10 per month.
Sponsorship	*The Guardian* currently has sponsorship deals with UNICEF, Unilever and Phillips. *The Guardian* has also sponsored Glastonbury Festival to appeal to their younger audience of millennials and their progressive values.
Partnership marketing	*The Guardian* has a content partnership with Yahoo, so they can distribute selected content across the UK, US, Canada, India and Singapore. This helps the paper secure a global reach and target the paper's growing number of mobile consumers.

Study tip

To develop your understanding of *The Guardian*'s audiences, request a press pack and find out as much as you can about *The Guardian*'s audience. You could organise your information into a table using the headings Demographics and Psychometrics.

Context

Cultural context:
The Guardian content is influenced by the cultural experiences and tastes of their audience, such as arts and culture, sports, fashion, cooking and travel.

Progressives People who are forward-thinking and advocate social reform.

Content and appeal of the paper

The stories featured in *The Guardian* reinforce the values and interests of their liberal audience, through the use of news values and selected stories, technical codes and language.

News values and selected stories

The Guardian front page (Figure 2.4) can be seen to use Harcup's news values in the stories that have been selected to attract the target audience.

Table 2.9 News values demonstrated on *The Guardian* front cover

	News value	Description of example from *The Guardian* cover	Appeals to the target audience interest in:
1	The power elite	• Prime minster Theresa May • Boris Johnson • England football manager Gareth Southgate	• Politics • Sports (4.2 million readers of *Guardian Sport*)
2	Celebrity	• Gareth Southgate	• Sports
3	Entertainment	• World Cup – Southgate as England manager and the sell line for the story on how to beat the Croatian football team	• Sports
4	Surprise	• Boris Johnson's resignation	• Politics
5	Bad news	• Impact of Johnson's resignation on Brexit talks for prime minister May • The England team facing Croatia in the World Cup	• Politics • Social issues • Sports
6	Good news	• Gareth Southgate's popularity • Boris Johnson's resignation	• Sports • Politics
7	Magnitude	• World Cup • Impact of Brexit negotiations on social and political issues with the UK in Europe and rest of the world	• Sport • Politics • Social issues
8	Relevance	• Brexit and British politics • England's performance in the World Cup	• Social issues • Politics • Sports
10	News agenda	• Lead story on *The Guardian's* view of how prime minister Theresa May has managed Johnson's resignation and what this means for Brexit	• Liberal, progressive, centre left news values • Politics • Social issues

Study tip

To practise analysis of Harcup's news values in unseen sources in the exam, analyse an unseen front cover of *The Guardian*. Identify as many news values as you can, noting which content on the front cover references the value. You could also identify how each one might appeal to the paper's target audience.

1. Sell lines in serif font

2. Mast head in serif font

3. Headline in serif font

4. Modes of address

5. Formal lexis

Figure 2.4 A *Guardian* front page

Use of technical codes and language

The technical codes and language used on the front cover also aims to ensure the paper, and the stories featured, appeal to the audience.

Technical code 1: Layout

- The layout organises the page in a straightforward, balanced and accessible way to reflect the paper's balanced journalism. This will appeal to the audience who like balance in the views expressed.
- The masthead on the top right takes up half of the page's width, branding the paper. The positioning of the masthead to the right of the page is unconventional in newspapers and suggests that this paper offers a different perspective.

Technical code 2: Sell-lines

- See annotation 1 on Figure 2.4 for examples of sell-lines. These help to sell the content inside the paper and the G2 supplement.
- They are usually selected to represent the range of content available. This issue mostly focuses on selling the sport stories inside the edition reflecting the predominance of the World Cup at the time that this edition was published; this is designed to appeal to the reader's values and interests at that time.

Technical code 3: Colours

Use of black, white, yellow, blue and red.

- The yellow and blue helps the cover lines stand out and appeal to the audience.
- The red pull quote helps the quotation, and implications of what it means, stand out to the reader.

Academic ideas

Hall 3: For more on applying this theory to audiences of *The Guardian*, see the grid on page 113.

Context

Social context: *The Guardian's* news values are influenced by social issues that affect the civic lives of their audience and will appeal to their social conscience.

Technical code 4: Font

- See annotations 2 and 3 on Figure 2.4. The serif font is traditional of broadsheet genre newspapers so that although *The Guardian* is now a tabloid, the use of serif font will appeal to readers who prefer to read quality journalism found in broadsheet papers.
- The style of this serif font is called Guardian headline, branding the paper.
- The consistent use and straightforwardness of the font not only aids the quick reading of extended writing in the lengthy lead article but will appeal to the audience by reinforcing the paper's straightforward journalism.

Language 1: Mode of address

- See annotation 4 on Figure 2.4. The mode of address is formal and serious in tone, even when discussing issues such as England's football manager, appealing to the educated audience.
- Words such as 'I' when quoting from figures referenced in the lead story helps to create a distance between the politicians and the reader so the paper appears objective and balanced.

Language 2: Lexis

- See Figure 2.5. Serious, formal vocabulary is used to help the content appeal to the audience in terms of their academic level, knowledge of language and expectation that the paper will provide quality, well-written journalism.

How audiences use and interpret media

Just like the readers of other news brands, *The Guardian* readers will use and interpret the content in the paper to fulfil certain uses or needs they have from reading news. If we apply the Uses and Gratification theory to the front cover in Figure 2.4, we can see how the audiences of *The Guardian* may use and interpret the paper's content.

Table 2.10 How *The Guardian* satisfies audience uses and gratification

Gratification or use of the media product	Example from print news to illustrate how audience use and gratification could be satisfied
Entertainment and diversion	• The reference to football and the image of Southgate helps satisfy the need for entertainment through sports and acts as a diversion.
Information and education	• The lead story is informative and educates the audience on a serious topic of national and political interest. It discusses some of the reasons for Johnson's resignation, what the implications of this are for the prime minister and how Brexit developments may progress so the reader is educated and kept up to date.
Social interaction	• The themes of the news stories selected on the front page could encourage interaction through discussion of politics, Brexit and sports.
Personal identity	• The reader could personally identify with the political 'centre left' news values or 'remain' preference reflected in the *Guardian*'s reporting of the Brexit story.

Print news: media language

The OCR specification identifies that in relation to print news and media audiences, learners should study:

Stark

Resignation

Rallying

Assent

Governed

Vanguard

Prevail

Figure 2.5 These words are taken from Figure 2.4 and illustrate the lexis used in the paper.

Study tip

To develop your understanding of the ways in which news content in *The Guardian* is made to appeal to audiences, look at two front covers from *The Guardian*. Analyse and note down how the technical codes and language are used to make the content appeal to the audience.

Academic ideas

Bandura 1: For more on applying this theory to audiences of *The Guardian*, see the grid on page 112.

Context

Political context: The paper's focus on social issues as well as national and global current affairs reflects the contemporary political climate and appeals to its politically aware audience.

- the elements of media language used in newspaper front covers such as locations, lighting, choice of camera shot, angle, typography, layout, address of content to the audience and editing as appropriate
- the ways in which the use of media language by news producers incorporates viewpoints and ideologies
- the codes and conventions of media language and how they are used to identify newspaper genres.

Codes and conventions of media language

In order to ensure the product's form and genre is recognisable, media producers follow certain codes and conventions in their use of media language.

Codes

- Codes are complex systems of signs that create meaning.
- Codes can be divided into two categories:
  - □ Technical codes
    - are the ways in which equipment is used to construct a media product so that it looks the way it does
    - help us identify how the newspaper front cover is constructed – what it looks like.
  - □ Symbolic codes help to communicate meaning, messages and values through the media language technical elements used in the construction of the front cover.

Conventions

- Conventions are the generally accepted way of doing something.
- There are general conventions in any medium such as the conventions of using a 'masthead' at the top of a print newspaper.
- Conventions can also be genre-specific.

Therefore, the use of technical codes and conventions are like rules that comprise what we would expect to see in a media product of a particular type:

- Producers follow these codes and conventions to make a product recognisable to the audience.
- Audiences look for codes and conventions to help recognise and select which media forms and genres they want to consume.

Newspaper genres

There are two genres or categories of UK national daily news brands:

- tabloid
- broadsheet.

Although their purpose is the same – to inform, influence and protect – their use of media language and technical elements helps to distinguish them as looking different and providing different kinds of news for their readers.

Knowledge check 33

How does *The Guardian*'s layout enable the content to appeal to their target audience?

Study tip

To identify the different uses *The Guardian* reader may be able to satisfy with the paper, look at a full edition. Read through the paper and select four stories that provide each of the four uses identified by Blumler, McQuail and Katz. Note down what the stories are and why they may satisfy that particular need in the audience.

Knowledge check 34

Which of Blumler, McQuail and Katz's uses is *The Guardian* reader most likely to satisfy from reading this newspaper?

Knowledge check 35

What are technical codes?

Tabloids

Tabloid newspapers were developed in the late nineteenth and early twentieth centuries:

- The *Daily Mail* (1896), although originally broadsheet in size, was recognised as the first tabloid-style newspaper in terms of its journalistic values.
- The *Daily Sketch* (1909) was the first tabloid-size newspaper.

By the early twentieth century, tabloid newspapers were established and became very popular with audiences so that by the 1950s, approximately 85 per cent of the British population were reading a tabloid paper daily.

Tabloid technical conventions:

- Compact in page size, smaller than a broadsheet
- Pages typically measure 11 x 17 inches (27.94 cm x 43.18 cm)
- Five columns across
- High ratio of images to text so that they are image-led
- Simple lexis
- Large headlines
- Personal and emotive mode of address.

The term 'tabloid journalism' refers to the type of stories selected and the way they are presented to the audience:

- Sensationalised and exaggerated versions of current events
- Emphasis on entertainment, with topics such as sensational crime stories, celebrity gossip and links with television features dominating their news
- Exclusive interviews with celebrities
- Focus on the personal impact of a story
- Emotional responses to the stories featured
- Use of binary oppositions to quickly position the audience to a specific viewpoint.

Tabloid news reporting can be described as soft news.

Broadsheets

Broadsheet newspapers were developed in the eighteenth century. The first examples were:

- *The Times* (1788)
- *The Observer* (1791).

Broadsheets developed in response to a government tax on the number of pages newspapers had. The bigger the size of the paper, the fewer pages were needed, so the owner paid less tax and the newspaper was cheaper to print. But few people could read to the standard required for these papers so they became associated with the well-educated.

Broadsheet technical conventions:

- Larger than a tabloid
- Pages typically measure 29.5 x 23.5 inches (74.93 cm x 59.69 cm)

Study tip

It is likely that at least one of your unseen sources will be a tabloid. To practise identifying the use of newspaper front page conventions, pick two tabloid front pages. Note the conventions used and see which ones both papers have in common.

Knowledge check 36

What does tabloid journalism mean?

- Six columns across, although some newer formats have five
- High ratio of text to image so they are text-led
- Formal lexis
- Headlines moderately sized
- Formal and authoritative mode of address.

The term 'quality' press refers to broadsheet journalism, the stories selected and the way they are presented to the audience:
- Serious reporting of national, global, political, social and business issues
- Emphasis on current affairs
- Focus on the social and cultural impact of a story nationally and globally
- Soft news and entertainment stories feature sports, arts and royal figures.

Broadsheet news reporting can be described as hard news.

These conventions suggest that tabloids and broadsheets are different in terms of:
- their size and the way they look
- the news values and quality of journalism applied.

Tabloidisation and changes to newspaper genre conventions

Tabloidisation refers to when:
- a newspaper is altered into a tabloid format size
- a newspaper takes on the journalistic values of a tabloid newspaper.

Economic pressures from reduced circulation sales and falling advertising revenue have led to broadsheets becoming tabloidised.

In order to cut printing costs and appeal to audiences who prefer the portability of tabloids for reading on public transport, a number of broadsheets have become tabloid in size:
- *The Times*
- *The Guardian*.

The following newspaper titles remain broadsheet in size:
- *The Daily Telegraph*
- the *Financial Times*.

This blurs the distinctions between tabloid and broadsheet newspaper conventions. This distinction is also complicated by the following issues:
- Some newspapers are broadsheet in size but their reporting borrows from the conventions of tabloid journalism, such as *The Daily Telegraph*.
- Some new tabloids, such as *The Guardian*, still provide serious news typical of a broadsheet.

This is known as **dual convergence**.

Study tip

To develop your understanding of the different genre conventions of tabloid and of broadsheet newspapers, and the blurring of these with tabloidisation, select one traditional tabloid, one new tabloid and one traditional broadsheet newspaper. Compare the conventions they use.

Knowledge check 37

What does quality press mean?

Dual convergence
Tabloids and broadsheets borrow conventions from each genre in the use of media language and values so they increasingly resemble one another.

Elements of media language used in front covers

The OCR specification stipulates the study of the following elements of media language conventions on newspaper front covers

Table 3.1 Media language conventions on front covers

Technical element	Conventional feature of print news	Description of the convention	Specific terms to look for in print news
Editing	Typography	Font sizes and styles affect how we read the words on the page and are used to identify which are most important: • **Serif** fonts are traditional in newspapers and are designed to help the reader digest large sections of content more easily. • **Sans serif** fonts have impact and can be read quickly.	Masthead Headline Sub-heading Skyline Byline Sell-line Cover line Jump line Caption Stand first Copy Bar code Pull quote Date line
	Layout	The placement and positioning of the content on the front page. Layout helps organise the content to identify what is most relevant on the page. Layout guides the reader's eye to the main points of coverage.	Columns Cropping Re-sizing Plugs or ears Anchors Lead story or splash Ratio of text to image Page furniture Gutter Page numbers
	Mode of address	The way in which the language in a newspaper addresses the reader. Mode of address can be emotive and conversational or formal and serious.	Lexis Hyperbole Rhetoric
Mise-en-scene	Locations	Which settings do we see in the images selected?	Interior v exterior National v global
	Lighting	The light source for the image selected.	Natural lighting High key Low key
Camera	Choice of camera shot	The distance of the camera from the main subject in the frame.	Mid shots Long shots Medium close-ups Main image
	Camera angle	The height of the camera in relation to the subject.	Eye level Low angle High angle

Serif A font with a stroke at the end of each letter traditionally used in broadsheets or literature to aid reading of large passages of text

Sans serif A font without a stroke, it appears modern and bold.

Anchors The use of an image next to text, either a caption or heading, anchors the image with meaning so that it positions the reader to think it means a particular thing.

The conventions of print news front pages are usually identified by their use of images, the way they have been edited and their layout on the page.

The layout or omission of conventions may be used differently to:
- identify the genre
- identify the individuality of each paper as a brand recognisably different to other newspapers.

How media language incorporates viewpoints and ideologies

Newspapers are believed to have a responsibility to inform and engage citizens so they are able to participate in democratic processes.

Journalistic values, and the way in which media language is used to incorporate viewpoints and ideologies, can be seen to have a fundamental impact on democratic societies, their values and attitudes.

Constructed media products

All media products are constructed:
- They are made by a producer.
- They have a specific intention to create a certain meaning.
- The producer aims for the audience to interpret and accept the meaning unquestioningly.
- Producers use different elements/conventions of media language to construct these meanings.

Producers of different news brands may use different elements of media language to communicate different ideas and viewpoints depending on the newspaper's journalistic values and political bias.

Constructed media representations can ensure that the meanings producers 'encode' in their products can be read and understood quickly. This means that conventions of media language are used as signs to communicate:
- the form and genre of the media product
- the political values and ideologies of the owner.

Semiotics

Semiotics is the study of making meaning. It looks at how 'signs' function as codes in our everyday lives and cultural products to communicate messages and values about our world and tell us or help us understand how we should live, behave and think within our society.

Every sign, for example a photo of a politician, is made up of two elements:

1 **Signifier** – another word for the sign itself; the image, word, etc.
2 **Signified** – this refers to the meaning associated with the sign/signifier. There are two levels of meaning that can be taken from the signified:
   - denotation – the actual meaning of the sign
   - connotation – additional meanings that attach to the sign and are socially and culturally developed and accepted.

For example:

Sign/signifier	A red rose
Denotation	A plant with thorny stems that has flowers
Connotation	A symbol of love and romance

Therefore, semiotics help identify that different signs have different meanings, often more than one. Importantly, these meanings might not be the real or original meaning of the sign but a meaning that has been attached to the sign over time in order to communicate specific ideas or values.

The use of connotations can also be referred to as myths. They are used to reinforce ideology and maintain **hegemony**.

The annotated front page in Figure 3.1, and the corresponding Table 3.2, illustrate how some of the technical conventions of media language used on the front cover are used to communicate meaning. Table 3.2 also shows what the messages and values from these technical signs and codes could be as well as how they may reinforce hegemony.

Figure 3.1 A *Daily Express* front page

Table 3.2 Analysis of technical conventions used and connotations found on the *Daily Express* cover (Figure 3.1)

Technical Convention (sign)	Description	Connotation (associated meaning/s)
Masthead	The title of the newspaper displayed on the front page.	The masthead connotes the *Daily Express* brings news quickly to readers every day; making it valuable, important and reliable.
Headline	The title given to the story; usually a brief, catchy summary of the main ideas and /or themes of the news item that encourages the reader to read the article.	The headline is a simple, straightforward statement; the word 'we're' connoting the paper and readers are unified. Its placement on top of the main image anchors the two and connotes the national significance of the result for the UK.

Hegemony The predominance of one social group over another to legitimise social norms. The idea of ideological hegemony is proposed in the work of Gramsci, a neo-Marxist, who looked at the way in which ideology was used to reinforce the social power, through economic and political systems, of the elite ruling class over the subject or working classes.

Knowledge check 38

What is the difference between denotation and connotation?

Knowledge check 39

List three media language conventions that are associated with typography.

Technical Convention (sign)	Description	Connotation (associated meaning/s)
Sub-heading	Usually shorter than the main headline and provide additional information about the story that will also appeal to the reader.	Two sub-headings quickly summarise the story, connoting the *Daily Express* is reliable and succinct with news.
Page furniture	Everything on the front page that is not a picture or text relating to news stories.	The use of page furniture helps to make the *Daily Express* front cover seem appealing to the reader with lots of content for them to engage with.
Splash	A large image and/or headline 'splashed' taking up the majority of the front page.	The text and images are splashed across over half of the cover, connoting the story's importance.
Main image	The dominant picture on the page filling up most of the front cover.	The Union Jack takes up half the page connoting nationalistic values of the paper and their views on the EU are important to the paper and their readers.
Copy	Also known as body text, this is the actual writing that makes up the article.	There is little copy on the front page, the story comprises just three columns of copy. This connotes that the *Daily Express* offers its readers brief summaries of news without going into much detail, conventional of a tabloid newspaper.
Lead story	The main story on the front page. It may be the only story or the one that takes up the most space. The lead story can also be called a splash.	Leaving the European Union, and its size on the page, connotes that this is the most important news of the day politically, culturally and socially.
Stand first	The first paragraph of a news story that summarises the whole story. It is usually bold and in a slightly larger font, so it stands out.	The stand first summarises the paper's point of view in relation to the main story and positions the audience to read the rest of the story from the same perspective, so that they accept the connotations and viewpoints offered by the paper.
Byline	The name of the article's author.	Macer Hall, the paper's politics editor, a white, middle class, British man, has written the article. This is authoritative and can be seen to be reinforcing the dominant voice in society of white, middle class, British men.
Plug	Small boxes or shapes, sometimes known as ears, which refer to other stories inside the newspaper.	The plug for the free Walker's sharing bag of crisps connotes that the paper is also one that shares things with its readers, thus valuing them.
Dateline	The date and year of the newspaper edition.	This connotes the stories are recent and therefore up to date and relevant.
Layout	How the paper is divided up into visual sections - from top to bottom and left to right. Masthead appears at the top with the main image and lead story taking up most of the front cover. Placement of the headline and captions on and underneath the image help to anchor meaning Remaining content is organised into column widths.	The content is divided in to 3 sections. The top section identifies the paper's brand, the middle part covers the headline and main image for the lead story. The bottom section is the smallest though it covers the actual news story. This layout anchors the brand with the main story and connotes that the *Daily Express* and lead story have impact and are bold and important.
Close up of power elite	Shot types such as close ups are used in images to help show detail and emotions when used to illustrate people within the corresponding news story.	Close ups of Cameron looking emotional and Johnson relieved may connote that the paper's values on Brexit are shared by Johnson and not Cameron.
Colour	Newspapers are typically black and white but use colour to help brand the news masthead and logo and to make the paper look more appealing to their reader.	Colour contrasts are eye catching. They connote the paper is interesting and engaging to appeal to the reader. The predominance of the red and white (very little blue shown) connotes the paper as nationalistic as red and white are the colours of the St George's flag.

Technical Convention (sign)	Description	Connotation (associated meaning/s)
Font	This is the style of the typeface (text) chosen by the newspaper. It can be serif (with a cursive at the end of each letter) or sans serif (without the cursive), emboldened, italicised, underlined and of a different font size.	Serif font is used for the title, headlines, caption and copy. It is a traditional font connoting the *Daily Express* is a traditional newspaper with traditional values. The sans serif font used on the strapline, plug, puff, skyline, sub-heading and caption, is modern and bold, connoting that the *Daily Express* is bold and reflects contemporary British values.
Logo	An image or graphic that visually represents the values of a news brand.	The logo of a knight in armour with the St George's cross on a shield refers to the Fourth Estate, connoting the paper's 'crusade for the truth' for its readers. It also connotes the *Daily Express'* nationalistic values.
Puff	A shape, often a circle or star, which is edited onto the front cover to stand out in contrast to the rest of the front page	The insertion of the price into a puff in the middle of the front page connotes that the newspaper is good value as the audience can access a range of news content at very little cost.
Other important technical conventions found on print news front covers but not in Figure 3.1:		
Pull quote	A quote from within the article, usually by the person in the image, is 'pulled' out and emphasised.	
Off lead	An article connected to the lead story but takes a different viewpoint or discusses a different topic related to the lead story	

To familiarise yourself with print newspaper front pages, select three or four and annotate each one to identify the placement of the media language conventions. Compare the layouts to see how the elements are organised on each front page.

What can the lead story and main image also be called if they take up the majority of the front page layout?

An exam question may ask you to show your understanding of how media language conventions, including genre, communicate meaning in an unseen front page. To practise, identify four conventions from a newspaper front page. Note down the meanings each one connotes. Write a paragraph for each example, first describing the conventions, then explaining the meaning conveyed.

Media language and set products – the *Daily Mail*

Newspaper genres

■ The *Daily Mail* is considered to be the first tabloid newspaper in the UK in terms of its journalism.

■ It was originally broadsheet in size until 1971 when it adopted the compact tabloid size.

■ The paper is considered to be a **mid-market tabloid**. It uses the generic conventions of layout and typography like most tabloids but also has the following genre conventions:

   □ It uses a combination of hard news and soft news stories.

   □ Hard news stories contain bias towards family values and British culture.

   □ It relies on a combination of images and text.

   □ Reporting can focus on the impact of the story on a family or its national impact.

   □ News features are sensationalised to attract audiences.

   □ Its mode of address and written style are less conversational and emotive than other tabloids.

   □ It uses binary oppositions to attract and position audiences.

   □ It influences and defends public opinion on social and political issues.

Elements of media language used in newspaper front covers

The annotated image in Figure 3.2 illustrates the use of technical elements and media language on the front page of the *Daily Mail*.

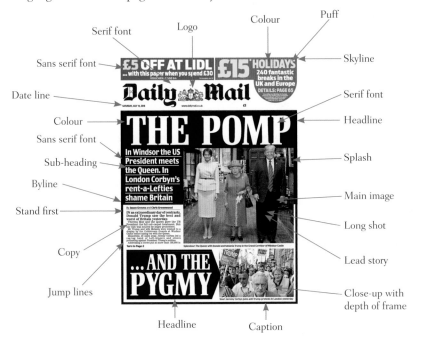

Figure 3.2 A *Daily Mail* front page

Table 3.3 also illustrates how the conventions of mid-market tabloids can be seen on this front cover of the *Daily Mail*.

Table 3.3 Conventions of mid-market tabloids seen on *Daily Mail* cover

Convention of mid-market tabloid	Example from the *Daily Mail* front cover
Uses a combination of hard news and soft news stories	The lead story is a hard news story in that it focuses on politics with Trump's visit and Jeremy Corbyn. The way it reports the story is soft as it uses emotive language and rhetoric.
Hard news stories contain bias towards family values and British culture	The image of Trump with the Queen to report a political event infers that the Queen, as the head of the royal family, is the bastion of British culture.
Relies on a combination of images and text but doesn't replace the text with images	There is very little copy but the layout of text and images creates a balance between the two. The headlines make the front cover very easy to read.
Reporting of stories can focus on the impact of the issue on the family or its national impact	Trump meeting the Queen reflects the national impact of his visit. The use of the word 'sour' in the caption suggests a negative national impact.
News features are sensationalised to attract audiences	The headline 'The pomp and the pygmy' sensationalises the story.

Mid-market tabloid A newspaper that offers a mix of both soft and hard news content in its coverage of news to appeal to its target audience.

Context

Cultural context: The Lidl advert and holiday offers advertised on the skyline are influenced by cultural trends in relation to shopping and tourism.

Knowledge check 41

What sub-genre of tabloid newspaper can the *Daily Mail* be defined as?

Academic ideas

Neale 3: For more on applying this theory to media language in the *Daily Mail*, see the grid on page 111.

Levi-Strauss 2: For more on applying this theory to media language in the *Daily Mail*, see the grid on page 111.

Convention of mid-market tabloid	Example from the *Daily Mail* front cover
Mode of address and written style is less conversational and emotive than tabloids	The use of language for the headline and the underlining of the sub-heading is emotive but informative.
Uses binary oppositions to attract and position audiences	The layout of the page and the headline 'The pomp and the pygmy' creates contrasts between Trump and Corbyn as good and bad respectively and positions them politically.
Influences and defends public opinion on social and political issues	The use of the words 'rent-a-leftie' and 'shame' in the sub-heading help to position the audience ideologically.

How media language incorporates viewpoints and ideologies

The use of technical conventions in the *Daily Mail* enables the editor to signify meaning and communicate the paper's conservative viewpoints and ideologies.

Table 3.4 identifies how some of the media language conventions used on the front page of the *Daily Mail* in Figure 3.2 can connote meaning:

Table 3.4 *Daily Mail* language conventions and their connotations

Technical convention (sign)	Connotation (associated meaning/s)
Masthead	The term 'mail' is associated with letters and news, so the size of the masthead and the meaning of the title connotes that the newspaper is a provider of the reader's daily news.
Byline	The article is written by two men, connoting a patriarchal point of view in the covering of the story. This is reinforced by the article, which focuses largely on Trump and Corbyn rather than the Queen and Trump's wife. This can be seen to be conveying the dominant view of many white, male, middle-class men.
Serif font	The serif font is used for the majority of the newspaper front cover, connoting traditional values.

Activity

1 Complete an analysis of the media language conventions used on the *Daily Mail* front cover in Figure 3.2.
2 For each media language convention not discussed in Table 3.4, consider the connotation offered and note your ideas down in a table or similar.
3 Use the examples in Table 3.4, and the analysis of connotations on the *Daily Express* front cover in Table 3.2, as a guide.

Media language and set products – *The Guardian*

Newspaper genres

- *The Guardian* historically was a broadsheet newspaper associated with serious journalism and hard news coverage requiring a well-educated reader.
- The paper adopted the compact tabloid size on 15 January 2018.

Study tip

To practise identifying the conventions of mid-market tabloids, select three *Daily Mail* front pages. Note down which conventions of mid-market tabloids are used across all three covers. Analyse the effect of each one.

Context

Cultural context: The selection of images and headlines reinforces the newspaper's ideological values regarding British cultural traditions.

Knowledge check 42

What combination of elements does the *Daily Mail* as a mid-market tabloid use in its news selection and reporting?

Academic ideas

Neale 2: For more on applying this theory to media language in the *Daily Mail*, see the grid on page 110.

- The newspaper made changes to the following conventions in the redesign to the new tabloid format:
  - ☐ masthead
  - ☐ colour palette
  - ☐ font
  - ☐ layout.
- The paper is still considered to offer quality journalism despite its change in size conventions although it does contain some soft news content, such as sports, food and lifestyle.

Elements of media language used in front covers

Activity

1 Trace *The Guardian* front page in Figure 3.3.
2 Label the image to match the technical conventions listed in Table 3.5. Refer to Figures 3.1 and 3.2 to help you.

Figure 3.3 A front page from *The Guardian*

How media language incorporates viewpoints and ideologies

The use of technical conventions in *The Guardian* enables the editor to communicate the paper's liberal viewpoints and values.

Table 3.5 identifies how some of the media language conventions used on the front page of *The Guardian* in Figure 3.3 can connote meaning.

Table 3.5 *The Guardian* language conventions and their connotations

Technical convention (sign)	Connotation (associated meaning/s)
Masthead	The term 'guardian' refers to someone who protects and defends, connoting the role of the press as the Fourth Estate. The simplicity of the masthead against the blue background connotes that the paper provides clear, serious journalism.
Splash/Lead story	The splash and lead story covers Trump's visit to the UK and refers to reported criticisms he made of May. The use of politics on the front page connotes that the paper is concerned with serious, hard news.
Main image	The long shot at a low angle positions a domineering-looking Trump in the centre of the image. Trump's hand on May's elbow looks as if he is controlling her and the situation, contrasting Trump's political power with May's lack of power. It also connotes traditional patriarchal views ascribed to Trump.
Headline	The headline stresses the informality and recklessness of Trump's comments. It also refers to Trump's belief that all news criticising him is fake news and connotes that he can't be taken seriously as a politician. It also connotes that *The Guardian*, in contrast, takes his comments seriously and is satirising him, reinforcing its liberal news values.
Byline	Reference to the journalists connotes that *The Guardian* is open-minded and provides equal opportunities to its news reporters so different voices can be heard.
Caption	This anchors meaning to the image by providing a description of what is happening in the photo. The reference to Chequers and the press conference connotes that the visit is following tradition and is possibly put on for PR.
Serif font	The use of serif font connotes traditional broadsheet journalism and indicates that whilst *The Guardian* is now a tabloid, it still provides the same quality journalism.
Edition dots	The edition dots at the foot of the page tell the reader that this is the third edition and is therefore very recent news, connoting the reliability of *The Guardian* as a brand.
Ear	The ear promotes the paper's supplements, connoting that the newspaper does not just contain serious hard news but also serves the lifestyle interests of its audience.
Layout	The layout of the page is divided into two main sections with a smaller section to the right. The largest element of the page is the lead story, which connotes that the reporting of news is the most important element for *The Guardian*. The layout is balanced and straightforward, connoting that the journalism is too.

Study tip

To prepare for an exam question assessing your understanding of the way media language communicates meaning in *The Guardian*, select a front page and using Table 3.5 as a guide, complete your own analysis of how the conventions create meaning on the front cover.

Academic ideas

Lévi-Strauss 2: For more on applying this theory to media language in *The Guardian*, see the grid on page 113.

Context

Cultural context: The use of language in the headlines reflect the cultural capital of *The Guardian* reader.

Academic ideas

Baudrillard 1: For more on applying this theory to media language in *The Guardian*, see the grid on page 113.

Neale 3: For more on applying this theory to media language in *The Guardian*, see the grid on page 113.

Context

Cultural context: *The Guardian's* content is influenced by the cultural trends, tastes and behaviour of their readers.

Print news: representation

Representation is the act of presenting an event, individual, social group or object in a certain way or from a particular point of view. It is *re-presenting*.

The representation of anything will always depend on the point of view and intention of the producer and will reflect their ideas and values as a result.

The OCR specification identifies that in relation to print news and representation, learners should study:

- the impact of industry contexts (for example, ownership) on the choices news producers make about how to represent events, issues, individuals and social groups
- the way events, issues, individuals and social groups are represented through processes of selection and combination, including a consideration of the choices news media make
- the positive and negative use of stereotypes by news media and how representations may invoke discourses and ideologies, and position audiences
- the ways in which representations constructed by news media make claims about realism.

What are social groups?

Social groupings share similar biological characteristics, lifestyle preferences, choices or values. They are a way in which people can be grouped by demographic or psychometric values.

For example:

- age
- gender
- class and social status
- ethnicity
- sexuality
- regional identity
- ability
- appearance, such as hair colour
- lifestyle interests
- political values
- profession
- regional location.

Within our society, there is a **dominant group** that holds positions of power within social institutions or owns the production of cultural products such as the news. Academic theorists such as van Zoonen, hooks, Hall, Butler and Gilroy would suggest that in general, members of this group have the following characteristics:

- middle-aged
- male
- middle class
- white
- capitalist
- Christian
- heterosexual
- able-bodied
- western
- university educated.

Using the ideas of hegemony and Althusser's concept of the **Ideological State Apparatus** (ISA), it could be argued that the dominant social group, by having access to power and means of communication, has control and influence over the way in which other social groups are seen and understood. Their social experience, beliefs and values are known as dominant ideology and it is from this perspective that all social groups will be influenced to experience the world around us.

Dominant group A sociological term used to refer to a social group that controls the value systems in any given society. They may not be the largest social group in terms of size but the group is made up of the social identities that hold social, political and economic power, privileges and social status. It is generally considered that the dominant social groups within our society - using the key markers of class, gender, age and ethnicity - are white, middle aged, middle class men as this group dominate our social, economic and political value systems.

Ideological State Apparatus This is a concept developed by the French cultural Marxist, Althusser. It refers to the social structures that are owned and used by the dominant group to reinforce and communicate dominant ideology so that they can retain social, political and economic power. He argues these structures work together to indoctrinate the subordinate groups into the belief systems and production practices of the ruling dominant class to further maintain their dominant social position and keep the subordinate groups subordinate.

Any individual that doesn't fit the characteristics of this dominant social group would be classed as 'other' or from a subordinate social group. But, these ideas are not always straightforward as an individual can be seen to fit into both dominant and subordinate groups simultaneously. For example a white British, working class woman would fall into the dominant ethnic group but also be in the subordinate class and gender group.

Importantly, the concept of dominant and subordinate groups doesn't mean that individuals with social identities that can be seen to fall within subordinate or minority groups are less important than those in the dominant group. Rather, it identifies - from a sociological viewpoint - that these subordinate groups have ideologically, less economic and political power and social status within society, than the dominant group. Therefore, these groups, as they are seen to be the binary opposition to the dominant identities and value system, are subject to face social discrimination, which can be communicated in media products through the representations of different social groups.

If we accept the idea of hegemony and the role of the ISA in communicating dominant ideology, this suggests that the representation of individuals and social groups will always involve bias towards the dominant group. This is for a number of reasons:

- The dominant group tends to include those who construct the representations in news content.
- The representation of social groups, positively or negatively, helps to maintain the social position of the dominant group.

The impact of industry contexts and choices news producers make about representation

Ownership, economic factors, news values, political bias and regulation all influence the choices made by editors when considering how they represent events, issues, individuals and social groups.

Ownership

The news industry in the UK is run by global or multinational cross-media converged companies or individual media barons. The owners are usually from the dominant social group in that they tend to be white, male and middle class.

Journalism is also an occupation whereby the dominant social group is in the majority and so the reporting of news can be influenced by its members' own social experience.

Knowledge check 43

Who make up the dominant group in our society?

Study Tip

To develop your understanding, and critical ideas around dominant and subordinate groups, use Levi-Strauss idea of binary oppositions to identify who you think are the dominant and subordinate identities within our society. List as many different binary pairs (opposites) as you can that you think could be relevant to our social identities, you could go as far to include education or occupations. For each one, identity the dominant and subordinate in the pair.

Economic factors

Newspapers are commodities that are made to be sold. The news industry functions by the socio-economic values of capitalism in that, while the purpose of the news is to inform, it is also to make profit for the owner. Newspapers must appeal to their audiences if they are to sell.

Tabloids rely on sensationalised, personal and emotive journalism with a predominance of news stories featuring celebrities or entertainment. This suggests that the genre of a newspaper, as a result of media language conventions and economic pressures, will affect the choices made by the editor in their representation of the news.

News values and political bias of the owner and editor

News values allow the editor, and journalists, to make very specific choices on how to represent events, issues, individuals and social groups. These will:

- reflect the genre of the paper
- use content that will reflect and appeal to their audience
- reinforce the political agenda of the newspaper to influence public thinking.

The majority of the British press are right wing and support the Conservative Party. This suggests, given their identification with the dominant group, that their right-wing, conservative values will be reflected in the majority of news representations in the UK.

Regulation

The self-regulatory approach for news reporting, of publish then punish, suggests that regulation has a limited impact on the choices made by editors and journalists on how they represent individuals and social groups.

Representation is about perspectives and viewpoints as opposed to accuracy of facts, suggesting that while representations may be distasteful, editors are allowed to print them if the factual information is accurate. This questions how effective regulation is if a negative representation of an individual or social group can only be upheld as a breach if the content is inaccurate.

Representation of different events and people is therefore complicated by the idea of a free press and the right to freedom of speech within a democracy.

How events, issues, individuals and social groups are represented through processes of selection and combination

Representation occurs as a result of:

- the processes of selecting news through gatekeeping
- the way different news features are selected and combined to either positively or negatively reinforce representations of individuals and/or social groups.

Processes of selection

Gatekeeping refers to the decision-making involved in selecting certain news stories and discarding others. These choices will usually be dependent on how the issues, events, individuals and social groups selected:

- will appeal to the target audience
- can be shaped to reflect a political agenda or viewpoints.

Knowledge check 44

How do economic factors influence the choices made by editors in the representations they select?

Study tip

To develop your understanding of the way events, issues, individuals and social groups are represented through processes of selection and combination, select two newspaper front pages. Identify for each the number of stories, the issues covered and the social groups represented or absent. How similar are the two front pages in their representation?

, is for this reason that different newspapers may report different daily news events in their papers.

It also explains why representations of the same event, issues, individuals or social groups in newspapers may be very different from paper to paper as each news brand has different audiences as well as ideological and political values.

The process of selection also involves the act of de-selection. When analysing a newspaper front cover it is important to ask not only which social identities and groups are represented, but who is left out and why this might be. Absence says as much about viewpoints as presence.

Processes of combination

Tabloid and broadsheet news genres are set apart by different conventions in the layout, selection and presentation of news. Therefore they may combine representations of events, issues, individuals or social groups differently.

Tabloid newspapers' front pages:

- may focus on a range of news stories that are represented in a similar way
- will usually reinforce common representations of the dominant group through celebrity or popular culture
- tend to repeat representations of individuals, groups or events from edition to edition so that the combination of stories and people represented becomes naturalised, expected and accepted.

Broadsheet newspapers' front pages:

- may focus on a range of news stories that feature different issues, events or social groups
- may question common representations of the dominant group to encourage the reader to question common stereotypes
- through the combination of content may aim to provide a range of perspectives in the representation of different issues, events, individuals and social groups.

Stereotypes, discourses, ideologies and audience positioning

This topic requires an understanding of the way in which:

- representations are constructed through the use of stereotypes in newspapers
- the use of positive and negative stereotyping communicates ideology to influence readers.

Stereotypes

A stereotype is a characterisation of an individual or social group that has a certain characteristic or feature.

Stereotypes can be seen to work as symbolic codes or signs. Stereotypes attach specific values or ideas to that group of people, which are generalised and largely inaccurate. But they become accepted in wider society due to the frequency with which they are used.

Stereotypes can be positive or negative, depending on:
- the individual, and the social group of the person who constructs the representation
- the social group that is being represented.

As touched up when discussing media language and the use of signs, Barthes would argue that these values attached to these social stereotypes are not real but 'myths' and serve to reinforce the ideology of the dominant group. Stereotypes work to support and reinforce the dominant groups in our society, so representations of white, middle-class, middle-aged, educated men are likely to be positive. In contrast, stereotypes of a minority or subordinate group tend to be negative and work to undervalue members of that group.

Common stereotypes include the following:

- Teenagers are rebellious and up to no good.
- Blonde women are unintelligent.
- Mothers are housewives and should complete all domestic duties in the house.
- Business men are intelligent white men.

Stereotypes are created by and widely used in the media industry for a number of reasons:

- They are quickly understood by audiences, whether they agree or disagree with the stereotype presented.
- They become shortcuts for introducing characters, groups of people or ideas about groups of people.

In using stereotypes, editors can represent social groups or events in a way that reinforces prejudice and generalised ideas about people within our society. Or they can be used to question these prejudices.

When thinking about the representation of social groups, and the related use of stereotypes, Daniel Chandler (*Media Representations* 2001) suggests the key markers of social identity are Class, Age, Gender and Ethnicity. He refers to these as the 'Cage of Identity', providing mnemonic with which to consider media representations of social groups and identities. When analysing representation in the news and in particular the use of stereotypes through textual analysis, it is useful to adopt Chandler's 'cage of identity' idea and develop the mnemonic to CAGED to look at the way different social groups are represented.

C	Class	E	Ethnicity
A	Age	D	Disability
G	Gender		

This mnemonic doesn't include sexuality, religion, occupation, education or regional identity, or other indicators of our social identities, which are all equally important social groups when analysing representation in newspapers. However, CAGED provides a starting point from which to analyse the representation of social stereotypes and identify:

- which are positive
- which are negative
- what messages are communicated as a result.

It is important to note that this approach explores ideologies of exclusion in relation to the representation of different social groups based upon the idea of there being a dominant group and in response to the concept of binary oppositions. This is just

Study tip

To develop your understanding of the representation of social groups, select two unseen front pages. List the different social groups referred to, explicitly or implicitly, using CAGED and include sexuality, religion, occupation, education level and regional identity. Note down how similar the front covers are in the social groups they represent.

one way to analyse representation and it is just a starting point. By identifying these social stereotypes and the messages and values they could be seen to communicate in relation to the dominant and subordinate groups, it allows us to identify and question discrimination, the 'myth' of representation and hegemony. Other approaches could consider ideologies of individualism and consumerism communicated in newspaper representations for example.

Table 4.1 summarises some of the general stereotypes for the CAGED social groups.

Table 4.1 Common stereotypes found in news media

Social group	Common stereotypes reflected in news media	Purpose of negative stereotype
Class	• The middle classes are the dominant group so are commonly represented in a positive way. • The working classes are stereotypically represented as uneducated, on benefits, consumers of popular culture, criminals, and so on.	To position the working classes as subordinate to the middle classes
Age	• Adults are the dominant group so are commonly represented in a positive way. • Youth are stereotypically represented as violent, rebellious and a threat to social order. • The elderly are stereotypically represented as dependent and weak. • Children are stereotypically represented as innocent and vulnerable.	To position youth, the elderly and children as subordinate to adults
Gender	• Men are the dominant group so are commonly represented in a positive way, especially if middle-class male adults, as strong, rational and in control. • Women are stereotypically represented as domesticated, emotional, nurturing and dependent.	To position women as subordinate to men
Ethnicity	• White British culture is the dominant culture so is represented positively. • Ethnic minorities are stereotypically represented as unadaptable, immigrants and, at times, criminals.	To position ethnic minority cultures as subordinate to the dominant white British culture
Disability	• Able-bodied is the dominant group so is represented positively. • The disabled are represented as dependent, vulnerable and immobile.	To position the disabled as subordinate to the dominant able-bodied group

Knowledge check 45

What are stereotypes? Why are they used in print newspapers?

What is dominant ideology?

Ideology is a system or structure of beliefs, values and ideas about the way in which we should live, behave and think in any given society.

Each society has a dominant group that establishes:

■ what our dominant values are
■ what the accepted (conventional) way of living should be.

What ideologies are invoked and how are audiences positioned?

Ideology refers to the beliefs and values that help to shape or structure a society. The use of positive and negative stereotypes in newspapers helps to communicate these beliefs and values. Representations are constructed to position social groups as inferior to the dominant group and attach a set of values to the different identities within that social group to influence behaviour and attitudes.

Negative representations of minority groups are contrasted with positive representations of dominant groups to reinforce the 'social status quo': the position of power that each group holds in society. So the dominant group always remains socially dominant and subordinate groups remain socially inferior.

The representations and stereotypes we see in the media, along with the messages and values associated with these stereotypes, can arguably therefore always work to keep the current dominant group in power, socially, politically, culturally and economically.

How representations constructed by news media make claims about realism

Representations found in the news are constructed, through a range of media language conventions, to present news stories as real.

Realism is the 'presentation' of something as if it were real and what we would expect to see in real life. For media forms that rely on real events, such as newspapers, the concept of realism is especially difficult to grasp. Although newspapers may report events that are happening or have happened in real life, the process of gatekeeping means the selection and manipulation of the information presents the newspaper's version of the 'real event' from a particular point of view that supports the editor's idea of how we should understand that event.

What is constructed realism?

Constructed realism is the idea that all media products and the content they portray – issues, events, individuals and social groups – are made or built using the technical codes of media language.

Therefore, constructed realism is the way in which a media product uses the technical elements of media language to create a product that looks real but is:
- a version of reality rather than the real thing
- constructed through a series of choices made by the editor and/or journalist.

Claims about realism

Given the intention of realism to pass as reality or as the real version of events, audiences tend to accept it as real. But, if we view realism as a selective process of reporting from a particular point of view using media language in a certain way, then we can see that realism is not real. It is a way of reinforcing particular viewpoints about news stories and making them appear real - what we referred to earlier as 'myths'.

Knowledge check 46

What is dominant ideology?

The constant repetition of similar representations and stereotypes, often across a range of mass media forms, helps these representations to become natural. This means audiences see them so frequently the representations become accepted as real. The ideology that is embedded in these representations is then also accepted.

Marxist theory refers to this as false consciousness and is the way in which the dominant groups in our society, and the owners of media industries, are able to hold onto their power without question.

Knowledge check 47

What is constructed realism?

Newspapers, through the use of representations and stereotypes, are therefore an important tool to help shape our society, the balance of power that different social groups have, and the way we think about individuals and their social identities through the process of constructed realism.

Representation and the set products – the *Daily Mail*

The impact of industry contexts and choices news producers make about representation

Jonathan Harmsworth, the *Daily Mail's* proprietor and main shareholder of the parent company DMG, can be seen to be part of the dominant social group. This experience can arguably inform the choices he makes about the news agenda of his paper.

The *Daily Mail's* former editor Paul Dacre and new editor Geordie Greig are also middle-class, middle-aged white men. The editorial values of the *Daily Mail* could therefore further reinforce the owner's values and impact on the choices made in the way events, issues and social groups are represented.

Economic issues around the genre, news values and political bias of the *Daily Mail* can be seen to be embedded in the choices made about how they represent events, issues, individuals and groups.

As a mid-market tabloid newspaper, the *Daily Mail* has a focus on reporting national current affairs alongside news stories featuring celebrities or entertainment. The representations of these events and social groups rely on:

- sensationalised, personal and emotive journalism
- prioritising positive representations of:
  - □ individuals in the dominant social group
  - □ traditional family values
  - □ British culture/nationalism
  - □ right-wing political ideology
  - □ the Conservative Party.
- the possible prioritising of potentially negative representations of minority groups, not just through the reporting of these groups but also by their absence.

Context

Social context: Social institutions such as family and education are represented in the *Daily Mail* from a traditional perspective to reinforce conservative values.

Knowledge check 48

Which social group are the *Daily Mail's* owner and editor part of? How will this affect the representations constructed in the paper?

Representation on the front page of the Daily Mail

In order to apply the OCR specification prompts, contexts and academic ideas to representation in the *Daily Mail*, it is useful to do so through the analysis of the front page given in Figure 3.2 on page 51.

How events, issues, individuals and social groups are represented through processes of selection and combination

Table 4.2 Methods of representation and their connotations

Representation on the front page	Selection/Combination of content	Connotations of this representation
Events	Two separate but connected events are represented: 1 Trump meeting the Queen 2 the anti-Trump demonstration. The headlines and images combine the two events so that their representation reinforces the paper's agenda.	Combining the two events creates meaning through the contrasts offered. A binary opposition is constructed to reinforce the *Mail*'s right-wing agenda, for which Trump could represent the dominant ideological view.
Issues	The issues represented are: 1 Trump's controversial visit to the UK 2 left-wing politics and the right to protest. Other issues it also infers but doesn't specifically address are the royal family, gender relations, capitalism and nationalism.	The selection of Trump's visit reinforces the *Mail*'s bias to the right and support of British culture, traditions and nationalism. The respectful representation of his visit reinforces the dominant group as good. The protest against Trump's visit is represented as a direct threat to right-wing politics. The sub-heading refers to the protest as a 'rent-a-leftie' mob, that 'shames' Britain, connoting that left-wing politics is not in the nation's interests.
Social groups	The predominant social group is white. While there is an equal distinction between men and women, there is no reference to the First Lady in the splash. The wide shot of the protest lacks cultural diversity and is made up mostly of men.	The selection of these images and use of language can be seen to be reinforcing white men as the dominant group within our society. The absence of minority groups in terms of the image or the references chosen can be seen to reinforce their lack of social power and that this is held by the dominant group.
Individuals	Trump, the Queen and Corbyn are represented as the three key individuals on this front cover. This selection is identified through the combined use of headlines, sub-heading and photos.	This representation combines a number of ideological values: • the relationship between the UK and USA, two capitalist countries with similar cultural values • the importance of British culture and the Queen • the threat of left-wing politics to right-wing agendas. Combining these images, headlines and sub-headings, the *Daily Mail* communicates a nationalistic political agenda with binary oppositions between good and bad.

Academic ideas

Hall 1: For more on applying this theory to representation in the *Daily Mail*, see the grid on page 110.

Academic ideas

hooks 1: For more on applying this theory to representation in the *Daily Mail*, see the grid on page 111.

Study tip

You may be asked to analyse representations on the front page of the *Daily Mail*. Using a table similar to Table 4.2, record your analysis of another front page. You can use each row of the table as paragraph content to help you write a practice essay.

Stereotypes, discourses, ideologies and audience positioning

In analysing the same front page using the CAGED approach to identifying the representation of social groups, we can see how representation in the *Daily Mail* constructs stereotypes to communicate ideology and position audiences.

Table 4.3 Positive and negative stereotypes according to CAGED group

CAGED element	Positive stereotypes	Negative stereotypes
Class	The middle classes are represented as the dominant class by the splash and images.	The term 'mob' is used in reference to the working class. This representation, together with the choice of shot of the protest, can be seen to stereotype them as unruly, out of control and a threat to middle-class values.
Age	Adults are represented as the dominant group, suggesting adults have social power and are in control of the national, economic and political issues within our society. The elderly, represented by the Queen, are shown in a positive way and in the centre of important issues and events.	Youth and children, by their absence, can be seen to be represented as unimportant in social issues and events, reinforcing dominant stereotypes about youth as irresponsible.
Gender	Whilst there is an even split in the genders portrayed, a bias can be seen towards stereotypical representations of men, supporting the gender balance in the ownership and editorial posts of the *Mail*. Trump's position in the foreground of the photo and Corbyn at the front of the protest can be seen to support stereotypical ideas that men are leaders. All four individuals are wearing stereotypically gendered clothes to reinforce traditional ideas about masculinity and femininity.	The Queen and First Lady are positioned slightly behind Trump, which can be seen to indicate their social position as inferior in relation to men, regardless of the social power they hold.
Ethnicity	British culture is stereotyped positively through representation of the Queen and reference in the headline to pomp, which refers to tradition and ceremony, reinforcing that idea that dominant British culture and associated traditions are important and the 'best' of the UK.	Minority cultures, through their absence, can be seen to be stereotypically represented as inferior to the dominant British culture. The use of the word 'pygmy' in the headline negatively stereotypes minority cultures as subordinate to British culture. The cropping of the image of Corbyn to look small, the anchoring of the word 'pygmy' in the headline next to him and the words 'shames Britain' stereotypes minority cultures negatively as a threat to British values.

Academic ideas

Van Zoonen 2: For more on applying this theory to representation in the *Daily Mail*, see the grid on page 111.

Context

Cultural context: The *Daily Mail* constructs and prioritises a traditional view of British culture as the dominant representation.

Social context: The *Daily Mail* is a product of capitalist culture and through the repetition of common stereotypes, positive and negative, it helps to reinforce the thinking of the dominant group.

CAGED element	Positive stereotypes	Negative stereotypes
Disability	The predominance of the visibly able-bodied is evidenced in the selection of individuals used on the front cover.	Individuals with disabilities, by their absence, can be seen to be stereotypically represented as inferior to those who are able-bodied.

How representations constructed by news media make claims about realism

The *Daily Mail* constructs representations, through the use of positive and negative stereotypes, to make claims about what is real. A reading of the key messages communicated by this front cover suggests that:

- British culture and values are important
- Donald Trump, as the US president, stands for and upholds the values of right-wing, Conservative, capitalist values and is a respectful friend to the UK
- British culture and values are under threat from left-wing groups
- Jeremy Corbyn is undignified and has little respect for British culture and tradition.

These messages are communicated to the reader as 'real' and truthful values through:

- the selective use and combination of events, issues, social groups and individuals
- the use of media language to construct and reinforce established stereotypes.

In this way, the *Daily Mail*, as a product, is able to reinforce both the values of the owner and editor, who are of the dominant group, and the dominant ideology to their target audience.

Representation and the set products – *The Guardian*

The impact of industry contexts and choices news producers make about representation

The Guardian's owner is the Scott Trust, which ensures *The Guardian* is protected from commercial influence and pressures in its reporting and commitment to progressive and liberal journalism. The Scott Trust board of directors is made up of representatives from different occupations and genders, but is largely white, British and middle-class. This suggests the ownership of *The Guardian* looks to support diversity in their viewpoints and representations of social groups, individuals, issues and events but from the perspective of the white middle classes.

The Guardian's editor invites columnists from a range of social groups to reflect the diversity found within contemporary British culture and to provide a voice for different perspectives. The editorial values of *The Guardian* therefore seek to reflect the values of the owner from a liberal middle-class viewpoint whilst providing opportunities for minority groups.

Traditionally a broadsheet genre paper, *The Guardian* has a focus on reporting national and global current affairs and civic issues that are of public interest. This suggests *The Guardian* seeks to represent social groups and issues objectively. However, the paper's editor will need to apply news values to their selection of stories and how they are represented.

Study tip

To further develop your understanding of the representation of positive and negative stereotypes in the *Daily Mail*, use the CAGED mnemonic to analyse several front pages. Also consider sexuality, religion, occupation, education level and regional identity, noting your analysis in a table like Table 4.3. What common stereotypes are repeated across the front covers?

Knowledge check 49

The Guardian's ownership, editorial staff and target audience fit into which social group?

The liberal approach to the way the paper chooses how to represent events, issues and people is reflected in its political bias, which is centre left. *The Guardian* will look to choose positive representations that support this political bias and be critical to the dominant political group.

However, *The Guardian* is made up of a largely white, middle-class, British and university educated staff, as are their target audience. This suggests that while the paper aims to construct positive representations of a range of events, issues, individuals and groups, the perspective of their reporting will always be with some bias from the dominant group because that is their experience.

Representation on the front page of The Guardian

It is useful practice to apply the representation concepts through the analysis of the Trump/May front page in Figure 3.3 on page 53.

How events, issues, individuals and social groups are represented through processes of selection and combination

Table 4.4 Methods of representation and their connotations

Representation on the front page	Selection/Combination of content	Connotations of this representation
Events	Trump's visit is selected as the lead story but his representation, through the main image and headline, is constructed as ridiculous.	This connotes *The Guardian*'s opinion of Trump, reflecting its centre-left agenda.
Issues	The issues inferred by the selection of the main image and article include: • the relevance of Trump's visit • relations between the UK and USA in light of Brexit • Trump's disdain of the press and reliance on fake news • May's political difficulties in a global arena.	The combination of main image, headline splash, copy and caption connotes that these issues are interconnected. This reinforces liberal worries about Trump's disregard for the press and control over global politics, including May's options in relation to Brexit. This connotes that the dominant group represents control by a few rather than the common good.
Social groups	The main image focuses on ethnicity and gender as social groups with Britain and America as the dominant ethnic cultures. Whilst May is in a stereotypically male role and wearing trousers, a male-gendered item, the photo selection sees Trump steering her away by the elbow. She looks unconfidently away from camera. The reference to content including sports and food relates to gendered interests, with men liking sport and women cooking.	Through the selection of the main image and the combination of the skyline and ear, *The Guardian* reinforces popular stereotypes of gender. However, the selected image invites us to question patriarchy.

Academic ideas

Gilroy 3: For more on applying this theory to representation in *The Guardian*, see the grid on page 114.

Gauntlett 1: For more on applying this theory to representation in *The Guardian*, see the grid on page 113.

Representation on the front page	Selection/Combination of content	Connotations of this representation
Individuals	Trump is represented as a domineering white, middle-aged man. The image shows him speaking to journalists with the headline presented as a quotation. Combining these technical codes can be seen to represent Trump as inept and controlling.

May is represented as unconfident and passive. She takes up less space than Trump in the selected image, which can be seen to represent a common stereotype of women as dependent and in need of male support. The headline addresses her from the perspective of Trump rather than directly. | Trump's representation questions common positive stereotypes we see of men and invites the reader to question Trump and his authority.

May's representation helps to implicitly reinforce the paper's political values. The image selection connotes that May isn't up to the job of prime minister and can be easily led by Trump. The use of common stereotypes helps *The Guardian* make a political statement that challenges the values without stating them directly, thus maintaining what appears to be objective journalism. |

Stereotypes, discourses, ideologies and audience positioning

In analysing the front cover in Figure 3.3 in relation to the CAGED social groups, we can see how representations in *The Guardian* construct or challenge stereotypes to communicate ideology and position audiences.

Table 4.5 Positive and negative stereotypes according to CAGED group

CAGED element	Positive stereotypes	Negative stereotypes
Class	The middle classes are represented as the dominant class with Trump and May in the splash, copy and image.

This selection reflects the middle-class identity of *The Guardian's* editor, journalists and target audience. | The absence of the working class on this front cover can be seen to reinforce the lack of social and political power that working classes have in the social and political arena. |
| Age | Adults are represented as the dominant group which can be seen to suggest adults have social power and are in control of national, economic and political issues within our society. | Youth, children and the elderly, by their absence, can be seen to be represented as voiceless in social issues and events. This reinforces dominant stereotypes about age and the belief that adults, in particular the middle-aged, make the important national decisions. |
| Gender | By indicating that the article is written by both a man and a woman, the byline identifies men and women as capable of the same jobs, subverting common stereotypes of male superiority. | Trump can be seen to be represented as a domineering white man with little respect for women. His representation can be seen as negative, challenging traditional representations of white, middle-class men. |

Study tip

You may be asked to analyse representations on the front page of *The Guardian*. To prepare, analyse the events, issues, social groups and individuals represented on a front page. Using a table like Table 4.4, record your analysis. You can use each row of the table as paragraph content to help you write paragraphs in an essay.

Academic ideas

Butler 2: For more on applying this theory to representation in *The Guardian*, see the grid on page 114.

CAGED element	Positive stereotypes	Negative stereotypes
Gender	Sport dominated by successful men is indicated by the reference to the English football team and souvenir issue. This contrasts with the female-stereotyped food magazine. The use of blue behind the sports players and pink behind the food also indicates gender stereotyping.	May can be seen to be represented as weak, subordinate and dependent on Trump, reinforcing common negative stereotypes about women.
Ethnicity	British culture as successful is stereotyped via the promotion of the souvenir magazine for the World Cup.	Minority cultures, through their absence, can be seen to be stereotypically represented as inferior to the dominant British culture. British culture is represented as a declining force. The image of Trump controlling May with the backdrop of the Union Jack and American flag strongly suggests American culture influences British culture today.
Disability	The stereotyping of the able-bodied as the dominant group can be seen to be evident in the image selection for this front page.	Individuals with visible disabilities, by their absence, can be seen to be stereotypically represented as inferior to those who are able-bodied.

How representations constructed by news media make claims about realism

The Guardian, just like the *Daily Mail*, constructs representations through the use of positive and negative stereotypes. In doing so, *The Guardian* seems to make claims about what is real and what we should think about real events in accordance with the paper's own beliefs and values. The key messages that seem to be communicated by this front cover are:

- Donald Trump, as the US president, has little respect for the British press and serious journalism.
- He cannot be taken seriously as the US president.
- Trump can be seen to influence British politics.
- He reinforces gender stereotypes attached to men and is controlling.
- Theresa May reinforces gender stereotypes attached to women and is passive and subordinate to Trump.
- British culture and values are under threat from the Trump administration, American politics and culture.

These messages are seen to be communicated to the reader as 'real' and truthful values through:

- the selective use and combination of events, issues, social groups and individuals
- the use of media language to construct and reinforce established stereotypes.

In this way *The Guardian* is seen to be able to reinforce the liberal and centre-left values of the owner and editor while encouraging their readers to question some of these representations.

Context

Social context:
The Guardian uses positive and negative stereotypes as shortcuts inviting the reader to question wider social stereotypes. This makes dominant ideology harder to reinforce.

Study tip

To further develop your understanding of the representation of positive and negative stereotypes in *The Guardian,* use the CAGED mnemonic to analyse several front pages. Also consider sexuality, religion, occupation, education level and regional identity, noting your analysis in a table like Table 4.5. What common stereotypes are repeated across the front covers?

Knowledge check 50

How are *The Guardian*'s messages to the reader communicated as real and truthful?

Online, social and participatory media

Introduction to online news

In your study of news as a media form, you also need to study news in relation to online, social and participatory media.

The study of online, social and participatory news media must address each of the theoretical frameworks, media contexts, academic ideas and arguments. You will also need to study these issues in relation to the set products.

Table 5.1 is a summary of the OCR specification coverage for Media Messages, Section A: Online, social and participatory media.

Table 5.1 OCR specification for Media Messages, Section A: Online, social and participatory media

Media forms	Online, social and participatory media	
Set media products	• The *MailOnline* website • *theguardian.com* website	Focus on industries and audiences
	• Two articles from the *MailOnline* website • Two articles from *theguardian.com* website	Focus on media language and representation
	Facebook, Twitter and Instagram feeds from the *Daily Mail* and *The Guardian*	
Media industries	✓	
Media audiences	✓	
Media language	✓	
Media representations	✓	
Media contexts	Historical, political, economic, social and cultural	
Academic ideas	✓	

The specification recommends that your study:

- illustrates the scope, scale and content of online news media
- considers how active each newspaper's social and participatory media feeds are, including which articles are featured and which generate the most audience participation.

Online media

By the 1990s, online media and the internet were becoming well established within daily life, with email and the ability to purchase and consume content from producers online.

Social media

Social media refers to a collective of online communication channels dedicated to communities, allowing them to interact, share and collaborate. The first social media site was Six Degrees in 1997.

Today, social media is an integral part of daily life used by owners and audiences of media, and has developed the relationship and interaction between the owner and audience of a product as well as the way in which media products, including the news, are produced, distributed, marketed and circulated.

Participatory media

Participatory media refers to the audience playing an active role in the process of collecting, reporting, analysing and sharing content. It can also refer to citizen journalism, whereby the audience report and contribute to news stories and information.

Participatory media permits a democratic media that is created and shared by citizens. Audiences are no longer simply the consumers of media products created and circulated by media owners and industries but actively participate in the production of ideas and content in a way that provides significant opportunities and development for public and social life on a national and global scale.

Knowledge check 51

Which set products must you analyse with focus on media language and representation in your study of online, social and participatory media?

Online news: industries

For the study of online, social and participatory media in relation to the news industry, the OCR specification indicates you must study the following:

- the significance of issues of ownership and economic factors, including the range of each newspaper's online content and the use of online monetisation
- the impact of digital convergence on the production, distribution and circulation of news organisations' offline and online offerings
- the impact of online news and social and participatory media on regulation.

Significant issues of ownership and economic factors

News ownership is usually by multinational conglomerates, media barons or trusts. And news, whether it is in print or online format, is a commodity that must make a profit for the owner.

As developments in technology have led to decreasing circulation sales of print news, owners are more reliant than ever on online media to drive revenues and income for the production of both print and online media.

The Print News section considered the issues around news ownership and the different economic pressures that owners face, such as:

- falling sales and loss of revenue from advertising
- different ownership types and the impact of off-setting loss with subsidiary brands
- how owners have identified solutions for increasing income in the current market.

For almost all news owners, online news is a vital part of the business that they seek to develop due to a number of factors.

Audiences continue to look to the internet and use **converged devices** to consume their news.

BBC News, Facebook and Google are the three largest sources of information online and present competition for the UK newspaper industry.

Converged devices
The integration of two or more different technologies into a single device, for example a desktop computer, mobile phone and social media sites.

Economic factors

Print news circulation had a clear revenue model in that the newspaper's income was derived from circulation sales and advertising revenue.

This economic model is less straightforward with online news as an actual point of sale does not exist. In addition, adverts are more successful when viewed in print news so revenue from online advertising was traditionally not enough on its own for owners to make a profit.

In order to address the need to increase revenue through their digital outlets to offset print losses, owners have to monetise online news. Table 5.2 identifies some of the ways in which online news has been monetised.

Table 5.2 Ways that online news has been monetised

Method of monetisation	Description
Paywalls	A feature of a website that requires payment before a user can access content. Some UK news outlets offer a soft paywall, so access to a limited number of articles or views is allowed before the reader must pay.
Subscription	A financial arrangement whereby the consumer pays in advance for regular access to content.
Donations	A donation is usually a one-off payment, usually to a charity, that is considered to be a gift.

Impact of digital convergence on the production, distribution and circulation of online news

Digital convergence refers to the coming together of a number of digital technologies into one product, space, technology or device.

Digital convergence and new media technology has had a huge impact on the newspaper industry. The widespread development of digital technology has influenced and developed the way in which news is produced, distributed and consumed by the audience.

In order to remain relevant for audiences and to tackle falling circulation sales of print news, national UK newspapers have had to move online. This move has some advantages for news owners in relation to the production, distribution and circulation of news, helping them to cut costs and reach a wider audience.

Production: News is produced on a computer and uploaded to the website. This reduces the costs of producing newspapers.

Distribution: Online news can be distributed digitally via the internet and on social networking sites. This is advantageous because it costs much less than physical distribution and reaches a global audience.

Circulation: Traditionally news is circulated through distribution and sold to the reader at a point of sale. With online news, digitally converged devices have led to changes in the way audiences consume and circulate the news.

Study tip

Some exam questions may assess your understanding of issues facing ownership due to digital convergence and online news. To ensure that you have examples to support your response, identify how each UK national daily newspaper has monetised its online news content. Organise your findings in a table.

Knowledge check 52

Why do owners monetise online news content?

The combination of print news and online news content for UK news outlets has been beneficial to owners, especially papers like *The Guardian* whose print sales have drastically decreased.

Impact of online news and social and participatory media on regulation

With the proliferation of digital technology and converged devices, the internet is one of the largest sources of news and information today.

There is no specific body that regulates the internet. Ofcom conducts research into regulation practices for the news industry that includes print and online content.

For those who are members, online news is currently regulated by IPSO, which investigates complaints about online printed material that may breech the editors' code.

The participatory nature of online news presents a problem for regulating news online because:

1   it is constantly changing and evolving from one minute to the next
2   it encourages participatory media so that not all content found on a news website is created by the paper's journalists but also by their readers.

In April 2018, the House of Lords Communication Committee began exploring the possibility of internet regulation in the UK. They are likely to recommend either greater self-regulation or legislation so that laws are in place to regulate online content and limit any harm it may cause to the public (the report was still being prepared at the time of writing this book).

Additionally, the internet has enabled a few companies to dominate the market for news and information production. This indicates that where print media is closely regulated to ensure there is plurality, the provision of online news content isn't regulated so closely.

In July 2013, the Department for Culture, Media and Sport conducted a consultation into media ownership and plurality. They found that:

- the internet provides access to a greater range of information, news and opinion than ever before
- after the BBC, Google and Facebook are the most used sources for news
- current regulations do not recognise online companies or public service news broadcasting in plurality and competition laws
- it is in the public interest that plurality laws should also include these types of news providers
- Ofcom and the Government are to work with the media industry on a new framework to decide what is appropriate for competition and plurality regulation.

Industries and the *MailOnline*

The *MailOnline*, also known as dailymail.co.uk, was launched in 2003 and made into a separately managed site in 2006. Combined with its print newspaper, the

Study tip

To develop your knowledge and understanding of digital convergence and news owners' online offerings, pick three news outlets and find out on which platforms you can access their content. Look at www.pamco.co.uk to discover how many people they reach on each platform.

Knowledge check 53

How has digital technology and convergence positively impacted the distribution of news content?

Study tip

If your understanding of online regulation is assessed in the exam, you will need to provide examples of instances where regulation has occurred to support your response. Go onto the IPSO website and look at the rulings section. Identify how many complaints have been made in response to online news outlets. What is a common feature of the complaints?

DMGT has a 20.1 per cent share of the market, making it leader in the UK news industry market.

Significant issues of ownership and economic factors

The *MailOnline* is owned by parent company DMGT, which is owned and run by proprietor Jonathan Harmsworth. As a multinational company with a portfolio of successful sister companies such the *Daily Mail*, the *Mail on Sunday* and *Metro*, the *MailOnline* has achieved significant success.

DMGT has adapted their paper to consumer preferences and has been successful in capitalising on new income revenues through their digital content.

DMGT offer *MailOnline* content on four different platforms:

1 desktop

2 mobile

3 tablet formats

4 social media.

These encourage audiences to access their content in different ways. They are also platforms for advertising.

Economically, DMGT has, to some extent, been able to continue the traditional model of raising income through advertising sales.

Due to its success as an online brand, digital advertising is profitable for the *MailOnline*.

- In 2017, revenue from advertising increased by 18 per cent to £26 million.
- In 2017, the *MailOnline*'s combined revenue was £119 million, an increase of £93 million from 2016.

This indicates just how successful DMGT are with their online brand. It also means that DMGT can remain very competitive in the market, as they don't have to introduce a paywall for their readers to access content. For readers, *MailOnline* content is still free.

Impact of digital convergence on the production, distribution and circulation of online news

In order to remain relevant and tackle their falling circulation sales of print news, the *Daily Mail* had to move online. This move, and subsequent rebranding as a separately managed site in 2006, had a number of advantages for the owners in relation to the production, distribution and circulation of the *Mail*'s content and values, helping them to cut costs, increase revenue and reach a wider audience.

Production

- The content featured on the website is exclusively for the *MailOnline* and is not published by the *Daily Mail*.
- The *MailOnline* employs over 800 people who post over 1,500 articles and 560 videos a day.
- While it is a separately managed site to the *Mail* and has a different editor, it retains the same conservative news values.

Knowledge check 54

Why is the participatory nature of online news problematic for regulators?

Academic ideas

Curran & Seaton 4: For more on applying this theory to industries in the *MailOnline*, see the grid on page 115.

Context

Economic context: The revenue made from the *MailOnline* offsets falling profits from the *Daily Mail* newspaper.

- The production of content features a broad mix of international news and mainly UK-focused coverage of sport, finance and travel.
- A major component is entertainment, celebrity and lifestyle news, and the site is dominated by images.

Distribution

- The *MailOnline* is distributed across digitally converged platforms with their website, mobile apps and social media content.
- The *MailOnline* also provides content on Snapchat.
- This reduces distribution costs, keeping down operating costs and enhancing the profit from advertising income.
- This enables a global reach for the brand which is distributed through their website and online content in the UK, the USA, Australia and India.
- This allows the *MailOnline* to attract younger audiences than the *Mail*'s print newspaper.

Circulation

- Since 2015, the *MailOnline* is considered to be the most visited English language news website in the world.
- Approximately one third of its daily traffic comes from the USA and Australia.
- The *MailOnline* has 15 million users accessing its content every day.
- It has 10 million Snapchat readers daily.
- The *MailOnline* Facebook page has 1 billion monthly video views.

The impact of digital convergence on the production, distribution and circulation of DMGT online offerings has been huge. It has enabled DMGT to address the threat of digital convergence in relation to the *Daily Mail* by creating an additional online brand that can take advantage of digitally converged devices and platforms to reach a wider, younger audience while still reflecting their conservative values and attracting advertising revenue.

Study tip

You may be asked to demonstrate your understanding of the impact of digital convergence on the *MailOnline* in the exam. Using the examples above and on page 73 write one paragraph each for production, distribution and circulation. Finish with a summary explaining the overall impact for the owner.

Impact of online news and social and participatory media on regulation

As a member of IPSO, the *MailOnline* is regulated by IPSO and individuals can make complaints through IPSO regarding content on any of the *MailOnline*'s platforms, which is written by the *MailOnline*.

Since 2015, IPSO has received 39 complaints against the *MailOnline*. Only two of these complaints identified that the *MailOnline* had breached the code of conduct.

However, IPSO can only regulate content produced by the *MailOnline* journalists, and given the participatory nature of the website and corresponding platforms, this means a large proportion of content isn't regulated.

Academic ideas

Hesmondhalgh 1: For more on applying this theory to industries in the *MailOnline*, see the grid on page 115.

Context

Cultural context: The global reach of the *MailOnline* enables the global spread of DMGT's cultural values.

Knowledge check 55

Has the impact of digital convergence been positive or negative for DMGT?

Academic ideas

Livingstone & Lunt 1: For more on applying this theory to industries in the *MailOnline*, see the grid on page 116.

One of the roles of the *MailOnline* journalists is to filter, edit and/or remove content that is deemed offensive, but the volume of user-generated content makes that difficult to do successfully.

This suggests a conflict between the impact of online news and social and participatory media on the regulation of the *MailOnline* content:

■ Minimal impact: although there is more room for invading privacy or publishing inaccurate information given the gossipy nature of the *MailOnline*'s content, this can be regulated by IPSO if it is posted by *MailOnline* journalists.

■ Significant impact: digitally converged media encourage often anonymous participation, sharing and commenting on content. This is largely self-regulated by the *MailOnline* staff and the readers of the *MailOnline* but the rigour in which this is completed is subjective.

Industries and *theguardian.com*

theguardian.com, formerly known as *The Guardian.co.uk*, was launched in 2008, developing *The Guardian*'s earlier news website *GuardianUnlimited*, which began in 1999.

Combined with their print newspaper and *The Observer*, GMG have risen from being the ninth largest newspaper in the UK, to now become the third largest in the world, according to the GMG chief executive, David Pemsel (July 2018).

Source: www.theguardian.com
/media/2018/jul/24/guardian-media-group-digital-revenues-outstrip-print-for-first-time.

This indicates that while their print news circulation is falling dramatically, *theguardian.com* is a highly successful product. *theguardian.com* has roughly 34.7 million monthly global users and country-specific online versions in Australia and the USA.

Significant issues of ownership and economic factors

theguardian.com is owned by parent company GMG, which is overseen by the Scott Trust. Its unique ownership by the Scott Trust means that ownership and economic factors cannot impact the content of the news provided, which provides progressive and liberal journalism.

However, the print news circulation of *The Guardian* is steadily decreasing, meaning that the owners must address economic issues if *The Guardian* brand is to survive.

GMG offer *theguardian.com* on four different platforms:

1 desktop
2 mobile
3 tablet formats
4 social media.

These encourage audiences to access their content in different ways. They are also platforms for marketing *The Guardian* brand.

The success of the online model is demonstrated in digital revenues achieved in 2017:

■ digital revenue of £108.6 million
■ an increase of 15 per cent in 2017
■ 50 per cent of GMG revenue.

Study tip

To collate examples to support a response to a question about regulation, go onto the IPSO website. Select three complaints against the *MailOnline*. Note down what they have in common and the outcome. You could also go to the *MailOnline* and select two articles. Note the type of comments users leave and the problems they could create for regulation.

Academic ideas

Curran & Seaton 3: For more on applying this theory to industries and *theguardian.com*, see the grid on page 116.

Context

Economic context: The revenue made from *theguardian.com* offsets falling profits from *The Guardian* newspaper.

Subsequently, revenue from *theguardian.com* is part of GMG's three-year plan to increase revenue for the company, so the owner is committed to addressing the changing consumption preferences of their audience and capitalising on revenue from the digital format.

In order to further supplement the income from digital advertising, readers can subscribe to digital editions from £11.99 per month with additional options to access app premium tiers and the iPad daily edition.

Impact of digital convergence on the production, distribution and circulation of online news

The Guardian has a long history of developing its content in response to digital convergence, with the first online version, *FringeWeb*, published in 1994 to document the Edinburgh fringe festival for its readers.

GMG's online content available for readers has developed consistently since 1994. Table 5.4 gives an overview of how *theguardian.com* has developed in response to digital convergence.

Table 5.4 Timeline of development of *theguardian.com*

Year	Online development of content
1994	*FringeWeb*
1999	*GuardianUnlimited*
2000	*GuardianUnlimited* is rebranded and extended to include greater content
2003	Paid-for website services launched that are ad-free editions of *GuardianUnlimited*
2004	Digital editions of the papers launched giving access to articles as they appeared in print
2006	A free comment section developed to encourage reader participation/sharing of ideas
2007	*Guardianamerica.com* was launched specifically for the US market
2008	*Guardian.co.uk* replaces *GuardianUnlimited* and becomes the first newspaper website to reach 20 million users per month
2009	*The Guardian* app for iPhone and iPod Touch is launched
2011	Guardian iPad app and apps for Android phones and windows are launched
2015	Global website *theguardian.com* is launched with versions for Australia and the USA

These developments suggest that GMG sees the benefit of adapting to digital convergence and providing a range of online content for the reader to access.

Production

- *theguardian.com* is an online version of the newspaper that retains the same liberal, progressive values as the print version.
- The website also offers additional features.
- *theguardian.com* is a core news site made up of niche sections covering subjects such as business, entertainment, technology, sport, arts and media.
- There is a substantial body of web features, such as the Opinion section and Guardian Soulmates, which enable a greater range of content compared to the print version.
- There is a rolling news service that is constantly updated by journalists.

Distribution

- *theguardian.com* is distributed across digitally converged platforms through their website, mobile and tablet apps and social media content.

Knowledge check 56

What percentage of GMG's revenue in 2017 was made up from *theguardian.com*?

Academic ideas

Hesmondhalgh 2: For more on applying this theory to industries and *theguardian.com*, see the grid on page 117.

Context

Cultural context: User-generated content from readers in the USA and Australia, as well as the UK, encourages the sharing of cultural identities and values.

- This reduces distribution costs, keeping down operating costs and enhancing profit from advertising income.
- *theguardian.com* has a global reach and also has country-specific online versions in Australia and the USA.
- *theguardian.com* content is also distributed through a partnership deal with Yahoo with users from the UK, the USA, Australia, India and Singapore accessing content.

Circulation
- *theguardian.com* has increased circulation by 25 per cent since 2015.
- *theguardian.com* has 34.7 million monthly global users.
- 1.15 million users access *theguardian.com* by mobile or tablet platforms.

The impact of digital convergence on the production, distribution and circulation of GMG online offerings has been significant. GMG have addressed the threat of digital convergence, historically building *The Guardian* brand online into a bigger and more successful digital platform.

Impact of online news and social and participatory media on regulation

GMG are not members of IPSO and therefore self-regulate across their titles and platforms. It is the role of the Readers' Editor to regulate both print and online content.

theguardian.com has a global reach of 140 million online users and therefore it isn't possible to regulate or respond to every user-generated content.

In deciding which complaints to prioritise, the Reader's Editor uses the following criteria:
- how serious the complaint is
- the likelihood that harm could occur
- the potential the content has to mislead
- the proximity of the person to the issue raised and whether it directly affects them
- how many readers have complained about the same feature
- the risk the complaint may have to the reputation of GMG, *The Guardian* newspaper and *theguardian.com*.

This creates a problem for the regulation of online news and suggests that online, social and participatory media have had a negative impact on regulation. But GMG and the Scott Trust are committed to a press that is self-regulated and free of legislative regulation.

Online news: audiences

For the study of social, online and participatory media in relation to media audiences, the OCR specification indicates that you must study the following:
- how audiences can be reached through different media technologies and platforms
- the content and appeal of online news content
- how audiences may use and interpret the same media in different ways.

Study tip

To demonstrate your understanding of the impact of digital convergence for news owners and online news in the exam, you must explain the impact of digital convergence on *theguardian.com*. Using the examples on pages 73 and 74, write one paragraph each for production, distribution and circulation. Finish with a summary explaining the overall impact for the owner.

Knowledge check 57

Has the impact of digital convergence been positive or negative for GMG?

How audiences can be reached through different media technologies and platforms

As a consequence of developments in digital technology, news owners can reach audiences through a range of different digitally converged platforms. Most UK national daily news outlets target their audiences through the following devices or technologies:

1 PC/desktop
2 mobile phone
3 mobile tablet
4 social media.

Academic ideas

Livingstone & Lunt 1: For more on applying this theory to industries and *theguardian.com*, see the grid on page 117.

Table 6.1 Audiences reached through different platforms

Online news platform	Audiences reached
PC/Desktop	• 20% of people read news brand content on a desktop weekly. Four million people access news content online daily via a desktop. • Men aged 35–54 consume the most online news content via a desktop.
Mobile phone and tablet	• 27 million adults access online news content via mobile phone platforms (this is half the UK population). • 18–34-year-olds make up one third of this reach; 56% of them are women. • 4.2 million 18–34-year-olds access news on their mobile phone or tablet daily. • Content is mostly consumed on mobile platforms in the morning between 6 a.m. and 10 a.m. • Their consumption of news outlets is part of their networked communication with people they engage with.
Social media	• 75% of users (26 million) read news outlets across social media platforms weekly. • Social media news brand content is mostly consumed between 5 p.m. and 10 p.m. • Social media news outlets have accumulated 920 million interactions altogether. • Facebook is the most popular social network with online news brand readers accumulating 856 million interactions.

Source: Adapted from www.newsworks.org.uk (2018)

These different devices and technologies enable owners to reach different segments of the market and at different times of day, allowing news owners to expand their market reach globally and demographically. The UK news brands, cumulatively, have the following reach by demographic across multi-platforms monthly:

- 84 per cent of men and women
- 88 per cent of 18–34-year-olds.

Media technologies and digital platforms allow news owners to reach a millennial audience who are less likely to read print news. For example, just less than half of 18–34-year-olds consume online news daily. This means news owners can reach a cross section of the population with a combined print and online circulation.

The ability to attain a wider audience reach across these platforms also has advantages for owners in terms of attracting advertisers, especially as online news readers engage differently with advertising when consuming their news. Online readers can be sold to advertisers as being:

- 30 per cent more likely to notice an advert on a news brand website than a standard website
- 27 per cent more likely to **ad-like** on a news brand website

Knowledge check 58

Which platform is the most popular with audiences for consuming online news content?

Ad-like Also known as approach, ad-liking is liking or clicking onto a digital advert on a website.

- 50 per cent more likely to engage in advertising
- 2.4 times more likely to consider a brand using video advertising more trustworthy if on a news brand website.

This suggests that digital advertising, while not as successful as advertising in print news, is still lucrative for owners and it is therefore essential to reach as wide an audience as possible across a range of platforms.

Reaching audiences through selection of content

News brand owners reach audiences by identifying and providing content that appeals to them. A clear advantage of online news over print news is the ability to identify which type of stories appeal to audiences. This is known as **click streaming**.

Evidence of click streaming can be found on sections of the news site usually titled 'most shared' or 'most popular'. This proves that users' searches are being monitored and the paper is able to update the website's content minute-by-minute so that the most popular type of news stories appear and make the news seem very current.

While this helps owners reach audiences, it also creates '**echo chambers**', meaning that audiences only receive more of the same to reinforce their current likes and preferences. This prevents cultural diversity and questions whether for commercial gain online news, in this sense, provides content that is in the public interest or simply provides content that the public are interested in.

Audiences and *MailOnline*

The MailOnline *audience*

The *MailOnline* is a separate company to the *Daily Mail* and provides separate content to the print newspaper. Subsequently, it can be seen to reach a slightly different demographic from the print newspaper, thus enabling DMGT to reach a wider market across their combined print and online platforms.

The *MailOnline* content is accessed by almost 13 million unique daily browsers across its platforms.

The *MailOnline* reader can be identified by the following demographics:

- 73.3 per cent aged 35+
- 26.7 per cent aged 15–25 compared to just 9.5 per cent for the *Daily Mail* print newspaper
- majority of the visits to the site are from the ABC1 socio-economic group.

Click stream The precise tracking of what users 'click on' and how long they spend on each online article.

Echo chambers A situation where a person only encounters beliefs and values that are consistent with their own. This allows existing values to be reinforced and amplified rather than the consideration of new or alternative ideas.

Study tip

To ensure you have a range of suitable examples to support your understanding of online news brand audiences, go to www. newsworks.org.uk. Click on fast facts and note down the useful points about the online reach of four news outlets of your choice.

Knowledge check 59

What is click streaming and what does it allow owners of news outlets to do?

Reaching audiences via different media technologies and platforms

The *MailOnline* enjoys considerable success and is the market leader in providing online news content across most of these platforms.

Table 6.2 Audiences reached by each platform used by *MailOnline*

Online news platform	Audiences reached
PC/Desktop	• 843,000 daily browsers • 6.5 million monthly browsers

Mobile phone and tablet	• 3.6 million mobile phone daily reach
	   − 2.3 million 35+
	   − 1.3 million 18–34
	• Smartphone reach is 2.9 million daily
	• Tablet reach is 775,000

Social media	• Facebook page/*DailyMail* has 14 million likes • Most successful news brand on Facebook with 264 million interactions between 2017 and 2018. • Approximately 1 billion video views per month on Facebook • Twitter profile @*MailOnline* has 2.2 million followers • Second most popular news brand content on Twitter with 10.4 million shares • 10 million Snapchat readers daily

Sources: *MailOnline* DMGT Investor briefing (1 February 2018)

The content and appeal of each of the set products

In their Investor Pack, DMGT argue that the success of the *MailOnline* is 'through the consistent application of core principles'. They define these as:

■ creating addictive and timely content

■ using data and analytics to tell us what is working

■ making **front door traffic** and engagement a priority

■ reinforcing the core *Daily Mail* brand across channels.

A further approach that demonstrates the brand's success in appealing to its audience is through their use of:

■ cheap, scalable video that tells stories originally

■ content to drive direct traffic to desktop and mobile homepages

■ discount codes.

When revising how the content appeals to the *MailOnline* audience, it is necessary to consider this in three ways:

1 selection of news content and stories using news values

2 use of technical codes

3 identification of what appeals to audiences.

Context

Cultural context: Recent trends in audience behaviour demonstrate a cultural preference for online media. This has led to changes in the consumption of print news, which will influence and affect the future of newspapers as a cultural product.

Front door traffic If 'traffic' is the term given to the number of people who view a website and engage in the content, then 'front door traffic' refers to encouraging readers to come directly to the newspaper's website rather than accessing its content via other sources. Such direct visits help attract advertisers for the news brand.

Context

Economic context: News platforms in free market capitalist societies are commodities, which are produced and distributed to be sold for profit.

Appeal of content through the use of news values and selected stories

The *MailOnline* website can be seen to use a number of Harcup's news values (see Table 2.3) in the stories that have been selected to attract the target audience. We can apply these to Figure 6.1.

Table 6.3 Harcup's news values used on the *MailOnline* website

News value	Description of example from the *MailOnline* website
Celebrity	• Ant McPartlin article • 'Don't Miss' sidebar
Entertainment	• Articles referring to TV programmes, celebrities and social media links
Surprise	• Exclusive lead story about imprisoned dentist
Bad news	• Exclusive lead story about imprisoned dentist • Ant McPartlin quitting TV until 2019
Good news	• 'Love Island' couple Meg and Wes are getting 'stronger and stronger' • Lots of celebrities on holiday
Relevance	Most of the stories reinforce British culture or attitudes, for example the British dentist lead story and the man being thrown off the plane in London.
Follow-up	Many of the entertainment and celebrity stories follow up TV shows and episodes to continue and extend the content from other sources
News agenda	*MailOnline*'s right-wing conservative agenda is reflected in: • British nurse imprisoned in Dubai for drinking glass of wine • Family demands council house after blowing £250,000

Figure 6.1 A *MailOnline* homepage

Appeal of content through use of technical codes

The use of technical codes and language also aim to ensure the website, and the stories featured, appeal to the audience.

Content guidance

Table 6.4 How technical codes and language are used to appeal to the audience

Method used to appeal to audience		Example of content from *MailOnline* website	Explanation of how it appeals to the audience
Technical codes	Layout	• The layout of the website features a banner at the top with a masthead and links to other pages. • This is followed by one lead story. • Underneath this is a stream of content made up of short articles that vary in theme. • The sidebar on the right-hand side is called 'Don't Miss' and is a scrolling stream of celebrity info. • Adverts are placed in banners at the top of the page and to the right. • Short videos appear at the bottom right of the page as you scroll down.	The layout provides so much content it is hard not to find something with appeal. The stream of articles in the main section of the website and the 'Don't Miss' side bar take time to scroll through. For readers interested in celebrity and entertainment, this will be a very appealing site.
	Colours	The use of colour repeats the house style of the *Daily Mail* newspaper with the same colour blue used on the links bar and on the font throughout.	For readers who are loyal to the *Daily Mail*, the same colour style reinforces the brand's core values so that the website works as an extension of the paper.
	Font	• The masthead uses the same font as the *Daily Mail* title font. • The headlines, subheadings and copy are in a sans serif font.	The branding of the masthead and website's name reinforces the *Mail*'s core values across the platforms, which will appeal to the loyal *Daily Mail* reader. Using sans serif font creates impact, looks modern and is very easy to read at a glance.
Language	Mode of address	The mode of address is conversational and informal.	This creates a familiarity with the reader, making the content easy to read.
	Lexis	Simple lexis is used to sum up the article's content in short headings.	This enables lots of content to be consumed with little effort from the reader. The lexis and use of language positions the meaning of each story.

Identification of what appeals to audiences

The *MailOnline* uses click streaming to analyse and use information regarding audience preferences and the types of stories that audiences engage with, using comments, shares and likes.

Evidence of click streaming taking place is seen by the use of two pieces of online content that encourages the audiences to click through to the selected articles:

1   Editor's Six of the Best – recommendations regarding what they should read in relation to the *Mail's* news values and political agenda

2   Most Shared Right Now – recommendations regarding what other *MailOnline* articles readers are interacting with to create a sense of participation and community on the website.

The results highlighted by these two sources informs the reader, and the *MailOnline*, that the most popular and shared stories across the site can range in focus from celebrity news to politics and from national and international stories in just 30 minutes. Therefore, a range of news content appeals to *MailOnline* readers and a story is made more popular when readers share why it appeals to them or what they think about it.

How audiences may use and interpret the same media in different ways

Blumler, Katz and McQuail's Uses and Gratification theory can help reveal how *MailOnline* audiences may use and interpret the website's content.

Table 6.5 How *MailOnline* satisfies audience use and gratification

Gratification or use of the media product	Example from *MailOnline* to illustrate how audience use and gratification could be satisfied
Entertainment and diversion	• The huge range of articles focusing on celebrity and the use of videos satisfy the audience's need to be entertained and diverted from day-to-day life.
Information and education	• While there is very little information or educational content, the *MailOnline* does offer some political and current affairs stories, providing information in a concise way that reinforces the *Mail's* news values and political agenda. • It could be argued that the celebrity stories are designed to inform the reader about particular celebrities.
Social interaction	• Social interaction is encouraged via a range of participatory media. This can be through liking on Facebook, Google+, Instagram, Pinterest, Snapchat and Twitter. • Articles on the website homepage enable comments so users can share and interact with others in response to a range of stories on the website.
Personal identity	• Stories are personalised and emotive, focusing on the impact of the story on an individual, their family or nationally. • For example the lead story of the dentist imprisoned in Dubai for drinking a glass of wine is accompanied by four pictures with her family, which will resonate with the reader demographic.

Audiences and *theguardian.com*

theguardian.com *audience*

theguardian.com is an extended version of *The Guardian* newspaper and provides the same and additional content to the print newspaper.

Academic ideas

Shirky 4: For more on applying this theory to audiences and the *MailOnline*, see the grid on page 116.

Academic ideas

Jenkins 1: For more on applying this theory to audiences and the *MailOnline*, see the grid on page 116.

Study tip

You may be asked to demonstrate your understanding of the appeal of online news content. Look at the *MailOnline* website and identify two different examples of content. Note down how each example could appeal to the audience in relation to at least one of Blumler, McQuail and Katz's Uses and Gratifications.

Academic ideas

Bandura 2: For more on applying this theory to audiences and *theguardian.com*, see the grid on page 116.

As a digital platform, it can be seen to reach a slightly different demographic than the print newspaper, thus enabling GMG to reach a wider market across their combined print and online platforms.

theguardian.com content has a daily multiplatform reach of over 4 million users. *theguardian.com* reader can be identified by the following demographics:

- 67 per cent aged 35+
- 33 per cent aged 15–34
- The majority of the audience fall into the ABC1 socio-economic demographic.

Reaching audiences via different media technologies and platforms

theguardian.com content aims to reach audiences across its digital platforms. These are PC/desktop, mobile phone, tablet and social media. It enjoys considerable success with its digital news provision and believes its audience to be very much 'consumers of content'.

Source: https://advertising.theguardian.com/audience

theguardian.com audience can be broken down into the following:

- 34.7 million monthly global unique users
- 24.2 million UK monthly cross-platform users.

theguardian.com is the market leader in providing online news content across PC/Desktop and Twitter platforms.

The content and appeal of each of the set products

When revising how online news content appeals to *theguardian.com* audience, it is necessary to consider this in three ways:

1 selection of news content and stories using news values

2 use of technical codes

3 identification of what appeals to audiences through click streaming.

Appeal of online content through the use of news values

Figure 6.3 A homepage from *theguardian.com*

theguardian.com website can be seen to use a number of Harcup's news values (see page 31 and Table 2.3) in the stories that have been selected to attract the target audience.

Table 6.6 Harcup's news values used on *theguardian.com*

News value	Description of example from *theguardian.com*
The power elite	• Arron Banks – business man and former UKIP and Brexit campaigner/donator • Boris Johnson
Celebrity	• Musician Ray BLK • Actor Steven Seagal
Entertainment	• Opinion section where readers can post comments
Surprise	• Arron Banks' ties with Russia and Brexit lead story • Steven Seagal's involvement in Russian/US negotiations
Bad news	• Youth violence in London • Sanctions Boris Johnson could face
Good news	• Interest rates to stay low
Magnitude	• Range of stories that have international and national appeal, e.g. Aaron Banks and Russia, Ray BLK and London violence, Boris Johnson
Relevance	• Range of content that addresses current affairs, politics, entertainment and culture means there will be some relevance to experiences of the reader in some way
Follow-up	• Brexit, Russia and US/Russian relations
News agenda	• Liberal, progressive centre-left agenda seen in reporting of Arron Banks and the Boris Johnson articles

Appeal of content through the use of technical codes

Table 6.7 How technical codes and language are used to appeal to the audience

Method used to appeal to audience		Example of content from *theguardian.com*	Explanation of how it appeals to the audience
Technical codes	Layout	Website content is organised into four consecutive sections that are methodical and easy to navigate. The first three sections are: • Headlines – this includes the masthead, links to pages, the weather, the lead story, up to seven or eight more feature headlines. • Spotlight – content focuses on contemporary cultural and social issues. • Opinion – this features opinion articles from journalists and guest writers, and also space for readers to comment and share.	The content is straightforward and easy to read and navigate given the way it is sectioned out, appealing to the audience who look to *theguardian.com* for balanced, straightforward news journalism.
	Colours	• The use of the masthead is also blue to extend and reinforce the blue branding identified on the newspaper's masthead. • The page tabs at the top of the page are identified in different colours to make them stand out. • Different coloured headings help to categorise each section.	The limited use of colour helps the content stand out and appear straightforward and easy to navigate. This will appeal to *theguardian.com* reader who will visit the site for serious news.

Context

Social context: The news reflects our society at the time it is produced; it shows what is happening in our country and the world, reflecting current social concerns and anxieties.

Academic ideas

Gerbner 2: For more on applying this theory to audiences and *theguardian.com*, see the grid on page 116.

Academic ideas

Hall 2: For more on applying this theory to audiences and *theguardian.com*, see the grid on page 117.

Context

Cultural context: Postmodern mixing of genres and 'implosion' is reflected in changing newspaper conventions and a greater representation of diversity.

Method used to appeal to audience		Example of content from *theguardian.com*	Explanation of how it appeals to the audience
Technical codes	Font	• The masthead has the same font as *The Guardian* newspaper. • The headlines, subheadings and copy are in a serif font.	The masthead's branding and the website's brand name reinforces *The Guardian*'s liberal, progressive values across their news content regardless of platform. The use of serif font reinforces the link between the online content and the print edition. It also appeals to broadsheet readers as the serif font is a convention of this genre.
Language	Mode of address	The mode of address is formal and serious across all of the website's content regardless of the section.	The mode of address will appeal to the website's educated, ABC1 audience.
Language	Lexis	The use of vocabulary is serious and formal.	It helps the content appeal to the audience in terms of their academic level, knowledge of language and expectation that the paper will provide quality, well-written journalism.

Study tip

To develop your analysis of the appeal of news content for audiences, pick two examples of content on *theguardian.com* homepage. Note down how these can be seen to appeal to the audience through the news values applied and the technical codes used.

Identification of what appeals to audiences

theguardian.com uses click streaming to analyse and use information regarding audience preferences and the types of stories they engage in by participating with comments, shares and likes.

On *theguardian.com* website, this feature is called 'Most viewed' and identifies that *theguardian.com* readers are most interested in stories ranging from culture, sports, politics and economics.

How audiences may use and interpret the same media in different ways

Using Blumler, Katz and McQuail's Uses and Gratification theory, we can see how the audiences of *theguardian.com* may use and interpret the website's content.

Table 6.8 How *theguardian.com* satisfies audience use and gratification

Gratification or use of the media product	Example from print news to illustrate how audience use and gratification could be satisfied
Entertainment and diversion	The inclusion of content regarding culture and sport provides entertainment and diversion.

Academic ideas

Shirky 4: For more on applying this theory to audiences and *theguardian.com*, see the grid on page 117.

Gratification or use of the media product	Example from print news to illustrate how audience use and gratification could be satisfied
Information and education	The focus of content in the 'headline' section is to inform and educate the audience on national and global current affairs, politics and economic news. The additional sections such as Spotlight and Comment inform the reader on socio-cultural issues and educate on a range of different points of view.
Social interaction	Social interaction is encouraged through the use of social media icons. Readers are encouraged to share articles through the share symbol. A range of articles also encourage comments from readers with the use of a speech bubble icon and colour to invite social interaction and for audiences to share their beliefs and ideas.
Personal identity	The range of content is focused on what is of public interest rather than the personalisation of stories. However, the range of themes and topics covered ensure there will be some content that the audience can personally identify with in some way. For example: • The Ray BLK interview and her views on London youth violence may offer personal identification with young readers or parents. • Readers who are homeowners may personally identify with the article on the Bank of England and interest rates.

Study tip

You may be asked to demonstrate your understanding of the appeal of online news content for audiences. Look at *theguardian.com* website homepage and identify three different types of content. Note down how each example could appeal to the audience in relation to at least one of Blumler, McQuail and Katz's Uses and Gratifications.

Online news: media language

The OCR specification identifies that, in relation to online, social and participatory news media, learners should study:

- the elements of media language used in online websites and social and participatory media such as locations, lighting, choice of camera shot, angle, typography, layout, address of content to the audience and editing and sound as appropriate
- how multiple meanings can be communicated across different news platforms and the impact of technology on media language (for example, post production editing of photos)
- the ways in which the use of media language by news producers incorporates viewpoints and ideologies.

Elements of media language used in online, social and participatory media products

Although online news borrows many conventions from print news, an online news product is different to the print edition because it is a different media form.

In terms of clear similarities shared by the online and print news versions, the website homepage will feature the name of the news brand just like the masthead on a newspaper. Online news articles rely on a conventional layout of text and images. They also use a similar, recognisable mode of address to that found in the print version. Additionally, the shot types, angles and locations used will be similar to print, as online versions use images to accompany the content.

However, online news also develops some of these shared conventions. For example, the homepage will have more headlines than a newspaper front page. It will also feature rolling or 'breaking news', which print editions cannot do.

Online newspapers also have additional media language elements. The website needs separate conventions, such as a navigation bar, and these identify it as an online media form. Additionally, online newspapers merge different communication elements from print, audio and video into one webpage.

These additional media language conventions provide a unique experience for the reader. The use of a range of borrowed and discrete media language conventions therefore ensures that the online versions:

- are identifiable as separate media forms
- offer news content that extends print news
- provide a further way to engage with the brand's news content.

Media language conventions of a website homepage

The annotated image in Figure 7.1 illustrates the use of media language technical conventions on a newspaper website homepage.

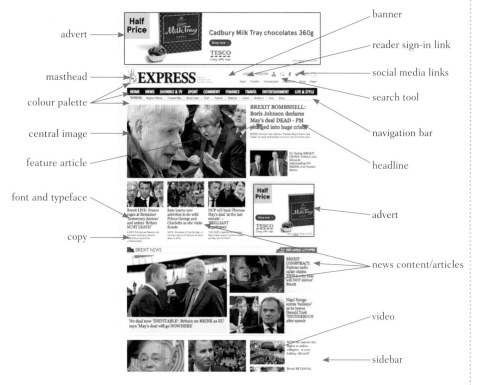

Figure 7.1 A homepage from the *Daily Express* website

Table 7.1 describes the media language conventions that are unique to news websites and those shared with print news, found on the news website homepage in Figure 7.1.

Table 7.1 Media language conventions

Media language element	Description of element
Banner	The section at the top of the website housing the masthead, navigation page links, sign in and search features.
Navigation bar	This runs across the bottom of the banner. They help the reader interact with and navigate across the content.
Social Media links	Icons that link to the social media accounts for the news brand. The reader can click on them and directly access the outlet's social media platforms.
Sidebar	A section to the right-hand side of the website. The sidebar contains several smaller news stories, images, copy and adverts.
Reader sign in link	Encourages audiences to feel a personal connection with the brand.
Search tool	Often identified by a magnifying glass symbol, provides the opportunity to actively navigate and find content.
Video advert	Moving image adverts introduce sound onto the website providing an audio-visual experience.
News content	News stories and articles; there are more on the website homepage than on a front cover. Scrolling down allows the reader to uncover more.
Copy	The copy is often just key points of the story, which are elaborated on if the reader clicks onto the story.
Headline	Headlines are short and direct on the website to provide a short, quick overview of the story and content.
Font and typeface	Typeface used is consistent across the website in a sans serif font making the short articles very easy to read.
Feature article	A key feature article larger than the other news content on the page. Feature articles are updated every few hours to keep the news content current and allow the reader to return.
Central images	Central images are used to support the feature article. These are larger than the ratio of copy to visually attract the reader to the story.
Advert	A banner advert, approximately the same size as the masthead, is featured above the start of the news content.
Masthead	The placement of the news brand's title – this retains the same font, typeface and look as on the print newspaper.
Colour palette	The three-colour house style used across print and online platforms to connect them as being the same news brand.
Additional conventions also found on News brand website homepages, although not on the *Daily Express* website homepage, are listed below.	
Comments button	Every news story has a comments button. This looks like a call out dialogue box. The number next to the button is the number of comments made.
Share link	An arrow symbol next to the comments section invites readers to actively participate by sharing content with others, further distributing the content.
Page links	Hyperlinks that categorise each story into a news topic, allowing the reader to access more of the same.

Media language conventions of a website article

Conventions in a website article are very similar to those used for an article in print news, as the annotated image in Figure 7.2 indicates.

Figure 7.2 An article from the *Daily Express* website

The key differences in the use of conventions in an online article compared to website homepage conventions are:

- social media links
- comments button
- reduced colour palette
- greater use of heading and sub-headings.

Media language conventions of social media news platforms

While Twitter and Facebook borrow media language elements from online news websites, their news content looks very different to print media. These social media platforms also use conventions to engage the audience and amplify the concept of belonging to an online community and participating through the media form.

Activity

Identify the media language conventions used by the *Daily Express*'s Twitter platforms.

1 Screenshot the image of the *Daily Express* Twitter platform, found at https://twitter.com/Daily_Express

2 Identify ten media language conventions used to construct the Twitter page, refer to Tables 7.1 and 7.2 to help you.

3 Annotate the page to show where these conventions are.

Study tip

It is useful to categorise the media language elements in online news content into specific categories; for example, banners, navigation and side bars relate to layout. Organise the conventions in Table 7.1 into uses of camera, editing, mise-en-scene and sound. Use the image in Figure 7.2 alongside Table 3.1 on page 46 to help you do this.

Knowledge check 62

Which conventions are used by both online news and print news articles?

Knowledge check 63

There is one key convention used by print, online websites and Facebook platforms that Twitter does not use. What is it?

Table 7.2 describes some of the media language conventions used by social and participatory news platforms.

Table 7.2 Media language conventions found in social and participatory news platforms

Media language element	Description of element
Banner	This is a shared convention with the news website. The banner allows the producer to visually personalise the space. It can sit with the masthead and news brand title. It can also use images that reflect the type of content that can be found in the paper and on the website.
Masthead	The masthead repeats the font, typeface colour and size of the masthead seen across all print and online platforms. This reinforces the brand and ensures it is recognisable regardless of the platform.
Profile picture	Enables personalisation by the brand. For producers it provides an opportunity to further brand their product. For example, the knight with sword logo becomes representative of the *Daily Express*.
User name	The news brand's user name is provided just under the profile image. This anchors the image with the name of the brand.
Sidebar	Facebook uses two sidebars, left and right. The sidebars are used to provide content that will encourage the audience to further participate rather than new content.
Caption	A caption helps to anchor meaning to an image underneath it. In Twitter posts, the caption works as a headline to inform the audience.
Image	Twitter and Facebook heavily rely on images as part of the content. These can be cropped differently on the two platforms to account for character restrictions.
Community	Numerous references are made to community features such as likes and followers. This helps to communicate the news brand's popularity to users.
Like, share, comment	Each post carries a like, share and comment button to invite audience participation.

How multiple meanings can be communicated across different news platforms

The proliferation of technology has considerably impacted the way in which multiple meanings can be communicated across different news platforms through the use of the same, but also additional, media language elements.

Where print news is considered a one-to-many media form, in that the content constructed by the producer is published for many people, online, social and participatory media provide a many-to-many approach in the way meaning is communicated across news platforms.

While the news is still produced and initially distributed by the news owner, social and participatory platforms that are linked to one another enable audiences to share their interpretation of meaning and put forward their own views. This encourages reader participation and the sharing of ideas and meaning.

Developments in technology such as the speeds for uploading technology and photo manipulation mean journalists can simultaneously upload the same story onto different online news platforms, adjusting layout and image sizes to suit the conventions of the media form.

Study tip

Select two news outlets. For each, screenshot the website, an article and social media platforms. Annotate the page to identify the use of conventions. Compare the conventions to identify how producers use media language conventions differently across each platform and brand.

Knowledge check 64

How does the inclusion, and placement, of the user name for the news brand help reinforce the brand and encourage audience participation? How is this a different experience to consuming print news?

Knowledge check 65

How can multiple meanings be communicated across different news platforms?

This enables multiple meanings to be communicated across numerous news platforms so news and meaning, become shared, globalised content.

The use of media language by news producers to incorporate viewpoints and ideologies

Like newspapers, social, online and participatory news media platforms are examples of constructed media that help producers 'encode' meaning or connotations in their products, which can be quickly understood by their audience.

Media language conventions work as signifiers of meaning so producers can incorporate viewpoints and ideologies across news content.

The headline and the main image of the online article in Figure 7.2 connote specific meanings. Table 7.3 suggests how it does this.

Table 7.3 Media language conventions and connotations

Media language convention	Possible meaning connoted
Headline	The headline focuses on and personalises the role of the Duchess of Cambridge as a parent and mother - a role that many of the readers will relate to. The words 'learns' and 'new activities' along with personalised references to two of her children and to visiting 'Scouts' connotates that Kate is a caring and responsible mother who is prepared to learn new things to help her children develop. The importance of Kate's abilities as a mother and her role in nurturing the future 'king' is reflected in the headline which specifically references 'Prince George' while his sister is simply referred to as 'Charlotte'. This could be interpreted as connoting that he has a greater social status and significance than his sister.
Main image	The main image is a montage of two different images of Kate, Duchess of Cambridge. One is a mid-shot and the other sees Kate in a medium close-up. This shot type helps to clearly identify her and creates a proximity between her as the subject of the story and the reader. It also connotes that she is relatable as she is seen to be happy, smiling, wearing a scout tie and engaging with and talking to her children. This positions her as approachable and caring, which can be argued to be reinforcing common gender stereotypes and connotations associated with women. However, it also helps to contradict traditional ideas about the royal family as aloof and superior. These images and connotations help the reader relate to and identify with the Duchess of Cambridge.

Study tip

You may be asked to demonstrate your understanding of how media language conventions, including genre, communicate meaning in online news platforms. To practise, identify four conventions from an online article. Note down the meanings each one connotes. Write a paragraph for each example, describing the conventions first, then explaining the meaning communicated.

Media language and the *MailOnline*

The *MailOnline* comprises different online, social and participatory media forms, and so uses media language conventions that are both shared and separate from the print version. However, the *MailOnline* continues the values of the *Daily Mail* print newspaper, and therefore will adopt particular media language elements to incorporate the brand's viewpoints and ideologies.

Elements of media language used in online, social and participatory media products

The use of media language conventions help to identify the *MailOnline*'s online, social and participatory platforms by:

- including media forms that are different from each other and also from the printed newspaper
- offering a different reading experience for their audience.

Activity

Identifying the media language conventions used by the *MailOnline*'s website, online and social media platforms.

1 Take screenshots of the following content:
   - *MailOnline* website homepage
   - the full feature article on the website homepage (click into the article to see this)
   - *MailOnline* Twitter page
   - *MailOnline* Facebook profile.

2 Annotate each of the screenshot pages, identifying which conventions have been used for each product. Use the content in Tables 7.1 and 7.2, and Figures 7.1 and 7.2 as examples to help you.

3 Compare the conventions and answer the following questions:
   (a) Which conventions found on the print newspaper front page are also used on the website homepage, in the article and on social media platforms?
   (b) Which media language conventions are used on the website, online article and social media platforms that aren't used in print newspapers?
   (c) Which media language conventions are the most successful in connecting the print, online and social media platforms as the same news brand?
   (d) Which media language conventions are used to tell audiences they can participate in the news content provided?

How media language incorporates viewpoints and ideologies

The use of media language by *MailOnline* journalists can help to reinforce the brand's values or to amplify viewpoints about wider social issues that their readers might have experienced.

This is achieved through the use of several media language elements:

- the use of language and mode of address in the headline
- the choice of the main image used
- the layout of the image and caption to anchor meaning
- the inclusion of comments buttons.

The article found at www.dailymail.co.uk/news/article-6078237/Father-standoff-Ryanair-cabin-crew-asked-free-pot-Pringles-delay.html and corresponding Table 7.4 identify how these media language elements help to connote certain viewpoints.

Context

Cultural context: News stories feature cultural events, traditions and behaviours that are considered important by audiences in their lived experience.

Table 7.4 Media language conventions and the meanings they connote

Media language convention	Possible meaning connoted
Headline	The headline is emotive: 'furious standoff' and 'four hour delay' connote that the passenger was unreasonably treated by the airline. The 'free pot of Pringles' juxtaposes the request with the length of wait to further reinforce the connotation. The words 'passenger' and 'cabin crew' creates a binary opposition, connoting that the passenger is the 'hero' in this situation who we should side with.
Main image	The choice of a selfie taken by the passenger personalises the story and connotes a sense of realism.
Caption	The caption's placement under the image anchors meaning, telling us who is in the image through factual information. This further reinforces realism connoting that this version is true.
Comments button	The comments button indicates 1,000 readers have responded, connoting that the story of the passenger's ordeal is of public interest and so sharing comments helps to reinforce or develop the viewpoints communicated in the story.

Study tip

To develop your skills in identifying how media language conventions incorporate viewpoints and ideology, select an online article from the *MailOnline*. Identify how the headline, image selected and one other element each connote a viewpoint or idea that positions the reader to react to the story in a certain way.

Media language and *theguardian.com*

While *theguardian.com* needs to construct online, social and participatory platforms that are recognisable as separate forms from each other and from the print newspaper, it must also show these are intrinsically connected to *The Guardian* newspaper in order to retain, and grow, its audience.

Media language used in online, social and participatory media products

Similarly to the *MailOnline*, *theguardian.com* is considered to be very successful in the production of news content online. Although the brand identity is very different to the *MailOnline*, *theguardian.com* utilises the same media language conventions of online, social and participatory media across its platforms.

Activity

Identify the media language conventions used by the *theguardian.com*'s website, online and social media platforms.

1 Take screenshots of the following content:
- *theguardian.com* website homepage
- the full feature article on the website homepage (click into the article to see this)
- *theguardian.com* Twitter page
- *theguardian.com* Facebook profile.

Context

Social context: News producers select different individuals and social groups in their news coverage and in their targeting of audiences, reflecting and adding to their visibility in society.

Academic ideas

Lévi-Strauss 2: For more on applying this theory to media language in the *MailOnline*, see the grid on page 115.

Barthes 1: For more on applying this theory to media language in the *MailOnline*, see the grid on page 114.

Baudrillard 2: For more on applying this theory to media language in the *MailOnline*, see the grid on page 116.

2 Annotate each of the screenshot pages, identifying which conventions have been used for each product. Use the content in Tables 7.1 and 7.2, and Figures 7.1 and 7.2 as examples to help you.

3 Compare the conventions and answer the following questions:

(a) Which conventions found on the print newspaper front page are also used on the website homepage, in the article and on social media platforms?

(b) Which media language conventions are used on the website, online article and social media platforms that aren't used in print newspapers?

(c) Which media language conventions are the most successful in connecting the print, online and social media platforms as the same news brand?

(d) Which media language conventions are used to tell audiences they can participate in the news content provided?

How media language incorporates viewpoints and ideologies

The use of media language by *theguardian.com* journalists helps to reinforce the brand's values and express viewpoints and ideologies regarding current affairs or wider social issues that will be of interest to their audience.

TheGuardian.com article found at www.theguardian.com/society/2018/aug/20/government-admits-role-in-birmingham-prison-failure-g4s and Table 7.5 indicate how media language elements can connote certain viewpoints. In this case, these are:

■ the use of language and mode of address in the headline
■ the choice of images used
■ the layout of the images to anchor meaning
■ the inclusion of the byline
■ the use of a comments button to encourage sharing of viewpoints.

Table 7.5 Media language conventions and their possible meanings

Media language convention	Possible meaning connoted
Headline	The use of the words 'government', 'admits' and 'failure' connotes the Government are to blame, inviting the reader to accept this ideological position that prisons are a political issue.
Images	The high key lighting and extreme long, wide-angled shot inside the prison makes the prison look sterile, impersonal and uninviting, connoting prison as a difficult and isolating place in which to live and work. The image of the minister smiling in an eye-level mid shot personalises the minister as responsible and the condition of prisons a political issue. The reader makes a direct connection between the juxtaposition of the two images and the article's viewpoint.

Context

Social context: News production reports on social issues such as current affairs, the economy, crime, unemployment, health and lifestyles.

Academic ideas

Barthes 1: For more on applying this theory to media language in *theguardian.com*, see the grid on page 116.

Context

Social context: The news reinforces and comments on other social institutions such as the Government.

Academic ideas

Baudrillard 2: For more on applying this theory to media language in *theguardian.com*, see the grid on page 117.

Todorov 2: For more on applying this theory to media language in *theguardian.com*, see the grid on page 116.

Media language convention	Possible meaning connoted
Byline	The byline indicates that the political editor is responsible for the article, further reinforcing the connotation that the issue of prisons is a social issue that requires government policy.
Comments button	Over 300 readers have shared the story, connoting that it is a topical social issue which readers feel strongly about.

Online news: representation

The OCR specification identifies that in relation to print news and representation, learners should study:

- the way events, issues, individuals and social groups are represented through processes of selection and combination, including a consideration of the choices news media make
- the impact of industry contexts (for example ownership) on the choices news producers make about how to represent events, issues, individuals and social groups
- the ways in which representations constructed by news media make claims about realism
- the positive and negative use of stereotypes by news media and how representations may invoke discourses and ideologies and position audiences.

Representations constructed in online news content tend to extend and reinforce the values, ideologies and viewpoint of the owner and the news brand in general. Ideas about the representations and ideologies constructed in online news platforms are similar to those seen in print news. The content on pages 55–61 of the Print News section is therefore also applicable to online representations.

However, compared to print news, online representations:

- have an immediate global reach
- use a greater combination of media language conventions, such as audio-visual communication as well as image and text, to construct and combine representations and ideological values
- are accessed differently by readers and can be discussed through social participation to identify alternative viewpoints that may be counter to the preferred meaning
- clearly reinforce ideologies of **individualism**, **globalisation** and **consumerism**.

This can be further explored by focusing on the constructed representations seen in the online, social and participatory media news content of the set products.

Study tip

Refer back to representation in the Print News section. Take notes on each sub-heading. Pick a UK national news brand and consider the representations offered across the print and online platforms on the same day. How similar are they? What differences are there?

Individualism A social theory that emphasises the worth of the individual over the social group. It is associated with capitalist ideals of free enterprise, the pursuit of profit and the right to self-realisation (fulfilment of a person's potential) and freedom.

Globalisation A process by which the world is becoming increasingly interconnected due to increased trade and cultural exchange. This has seen greater trade and freer movement of capital, goods and services, with the most successful companies being multinationals.

Consumerism Encourages the acquisition of goods and services in ever increasing amounts. Economic policies emphasise consumption and are linked to the idea of individualism with consumption as the free choice of the consumer. It cuts across social groups such as religion, age, gender and ethnicity in focusing on the interests of the consumer.

Representation and the *MailOnline*

The impact of industry contexts and the choices made about representation

DMGT is the parent company of the *MailOnline*. While the *MailOnline* is a separate company to the *Daily Mail*, the values seen in the print newspaper are extended across the online platform, as is the need to minimise risk and extend profit. The representations offered in the *MailOnline* therefore not only reflect the values and agenda of DMGT main shareholder, but must also appeal to a global audience for the website to have global reach and maximise profit.

Economic issues around genre, news values and the political bias of the *MailOnline* are embedded in the choices made about how it represents events, issues, individuals and groups.

As an online tabloid news provider, the *MailOnline* focuses on reporting global human interest stories featuring celebrities and entertainment. The representations of these events, social groups and individuals rely on:

- sensationalised, personal and emotive journalism
- the possible prioritising of positive representations of:
  - □ individuals in the family group
  - □ traditional family values
  - □ global, westernised cultural values
  - □ a right-wing political ideology
  - □ the values of consumerism and individualism
- the possible prioritising of negative representations of minority groups, not just through the reporting style, but also by their absence.

According to MailMetroMedia, the *MailOnline* provides engaging picture-first content that is easily accessible across a number of devices.
(Adapted from: www.MailMetroMedia.co.uk)

Online news platforms are therefore commodities made for consumption, thus reinforcing globalisation, individualism and consumerism as ideologies within the content they select.

The promotion of consumerism in this globalised context enables the *MailOnline* to provide a specific type of online news that is distinct from its print version and other online news brand platforms so that it is attractive for its audience and advertisers.

This marketing decision has led to the *MailOnline* becoming the most visited English language news website in the world. It has 27 million monthly unique visitors. The average time spent on the website is 3.5 times longer than any other news brand. (Figures sourced from: www.MailMetroMedia.co.uk).

This indicates that the drive to pursue profit, along with the use of media language conventions can influence the choices made by the *MailOnline*'s editor in the news selected and the representations offered.

Knowledge check 66

What is different about online news representations compared to print news?

Context

Economic context: Ownership models are moving to cross-media converged companies with global reach and a focus on profit.

Cultural context: Reading news content is a cultural trend embedded in the behaviours of the British public.

Knowledge check 67

What is different about the *MailOnline* representations compared to the *Daily Mail*?

How events, issues, individuals and social groups are represented through processes of selection and combination

In order to apply the OCR specification prompts, contexts and academic ideas to representation, it is useful to analyse the homepage from the *MailOnline*, Figure 6.1 on page 81. Please refer to Figure 6.1 when studying Table 8.1.

Table 8.1 Connotations of representation on the *MailOnline* homepage

Representation on website homepage	Selection/Combination of content	Connotations of this representation
Events	There are 11 stories featured in the top section of the homepage to demonstrate that content from a number of events has been selected. The main events referred to are: • the arrest of the British dentist in UAE after drinking a glass of wine • a family demanding a council house after spending their inheritance.	• The importance of the selected events is signified by their size and positioning on the homepage, reinforcing the dominant ideological values of the *MailOnline*. • Outrage at the arrest of the dentist reinforces traditional Western values regarding freedom and liberty. • The family 'demanding' a council house constructs a negative representation of the working classes and can be argued as reinforcing the *Mail* brand's traditional, conservative values that promote individualism.
Issues	Issues represented are: • Western ideological values • social benefit • celebrity culture • family values.	The selection and combination of these issues across the homepage connotes a white, Western, conservative and traditional perspective, also seen in the *Daily Mail*, despite the *MailOnline*'s global audience.
Social groups	The predominant social group is of white and Western ethnicity. There are also representations of gender, class and age.	Common stereotypes are constructed about those who have social power. Stereotypical representations of class, gender and ethnicity are evident: • Ant and Dec can be seen to be presented as successful white men, connoted by their suits, in contrast to the t-shirted man demanding a council house, who can be seen to be irresponsible. • The representation of the female dentist focuses on her role as a mother not her occupation; other female representations on the homepage, such as the stars of *Love Island* and Britney Spears, could be argued to be objectified in terms of physical appearance.
Social groups		Such representations offer shortcuts for the audience to quickly consume connotations associated with these stereotypes while reinforcing the *MailOnline*'s ideological values of exclusion, individualism and consumption.
Individuals	The individuals presented on the homepage range from the everyday person, such as the dentist and the flight passenger, to celebrities. A greater ratio of celebrities are presented, with the sidebar offering a scrolling list of individual celebrity news content.	The celebrities selected are relevant to the *MailOnline*'s national and global cultural interests, positioning the audience to consume a range of cultural products. The human interest stories are generic and can appeal across cultural boundaries to the global audience.

Stereotypes, discourses, ideologies and audience position

In analysing the selection of news content on the *MailOnline* website, and the representations offered, a number of stereotypes, discourses and ideologies can be identified that position the audience to accept a preferred response.

When discussing the representations constructed in the *Daily Mail* newspaper, the CAGED mnemonic was used to identify the positive and negative stereotypes used in the paper and how these communicated ideologies of exclusion in relation to social groups such as class, age, gender and so on. This is also applicable for representations found in the *MailOnline*.

Ideologies of globalisation, individualism and consumerism are also fundamental when considering online representations, so it is helpful to analyse how these are represented on the *MailOnline*'s homepage in Figure 6.1.

Table 8.2 Ideologies represented on the *MailOnline*'s homepage

Ideology	Content selected for *MailOnline* homepage to represent the ideology	Preferred meaning
Globalisation	Social media icons at the top of the sidebar make reference to the inter-connected processes that structure our world and the global reach of the *MailOnline*.	These representations encode the idea that globalisation is positive by allowing audiences to be interconnected, creating communities of like-minded people and access to a range of content from around the world. The repetition of content
	The celebrity story featuring Britney Spears and the video of a jaguar attacking a crocodile, along with the human interest stories of the jailed British dentist and the Indian father, all represent the freer movement of culture, people, goods and services.	that supports globalisation naturalises it, providing a preferred reading that it is for social and cultural good, while simultaneously benefiting the *MailOnline* and allowing DMGT to grow their global reach.

Content guidance

Ideology	Content selected for *MailOnline* homepage to represent the ideology	Preferred meaning
Individualism	The main story of the British dentist arrested in Dubai makes reference to her losing her individual freedom. The social media icons reinforce individualism as an ideology in that they promote individual expression and the right to freedom of speech. The story of the family demanding a council house highlights the contrasts between the individual over the social, with the negative account of his excessive consumption seen as a drain on individual taxes to provide social benefit.	Representations of individualism are encoded through the use of images, headlines and selection of stories. The collective preferred meaning across the content is that individualism, and value of the individual rather than the social, are important. The restricting of individual personal freedoms and draining of individual resources through aspects such as social housing are represented negatively. This helps to reinforce the *MailOnline*'s capitalist values of free enterprise, pursuit of profit and freedom of speech.
Consumerism	It can be argued that every item on the homepage promotes the ideology of consumerism in some way: • Digital adverts promote consumption of goods, services and holidays. • News stories selected focus on the dentist holidaying (a form of consumerism), as does the story of the father ordered off a plane. The family demanding a house story highlights excessive consumption of material goods at the expense of their disabled children. The story of Ant McPartlin, including the sidebar content, focuses on the consumption of celebrity culture. • Social media icons encourage the sharing of news content to promote further consumption through the act of prosumption, creating online communities that consume news content and sharing ideas.	The combination of this range of content encodes a positive representation of consumerism as a cultural attitude and behaviour. The naturalisation of consumerism is achieved through the repetition of acts of consumption – reading the stories, sharing comments and clicking on adverts _ and also in the selection of stories that feature consumption as part of the subjects' everyday lives. This encodes a preferred reading that consumerism is good, natural and should be encouraged, thus benefiting not only the *MailOnline* but the content, goods, services and cultural products featured and advertised on the homepage.

Academic ideas

Hall 1: For more on applying this theory to representation in the *MailOnline*, see the grid on page 114.

Prosumption The act of consuming and producing content. From the term 'prosumer', referring to a consumer involved in designing, customising, editing and sharing products for their own needs.

How representations constructed by news media make claims about realism

The *MailOnline* constructs representations through the use of positive and negative stereotypes, reinforcement of traditionalist values and wider ideological values. The key ideological messages communicated on its website are:

Dominant groups have social power: Common positive and negative stereotypes regarding age, class, gender, ethnicity and disability are reproduced to reinforce and naturalise ideologies of exclusion.

Individualism is important: The representations offered suggest readers should prioritise individual needs over the social, with social media being a way of communicating individual ideas, freedom of speech and sharing with like-minded people.

Globalisation benefits society: It allows access to a greater range of content and an increase in knowledge while in reality it provides a global audience which allows DMGT to continue to grow and profit.

Consumerism is natural: The *MailOnline*'s representations suggest readers' daily lives are structured around acts of consumption, whether they be the physical consumption of material goods and services or the consumption and prosumption of content.

These messages are communicated to readers as 'real' and truthful values through:

- the selective use and combination of events, issues, social groups and individuals seen in the stories featured
- the use of media language conventions
- the vast range of content which ideologically positions the audience to actively accept common stereotypes, globalisation, individualism and consumerism.

Representation and *theguardian.com*

The impact of industry contexts and the choices made about representation

theguardian.com is an extension of *The Guardian* print newspaper and so the same news stories, along with additional content, are available on the website. The values of the print newspaper are extended across the online platform. *theguardian.com* has enabled GMG to cut costs, minimise risk and extend profit. However, because the Scott Trust is the parent owner and oversees the editorial processes of *theguardian.com*, it could be argued that these benefits have not been at the expense of quality journalism or the representations offered.

As well as reflecting the values of the Scott Trust, representations constructed in *theguardian.com* must also appeal to a worldwide audience to achieve global reach and maximise profit.

As an online tabloid news provider, *theguardian.com* would be expected to report global human interest stories, featuring celebrities and entertainment. However, when looking at *theguardian.com*, it is difficult to identify the platform as a tabloid when compared to *thesun.com* or the *MailOnline*.

Study tip

Select one article from the *MailOnline*, its Facebook page and its Twitter page. Identify how the ideologies of globalisation, individualism and consumerism are represented through this selection of content. Make a table similar to Table 8.2 to record your findings.

Knowledge check 68

What are the main ideological messages communicated by the *MailOnline*?

Its representations of events, social groups and individuals rely on:

- balanced, liberal journalism
- prioritising public interest stories that represent the following issues:
  - politics and current affairs
  - social welfare
  - the arts, culture, sports and lifestyle
  - global, westernised cultural values
  - representative diversity of social groups
  - a centre-left political ideology.

Online news makes up an important part of the news industry and is a social institution. It is highly visible in our day-to-day lives and run by owners in dominant social positions, who are able to shape and influence thought. *theguardian.com* is therefore an important platform for the outlet to express its values through representations that contrast with other competing outlets in the market.

Nevertheless, whilst *theguardian.com* may offer a different viewpoint to online news platforms such as the *MailOnline*, it is still made for consumption, thus reinforcing globalisation, individualism and consumerism as ideologies. However, the representation of these ideologies may be more implicit than those demonstrated in the *MailOnline*.

Consumerism enables GMG to extend the content from *The Guardian* across its online news platforms, building on its brand values via a loyal audience who are encouraged to continue consuming the brand. This has increased traffic to the site and improved revenue for GMG, suggesting the representations offered are attractive to its audience and subsequently to advertisers. This indicates that the need to increase profit doesn't have to be at the expense of finding new readers with different news content.

How events, issues, individuals and social groups are represented through processes of selection and combination

In order to apply the OCR specification prompts, contexts and academic ideas to representation, it is useful to analyse the homepage from *theguardian.com* (see Figure 6.3).

Table 8.3 Connotations of representation on *theguardian.com* homepage

Representation on website homepage	Selection/Combination of content	Connotations of this representation
Events	The homepage covers a number of recent events: • Russian involvement in the Brexit run-up • an airstrike in Yemen • Boris Johnson's resignation • Ben Stokes' affray trial • Argentina abortion vote.	The selection of these events connotes that *theguardian.com* covers hard news, with politics and current affairs featuring in the top 'headline' section of the website layout.
Issues	The homepage covers an extensive range of issues: politics, racism, housing, global current affairs, finance, youth violence, film, the environment, activism, health.	The coverage of these issues signifies that *theguardian.com* is socially and politically aware, representing issues that are in the public interest and will appeal to the target audience's values. The range of issues chosen also encourages consumption of the news content.

Knowledge check 69

Why are the representations found in *theguardian.com* the same as those in the print edition?

Representation on website homepage	Selection/Combination of content	Connotations of this representation
Social groups	The social groups included on the homepage include: • middle-aged white British men • young black British women • middle-aged Muslim men • middle-aged white British women.	The inclusion of a range of social groups offers some representation of the diversity found within contemporary culture and aims to provide a number of voices. However, the representation of white middle-aged men, with Arron Banks and Boris Johnson (who features twice), dominates the 'headline' section of the homepage that is seen first by the viewer, reinforcing the idea of the political power of this social group.
Individuals	Individuals represented include: • Arron Banks • Boris Johnson • Ben Stokes • Ray BLK • Steven Seagal • Jamil Dehlavi.	With the exception of Ray BLK, the individuals featured on the homepage are all men. The connotations constructed here are that men are socially and culturally privileged, thus reinforcing dominant ideological values within our patriarchal society. However, Dal Babu, the British Asian former Metropolitan Police Chief Superintendent is a guest writer and many of the journalists featured on the homepage are women so that, although journalism as a profession is dominated by the white middle classes, *theguardian.com* possibly aims to provide some diversity in the writing of its content.

Academic ideas

hooks 1: For more on applying this theory to representation in *theguardian.com*, see the grid on page 117.

Van Zoonen 3: For more on applying this theory to representation in *theguardian.com*, see the grid on page 117.

Stereotypes, discourses, ideologies and audience position

In analysing the selection of news content on *theguardian.com*, and the representations offered, a number of stereotypes, discourses and ideologies can be identified that position the audience to accept a preferred response.

When discussing the representations constructed in *The Guardian* newspaper, the CAGED mnemonic was used to identify the positive and negative stereotypes used and how these communicated ideologies of exclusion in relation to social groups such as class, age, gender and so on. This is also applicable for representations found in *theguardian.com*.

Study tip

Analyse the positive and negative use of stereotypes across social groups on *theguardian.com*'s homepage. Use Tables 4.1, 4.3 and 4.5 and the CAGED mnemonic to help you. Also consider representations of sexuality, religion and regional location where possible.

Ideologies of globalisation, individualism and consumerism are also fundamental when considering online representations, so it is helpful to analyse how these are represented on *theguardian.com*'s homepage (Figure 6.3).

Context

Social context: The production and circulation of news socialises us into learning what is important and how we can think about different events, issues, social groups and people. To do this effectively it must reflect other socialising institutions.

Content guidance

Table 8.4 Ideologies represented on *theguardian.com*'s homepage

Ideology	Content selected for *theguardian.com* homepage to represent the ideology	Preferred meaning
Globalisation	The content on the homepage has a greater ratio of news relating to national current affairs, culture and politics. Content is also selected that represents ideas of globalisation: articles on the Yemen, Argentina, the Pakistani Film Industry, Russia/US relations, global activism and Brexit are all global in their focus. The comment boxes to the side of some of the articles make reference to the inter-connected processes that structure our world and the potential global reach of *theguardian.com*.	These representations encode the idea that globalisation is positive, enabling audiences to feel interconnected, to create communities with like-minded people through comments sections. The content that focuses on global issues breaks down geographical boundaries between the topic and the reader, giving a preferred reading that knowledge of wider social and cultural issues is crucial in today's globalised world.
Individualism	Individualism, in particular the promotion of individual expression and the freedom of speech, is evident on the 'opinions' section of the homepage, which features six articles from different writers on a range of socio-cultural and political issues. The main story on Aaron Bank's relationship with Russia refers to individualism in terms of capitalist values of free enterprise and the pursuit of profit for self-realisation.	The preferred meaning is that individualism is complex. Freedom of speech and self-expression is promoted in the Opinion features but, as shown in the activism story, *theguardian.com* also believes that individualism and social good can be linked. These support the outlet's progressive, liberal values. Contrastingly, the preferred meaning of the Aaron Banks story is that free enterprise in the pursuit of individual profit leads to corruption, negatively impacting society, and so is questionable. This supports the outlet's political values.
Consumerism	Representations of consumption are evident on this page although obvious consumption is implicit: • Digital adverts: banner ad at the top of the page; advert for *The Guardian* Masterclasses; advert for Travelodge. • News stories selected: some signify consumerism as an everyday practice in our society: article on interest rates, feature on the falling pound, cultural consumption in relation to the film and music industries. • Comment boxes: call out icons invite the consumption and sharing of news and ideas. Also, all the content selected on the website is only relevant if it is consumed by the reader.	The preferred meaning is that consumerism is an established part of our daily social and cultural lives. The ideas of consumerism are evident in the issues covered by some of the news stories selected, promoting the consumption of knowledge to acquire **cultural capital**, thus reflecting the liberal values of the outlet and the university educated, middle-class status of its journalists and readers. This preferred meaning also enables *theguardian.com* to promote its journalism and outlet across a global platform, thus benefiting the outlet.

Academic ideas

Gilroy 3: For more on applying this theory to representation in *theguardian.com*, see the grid on page 117.

Context

Political context: News outlets have a left-wing, centrist or right-wing political agenda in their news. In times of political conflict, such as Brexit, these differences in agendas will increase.

Academic ideas

Hall 2: For more on applying this theory to representation in *theguardian.com*, see the grid on page 116.

Cultural capital

The accumulation of knowledge in relation to culture, social and political issues, behaviour, dress, and taste. It is usually acquired through educational development. It is connected to, and can help change, someone's socio-economic status.

How representations constructed by news media make claims about realism

Theguardian.com, as a media product, constructs representations through the use of positive and negative stereotypes and reinforcement of liberal values. The key ideological messages communicated on its website are:

Dominant groups have social power: While there is some diversity in the social groups represented on *theguardian.com* homepage, the individual representations of white, middle-aged, middle-class men dominate the social, cultural and political stories selected, which can be seen to be reinforcing the power and visibility the dominant group continue to have.

Individualism is complicated: Freedom of speech and self-expression are celebrated and seen as important aspects of the human experience. But, individualism also favours the individual over the social, and individual profit to aid self-realisation. These latter ideological features contradict *theguardian.com*'s centre-left political bias and its liberal journalism that prioritises stories that are for the public interest and social good.

Globalisation benefits society: Globalisation is represented as enabling access to develop knowledge about the world, allowing readers interconnection with a wider community to share knowledge, ideas and values. This presents an outward-looking, non-isolationist attitude of care about and engagement with issues of the world.

Consumerism as part of everyday social and cultural life: *theguardian.com*'s representations of consumerism are embedded within the consumption of news as knowledge that can develop readers individually and socially rather than conspicuous, material consumption of physical goods or services.

These messages are communicated to readers as 'real' and truthful values through:

- the selective use and combination of events, issues, social groups and individuals seen in the stories featured
- the use of media language conventions
- the range and layout of content, which positions the audience ideologically to actively accept *theguardian.com*'s viewpoint with regard to political, social and cultural issues including their preferred readings for ideologies such as consumerism, individualism and globalisation.

Although the representations of issues, events, social groups and individuals in *theguardian.com* and the *MailOnline* differ to reflect the values and political bias of each set product, their representation of wider ideologies, such as globalisation, individualism and consumerism, which currently structure the experience of our everyday lives, are similar. This is because they are both products of the same historical, political, social, cultural and economic contexts. They need to be relevant, attract their audience and continue to function as successful businesses.

Study tip

Select one article from *theguardian.com*, its Facebook page and its Twitter page. Identify how the ideologies of globalisation, individualism and consumerism are represented through the selection of content. Make a table similar to Table 8.4 to record your findings.

Study tip

To practise making comparisons of the two set products, visit the website homepages of the *MailOnline* and *theguardian. com*. Identify three differences in the representation of the issues, events, social groups and individuals presented. To develop your knowledge further, repeat the comparison, but this time using a news article from each website.

Knowledge check 70

What are the main ideological messages communicated by *theguardian.com*?

Contexts grid

Context	Print news industry
Historical	<ul><li>Newspapers are one of the oldest media forms.</li><li>Print news in the UK dates back to the seventeenth century.</li><li>Mass readership of newspapers arose in Britain in the late nineteenth to early twentieth century with the extension of education and the vote, the increase in mass consumption and the growth of urban popular culture (e.g. music halls).</li><li>The contemporary printed press has been shaped by historical developments in technology, which have impacted on the way news is produced, distributed and circulated.</li><li>Since the 1980s, the digital age has impacted the printed press to the extent that the industry has had to change in response.</li></ul>
Economic	<ul><li>The British news industry contributes significantly to the British economy.</li><li>Newspapers in free market capitalist societies are commodities which are produced and distributed to be sold for profit.</li><li>Technological advances have impacted on the circulation of print news, as audiences prefer not to buy newspapers but to source information online.</li><li>The economic structure and funding of the production and distribution of newspapers relies on circulation sales and advertising revenue from print; the latter relies on a consumerist economy.</li><li>The current funding models in place must be reviewed if UK newspapers are to survive.</li><li>Ownership models are moving from trust and proprietor companies to cross-media converged companies with global reach and a focus on profit.</li><li>Ownership of market shares has to be monitored to ensure competition and plurality in the news industry.</li></ul>
Political	<ul><li>A free press, self-regulation and the Fourth Estate are important in democratic societies.</li><li>Protective coverage gives editors power over information that reaches mass audiences.</li><li>Newspapers reflect political bias and have a left-wing, centrist or right-wing political agenda in the production of news. In times of political conflict (e.g. Brexit) these differences will be increased.</li><li>Owners and editors support key political figures and reflect their political values in their news reporting, often owning newspapers to gain political influence.</li><li>Politicians will test the reaction of the press to policies before deciding to continue with them (e.g. the 'dementia tax' was dropped once this name was coined by the press).</li><li>Reporting on government and opposition policy and elections can influence readers, so political outcomes and national decisions benefit the political parties that are supported by the newspaper's owners.</li><li>Government legislation, reviews and policy affect ownership, practice and the regulation of the news in the UK.</li><li>Government can review the ownership of news titles every 4–5 years to ensure plurality in the market.</li><li>Government can intervene to prevent mergers/deals if news owners have a majority market share of print news.</li></ul>
Social	<ul><li>Gatekeeping the production, distribution and circulation of news means it is a socially constructed product by *owners* and journalists.</li><li>The news industry is a social institution, highly visible in our day-to-day lives and run by owners who are in dominant social positions.</li><li>The news reflects our society at the time it is produced; it shows what is happening in our country and the world, and it reflects current social concerns and anxieties, including those caused by social change.</li><li>The news reinforces and comments on other social institutions such as law, government, finance, family, religion, education and media.</li><li>News production reports on social issues such as current affairs, the economy, crime, employment, poverty, health, lifestyles and entertainment.</li></ul>

Context	Print news industry
Social	• News production selects and deselects different individuals and social groups in their news coverage and in their targeting of audiences, reflecting and adding to their visibility in society. • The production and circulation of news socialises us into learning what is important and how we can think about different events, issues, individuals and social groups. To do this effectively the news must reflect other socialising institutions such as the family and education. • News ownership and production shapes our social consciousness.
Cultural	• Concentrated news ownership in the UK supports a one-dimensional, conservative view of British culture which reinforces cultural norms. • Postmodern mixing of genres and 'implosion' is reflected in changing newspaper conventions and greater representation of diversity. • News stories feature cultural events, traditions and behaviours that are considered important by audiences in their lived experience. • Reading news content every day is a cultural trend embedded in the behaviours of the British public. • Increasing consumerism means that audiences expect more entertainment from newspapers and accept more marketing, e.g. self-promotion and sponsorship, in newspapers. • Recent trends in audience behaviour demonstrate a cultural preference for online media. This has led to changes in the consumption of print news, which will influence and affect the future of newspapers as a cultural product as audiences expect 'participatory culture'.

Academic ideas: summaries and set product grids

Theory summaries

Industries

Curran and Seaton: Power and media industries

1 Patterns of ownership and control are important in how the media functions.

2 Media industries are **capitalist** and aim to increase concentration of ownership; this leads to a narrowing of opinions represented in the press, affecting plurality.

3 Owners pursue profit at the expense of quality or creativity.

4 The impact of the internet on the ownership of news is nominal and it is still controlled by an **oligarchy**.

Hesmondhalgh: Cultural industries

1 Cultural industries follow a capitalist pattern of increasing concentration and integration so production is owned and controlled by a few conglomerates.

2 Risk is seen in terms of loss of money. Risk is high because production costs are high.

3 Companies rely on repetition to minimise risk and cover failure. Repeated formats are easily recognisable to audiences and use copyright laws to protect products from reproduction and piracy.

Capitalist A person or company who uses their wealth to invest in a service or industry with the sole intention of creating profit.

Oligarchy A small group of people who have control.

Livingstone and Lunt: Regulation

1   Consumers are individuals who seek private benefits from the media and require regulation to protect them from damage by the media. Citizens are social, seek public or social benefits from the media and require regulation to promote public interest.

2   Regulation in the UK is under threat by increasingly globalised industries due to technological convergence.

Audiences

Bandura: Media effects

1   The media influence people directly.

2   The media can influence directly or indirectly, through related platforms such as social media, so we can become influenced by the media without being exposed to them.

Gerbner: Cultivation theory

1   Exposure to particular media forms, genres or content over long periods of time can cultivate and shape our behaviour.

2   Repetition of negative media messages and values are likely to create 'mean world syndrome', which leads to the mistrust and fear of others within our society.

Hall: Reception theory

1   There is an encoding/decoding model explaining the relationship between producer, media product and audience in creating meaning.

2   Media producers encode products with a preferred meaning.

3   Each audience member can decode meaning in one of three ways:
    (a) Dominant reading – accepts the preferred meaning and ideological assumptions encoded by the producer
    (b) Negotiated reading – some of the decoded message is accepted but the audience disagrees with aspects of the encoded meaning so negotiates their reading to fit their experiences and values
    (c) Oppositional reading – both the preferred meaning and any ideological assumptions encoded in the product are rejected.

Jenkins: Fandom

1   New media have enabled participatory culture where audiences are active.

2   Participatory audiences create online communities using new media forms to develop or influence how media is consumed.

Shirky: End of audience

1   Traditional media are shaped by centralised producers.

2   Audiences were seen as a mass of people with predictable behaviours.

3   Audience behaviour is now variable; they are prosumers who can create and shape their own content.

4   User-generated content creates emotional connections.

Media language

Barthes: Semiology

1 Denotations can signify connotations, associated meanings for the same sign.

2 Denotations and connotations are organised into myths.

3 Myths create an ideological meaning and help ideology feel natural, real and acceptable.

Todorov: Narratology

1 Narratives can be seen to move from a state of **equilibrium** to **disequilibrium**, to resolution, to a new equilibrium.

2 The narrative structure, the characters we see within it and the role they play help to reinforce ideological values.

Neale: Genre theory

1 Genres change or decline in popularity.

2 There is a process through which generic codes and conventions are shared by producers and audiences through the repetition of conventions in media products.

3 Genres aren't fixed but are constantly evolving; they can become **hybrids**, playing with genre codes and conventions from other genres.

Lévi-Strauss: Structuralism

1 This is the study of hidden rules that shape a **structure** to communicate ideology or myths.

2 We understand the world and our place within it based on **binary** oppositions. For example, night and day. We know it's not night if it's day.

Baudrillard: Postmodernism

1 **Postmodern** society is concerned with hyper-real simulations, play of signs and images.

2 Social distinctions are no longer rigid; differences in class, gender, politics and culture become **simulations**.

Representation

Hall: Representation

1 Through stereotyping and the communication of ideology, those in power try to fix the meaning of a representation to a preferred reading that suggests there can only be one true meaning.

2 There are many meanings a representation can generate so preferred readings can be contested.

3 Meaning is created by a representation, but it isn't just by what is present but also by what is absent and different.

4 Stereotypes, and the way they are constructed, should be pulled apart and deconstructed to identify what they tell us about ideology.

Equilibrium A sense of balance and order

Disequilibrium When a sense of balance and order is disrupted. In narrative film and TV drama, this would require the protagonist to find a resolution to bring the balance back to equilibrium.

Hybrid When two conventions or characteristics are combined into one to create a new product.

Structure The way in which things are organised. In TV drama it could be the structure of the narrative or for new stories the order the events of the story are written in. Social structure refers to institutions like family, religion, education and media that are important in organising our daily lives.

Binary Having two parts or halves.

Postmodern Of an era that occurred as a response to, and alongside, Modernism in the second half of the twentieth century. A cultural movement reflected in the arts, architecture and film, it is characterised by conventions and features that set it apart from modern ideology and products.

Simulations Imitations or copies of something.

Gauntlett: Identity

1 The media have an important but complex relationship with identities.

2 There are many diverse and contradictory messages that individuals can use to think through their identity and how to express themselves.

Van Zoonen: Feminist theory

1 Women's bodies are represented as objects.

2 Ideas of femininity and masculinity are constructed in our performances of these roles.

3 Gender is what we do rather than who we are and changes meaning depending on cultural and historical contexts.

bell hooks: Feminist theory

1 Intersectionality refers to the coming together of gender, race, class and sexuality to create a white supremacist capitalist patriarchy, which dominates media representations.

2 Women should develop an oppositional gaze that refuses to identify with characters that reinforce patriarchal ideology and politicises the gaze. This is particularly important for Black women.

Butler: Gender performativity

1 Gender is created in response to our performance of gender roles.

2 We learn how to perform gender roles through repetition and ritual so it becomes naturalised.

Gilroy: Ethnicity and post-colonialism

1 The Black Atlantic is a transatlantic culture that is simultaneously African, American, Caribbean and British.

2 Britain has failed to mourn its loss of empire, creating post-colonial melancholia, leading to a version of British colonial history that criminalises immigrants.

3 Representations support a belief in the inherent superiority of white western civilisation.

Application of academic theories to print news

Daily Mail

Industries: theories and examples	Audiences: theories and examples	Media language: theories and examples	Representation: theories and examples
Curran & Seaton 1: The historical ownership of the paper by the Rothermere family since 1896 repeats the paper's ownership pattern.	**Bandura 1:** The use of language through mode of address and lexis influences the audience to accept the *Daily Mail*'s news values.	**Neale 2:** The masthead and use of splash with strongly worded headlines to anchor images of the powerful elite are repeated conventions used by the *Mail* to identify the paper as a brand its readers will be familiar with and expect.	**Hall 1:** The editor constructs contrasts in the stereotypes to represent opposing political views. In positioning the stereotypes as good and bad, the *Daily Mail* fixes a preferred reading to right-wing politics as good and left-wing politics as bad.

Industries: theories and examples	Audiences: theories and examples	Media language: theories and examples	Representation: theories and examples
Curran & Seaton 2: The market share enjoyed by the DMG Media outlets reinforces the Conservative political agenda of the *Daily Mail* across these news titles to a large audience. 73% of *Daily Mail* readers vote Conservative.	**Bandura 2:** The concentration of ideas and values across the *Mail*'s news platforms (print and online) implicitly influences the reader to accept the news values in their content.	**Neale 3:** As a middle market tabloid the *Mail*'s focus on politics and current affairs borrows from the hard news reporting we expect of broadsheet newspapers. But the headlines are more conventional of a popular tabloid.	**Hall 3:** Representation of the dominant group as white, male, middle class, middle-aged and right wing can be seen to reinforce the paper's political agenda. The absence of minority groups can be interpreted as reinforcing their lack of power in the social and political arena.
Curran & Seaton 3: The paper's news values support populist news reporting that relies on sensational and personalised news reporting.	**Gerbner 2:** The *Daily Mail*'s headlines are often sensationalised with strong, emotive language and a preference for negative news values when selecting stories. This can influence its audience to mistrust others and believe social developments will have a negative impact on them.	**Lévi-Strauss 2:** The use of images and the headline creates a binary opposition between Trump and Corbyn as hero vs villain; good vs bad. Opposition between man vs woman with subordination of women to men in the image is evident. These binary oppositions reinforce ideologies about politics, morals and patriarchy.	**Gauntlett 1:** The *Daily Mail* provides a traditional, conservative view of what it means to be British, a man or a woman in contemporary culture. Representations like these provide an identity that the *Daily Mail* reader can accept, adopt or decide to discard.
Hesmondhalgh 1: DMGT as the parent company and DMG Media as its news subsidiary, allows the Rothermere family to integrate a number of outlets and services, in addition to the *Daily Mail*, reducing competition.	**Hall 2:** The *Daily Mail* encode their ideology through the selection of stories, use of language, images selected, layout and font style. This helps the editor communicate the paper's viewpoint.	**Baudrillard 2:** The *Daily Mail* challenges this view as its description of Trump's meeting with the Queen as 'pomp' reinforces a singular view of what is important about British culture and who it involves. This is contrasted with the description of Corbyn as a 'pygmy' and part of a 'Leftie mob' to suggest that alternative viewpoints aren't acceptable or relevant.	**Van Zoonen 2:** The *Daily Mail* can be seen to reinforce traditional gender roles in terms of occupation, activities, events and the way we look. Trump and Corbyn are presented in stereotypically masculine roles. Trump visiting the Queen and Corbyn rallying the left-wing demonstration portrays men as socially active and powerful. Women are arguably represented as passive and part of the ceremony.
Hesmondhalgh 2: Printing and distributing the *Daily Mail* is expensive. Increasing the digital outlets and closing printing plants, such as Didcot, helps DMG Media to reduce risk.	**Hall 3:** The *Daily Mail* reader is likely to accept its preferred reading as the majority of its readers are politically aligned to the paper, which is one reason why they buy it. However, as the paper has a mass audience, not all readers will accept the preferred reading of some stories, such as their reporting of immigration, and may take a negotiated or oppositional reading to views expressed.		**hooks 1:** The *Daily Mail* can be seen to represent the values of a white supremacist capitalist culture. It is owned by a white, male, middle-aged man who makes considerable profit from the paper, which uses editorial news values which can be argued to reinforce and support dominant positive stereotypes of white, middle-class, heterosexual men.

Industries: theories and examples	Audiences: theories and examples	Media language: theories and examples	Representation: theories and examples
Livingstone & Lunt 1: The *Daily Mail* is a member of IPSO. Seventeen cases were brought against the *Daily Mail* in respect of claims of inaccuracy, invasion of privacy and intrusion.	**Jenkins 1:** The *Daily Mail* has a loyal readership who trust the outlet, creating a community of like-minded people. While the paper can only invite audience participation through purchase of the paper or via letters, the *MailOnline* is a platform where the *Mail*'s readers can actively share and comment on the news.		**Butler 2:** The *Daily Mail*'s repetition of common gender roles – the passivity of the First Lady and the Queen can be seen to be contrasted with the dominance of Trump and Corbyn 'leading' the 'mob' – helps to naturalise behaviour so men and women learn how to behave and the roles they must adopt.
	Shirky 2: The *Daily Mail* has a mass audience with predictable behaviours, which the MailMetroMedia presents on a fact sheet, to help attract advertisers for the paper.		**Gilroy 3:** The *Daily Mail* arguably reinforces the superiority of white Western civilisation through its owner and journalists, the dominance of white men in lead stories and the political values of the newspaper.

The Guardian

Industries: theories and examples	Audiences: theories and examples	Media language: theories and examples	Representation: theories and examples
Curran & Seaton 1: The historical ownership of *The Guardian* by the Scott Trust ensures ownership and control do not affect the journalistic values of the paper.	**Bandura 1:** The use of language through mode of address and lexis influences the audience to accept *The Guardian*'s news values.	**Barthes 3:** The headline implicitly criticises Trump, so when juxtaposed above the image it anchors a message that Trump's position as president and his traditionalist values aren't acceptable. Thus *The Guardian* invites the reader to question the myth.	**Hall 1:** *The Guardian*'s representation of Trump as domineering and comical reinforces liberal political views. Selective use of the image anchored by the headline creates a preferred reading of Trump as inadequate and disrespectful of May and the press.
Curran & Seaton 2: *The Guardian* aims to provide a voice for different perspectives, which can be seen as an alternative to the narrowing of opinions presented by the few companies controlling the market.	**Bandura 2:** The concentration of ideas and values across *The Guardian*'s news platforms (print, mobile and online) implicitly influences the reader to accept the news values in their content.	**Todorov 2:** Trump is positioned as the villain, challenging ideological values as we would usually expect the white, middle-class male, especially of a political elite, to be the hero.	**Hall 3:** Representations of the dominant group and gender, seen through the headline, skyline and image implicitly reinforce stereotypes. The absence of minority groups can be seen to indicate their lack of power in the social and political arena.

Industries: theories and examples	Audiences: theories and examples	Media language: theories and examples	Representation: theories and examples
Curran & Seaton 3: The Scott Trust aims to ensure that the quality and creativity of the paper's journalism aren't affected by commercial pressure. The transition to tabloid and development of online platforms of the outlet illustrates the need for companies to adapt in order to be financially solvent and survive.	**Gerbner 2:** *The Guardian* aims to provide balanced news reporting and offer different perspectives on topics. This would suggest that its audience would be unlikely to develop mean world syndrome as they will encounter a range of ideas to help process and make sense of negative events.	**Neale 3:** The transition of *The Guardian* to a tabloid is by size only; the journalistic values of the paper remain the same as those of its broadsheet roots. In doing this, the paper uses conventions of both tabloid and broadsheet genres so becomes a hybrid of the two.	**Gauntlett 1:** The choice of image and headline presents a preferred meaning of Trump and May that questions right-wing politics. This invites readers to question the ideology behind the identity of this group. May as prime minister fulfils a role linked with men, possibly developing the identities women can have today.
Hesmondhalgh 1: *The Guardian* newspaper has struggled to survive in a competitive market dominated by a few global media conglomerates. Circulation dropped 13.1% in 2018.	**Hall 2:** *The Guardian* encodes ideology through news selection, use of language, images, layout and font style. This helps the editor communicate the paper's viewpoint.	**Levi-Strauss 2:** The use of image and headline creates a binary opposition between May and Trump as hero vs villain, good vs bad and woman vs man with May subordinate to Trump. These binary oppositions help *The Guardian* influence its readers to question ideological views about morals and patriarchy.	**Van Zoonen 2:** In the main image, Trump and May are presented as similar regardless of their gender; both are in a role that assumes principal power over their countries and both are wearing suits. But the choice of image, with Trump steering May by her elbow, and the proportion of headline and copy devoted to Trump, could be seen to suggest the privileged role that men hold in patriarchal society.
Hesmondhalgh 2: Printing and distributing the paper is expensive. Developing the digital outlet, transitioning to a tabloid-sized paper and identifying other revenue streams helps GMG reduce risk.	**Hall 3:** *The Guardian* reader is likely to accept the preferred reading of the paper as its readers are politically aligned to the paper. However, as some of the paper's audience are reformers and explorers, they may have alternative or new points of view so may take a negotiated or oppositional reading instead.	**Baudrillard 1:** The concept of what is real or fake news leads us to question what is news and what isn't. The reference to fake news on the front cover of *The Guardian* is ironic and self-reflexive, as it is highlighting the concept of fake news through its own conventions (the headline) as a news provider. It also highlights the idea of Trump as a 'hyper-real' president.	**hooks 1:** The representation of the white supremacist capitalist Western patriarchy can be seen to be evident through the main image and the national flags in the background. It being the only story on the front page reinforces this. But the preferred reading doesn't support the dominant group's values – the headline is close to mocking patriarchy.

Industries: theories and examples	Audiences: theories and examples	Media language: theories and examples	Representation: theories and examples
Livingstone & Lunt 1: *The Guardian* self-regulates, refusing to join IPSO or IMPRESS, which the paper perceives as unethical and ineffective regulation. *The Guardian* will protect whistle blowers and run their stories if they are in the public interest.	**Jenkins 1:** *The Guardian* has a loyal readership who trust the outlet, but many of its audiences are digital natives and explorers so prefer to access the paper on mobile platforms where they can be culturally and physically active in their reading.		**Butler 2:** The representation of May arguably reinforces the idea of the subordination of women in patriarchal society, so that despite her privileged position, she is still subordinate to Trump. This reinforces the ritual of the behaviour between men and women which therefore feels naturalised.
	Shirky 2: *The Guardian* views its audience as having different perspectives and interests, supported by the range of content provided across the newspaper and supplements. But to attract advertisers, *The Guardian* has to reduce its audience to statistics and identify predictable behaviour.		**Gilroy 3:** The superiority of white Western civilisation can be seen to be represented through *The Guardian*'s owner and journalists: the use of a white, middle-aged man and woman in the lead story and the image selection with flags of the US and UK reinforces Western supremacy. But the headline anchors a preferred meaning that questions this superiority, inviting readers to query stereotypes of the dominant group in the media.

Application of academic theories to online news

MailOnline

Industries: theories and examples	Audiences: theories and examples	Media language: theories and examples	Representation: theories and examples
Curran & Seaton 3: *MailOnline* has posted an increase in its revenue of £93 million in 2017. This is achieved through a formula of news content that focuses on celebrity, entertainment and lifestyle.	**Bandura 2:** *MailOnline*, across its digital platforms and the *Daily Mail* newspaper, continues to express and reinforce the *Mail*'s core values and its right-wing news agenda. This can influence the audience indirectly, as accessing *MailOnline* content on Facebook still reinforces the same values as if content were accessed through the website.	**Barthes 1:** The combined use of media language elements such as the headline, choice of main image and juxtaposition of the image and caption, work as signs to connote that the passenger had been unfairly treated by cabin crew, positioning the reader to accept the story as real and sympathise with the passenger.	**Hall 1:** Through the selection of content, repetition of issues and ideological values, the *MailOnline* encodes a preferred reading across the website to fix their news values and viewpoint as the correct and natural meaning.

Industries: theories and examples	Audiences: theories and examples	Media language: theories and examples	Representation: theories and examples
Curran & Seaton 4: Through the *MailOnline*, DMGT has become the UK's leading news outlet, enjoying a 20.1% share of the market as a result. This means that only a few multinational companies still control the news industry in the UK.	**Gerbner 2:** The choice of news stories personalises events and issues and the use of hyperbole sensationalises events. This could make *MailOnline* readers more susceptible to believing negative events are happening more frequently and could happen to them.	**Todorov 2:** The article has a beginning and middle, which are clearly communicated through the use of the language and layout of the headline. These construct the passenger as playing the role of hero and the cabin crew as villains so the viewpoint that he was harshly treated can be reinforced.	**Gauntlett 2:** The content on the website offers a mix of representations that readers can use to inform their identity. For example, those offered in the celebrity sidebar may appeal to some readers in shaping their own personal identity or be rejected by others depending on their personal values.
Hesmondhalgh 1: *MailOnline* enables global distribution and circulation, extending DMGT's reach. Production of news content for the paper, whilst separate to the *Daily Mail*, follows its conservative and traditional news values and allows such news to be repeated on a larger scale.	**Hall 2:** The vast number and repetition of celebrity and entertainment stories, along with short headlines, lack of copy and constant uploading of content, encodes a preferred meaning that celebrity culture is important and interesting.	**Neale 2:** The article shares conventions with online and print news reporting so that the audience is clear of the media form and that the content is newsworthy and reliable. This is achieved through the repetition of headlines and choice of image, captions, byline and copy.	**Van Zoonen 1:** The representation of women, in particular female celebrities, can be seen to be negative. For example, stories of Megan from *Love Island* and Britney Spears select images of both women in revealing costumes, which can be interpreted as sexualising and objectifying them.
Hesmondhalgh 2: Development of the *MailOnline* outlet has reduced risk significantly for DMGT. Production costs are low and advertising revenue is profitable for the company.	**Hall 3:** The *MailOnline* attracts a mass audience and not all of its readers share the same values and beliefs so they will decode meaning differently. Comments from readers in response to stories show how meanings are decoded and help identify how many readers share the *MailOnline* preferred reading.	**Levi-Strauss 2:** The news article sets up a clear binary opposition between the passenger and the cabin crew. A number of binary oppositions are created: hero vs villain; individual vs corporate owner; good vs bad. These communicate ideological values and lead the reader to favour the passenger.	**hooks 1:** The combination of stories selected and the use of common negative and positive stereotypes of different social groups, such as the story of the white British dentist detained in the UAE and the representation of consumerism and individualism as valued ideologies, arguably reinforces a capitalist patriarchy.

Industries: theories and examples	Audiences: theories and examples	Media language: theories and examples	Representation: theories and examples
Livingstone & Lunt 1: The proliferation of celebrity, entertainment and gossip-driven news content leads to individuals requiring protection from online news content. The *MailOnline* has more than twice the number of complaints made against it than the *Daily Mail* newspaper. This suggests that online news content is less rigorous in adhering to the editor's code of conduct than print news. Additionally, user-generated content cannot be regulated.	**Jenkins 1:** *MailOnline* readers are encouraged to participate and be active in their consumption of content. For each story users are encouraged to share, like or comment on the content.	**Baudrillard 2:** Comments, share and like buttons help transcend social barriers. Whilst the social distinction between the passenger as individual and cabin crew as corporate is evident in the headline and copy, the comments feature allows all people regardless of social class, gender, politics and culture to participate. They are simulations in that they don't exist in the comments section in a material form but an identity, through what they comment, can be created.	**Butler 1:** The selection of stories and the representations of gender that they seem to offer, for example that men should be providers, women should be mothers etc. can be seen to reinforce traditional gender stereotypes in the *MailOnline* that naturalise our performance of these roles.
Livingstone & Lunt 2: The *MailOnline* is a global outlet with significant traffic from Australia and the USA, suggesting digital and media convergence lead to plurality issues: companies such as DMGT, along with the BBC, Facebook and Google, are able to dominate the news market.	**Shirky 4:** In sharing stories and posting comments, users can create emotional connections, both positive and negative, with others.		**Gilroy 3:** Although the *MailOnline* is a global outlet, the content selected, representations offered and the events, issues, individuals and groups absent from the news platform arguably reflect a bias towards a white, Western experience of the world.

theguardian.com

Industries: theories and examples	Audiences: theories and examples	Media language: theories and examples	Representation: theories and examples
Curran & Seaton 3: Whilst GMG need to make a profit in order to survive, the Scott Trust separates the commercial arm from journalism, so that the owners do not pursue profit at the expense of quality journalism.	**Bandura 2:** The combination of digital multiplatforms and print enable *The Guardian* outlet to reinforce and therefore influence readers in a number of different ways without the reader directly viewing the main website or app.	**Barthes 1:** The particular use of the words 'government' and 'failure' in the headline connote that the Government are at fault for the condition of prisons, thus quickly establishing the journalist's ideological position to the topic.	**Hall 2:** While *theguardian.com* encodes a preferred meaning, the reader can contest this if they don't agree with it. However it is likely that *theguardian.com* readers are aligned to the values of the outlet so will accept the reading.
Curran & Seaton 4: The internet has allowed *theguardian.com* to increase its market share of the news industry. This allows GMG to become a political voice different to the right-wing values of those in control.	**Gerbner 2:** The reporting of 'bad news' in *theguardian.com* is balanced with good news and the use of opinion columns helps to provide liberal perspectives to reduce fear of others within our society.	**Todorov 2:** The use of headline, images and copy constructs a disequilibrium in the prison service as a result of government failures. *theguardian.com*'s political bias is reinforced along with the view that the Conservative Party isn't committed to developing social institutions and welfare.	**Gauntlett 2:** The issues covered by the content include both dominant and minority social groups, providing some diversity in the representations and identities constructed across the homepage to offer a range of messages for the audience to process in response to their own identity and interests.

Industries: theories and examples	Audiences: theories and examples	Media language: theories and examples	Representation: theories and examples
Hesmondhalgh 1: GMG have developed *theguardian.com* and digital platforms on which online news can be accessed to increase their share in the market in response to competition from other news owners.	**Hall 2:** The layout and selection of content that focuses on current affairs, culture, sport and opinion constructs a preferred reading that news is balanced and varied, addressing a range of issues across all aspects of our social and cultural lives.	**Neale 2:** *theguardian. com* article repeats the familiar conventions of a print news article with headline, byline, main image and copy extending the paper's journalistic values. It also repeats the conventions of comments and participatory logos to identify it as an online form that encourages reader participation.	**Van Zoonen 3:** The representation of white middle-class men in positions of social and political power can be seen to reinforce traditional gender roles, but the proportion of female writers on the homepage indicates that gender roles can change in response to cultural and historical contexts.
Hesmondhalgh 2: The risks presented by *theguardian.com* are lower than those presented by *The Guardian* print edition. The online editions reduce cost and attract a greater number of users to enable an increased revenue so that the digital revenue comprised 50% of GMG's income in 2017.	**Hall 3:** *theguardian.com* attracts a mass audience and not all of its readers will share the same values, experiences and beliefs so the way they decode meaning will be different. The comments made by readers help identify how they decode the preferred reading in articles and whether or not they agree.	**Levi-Strauss 2:** A binary opposition between the Government and the prison system is constructed. In this way *theguardian.com* identifies the Government as villain and social institutions as heroes that are beneficial for social development. This supports their political agenda.	**hooks 1:** Although *theguardian.com* offers some diversity in the representations constructed, the repetition of Johnson's resignation and the Arron Banks lead story arguably identifies that a white supremacist capitalist patriarchy still dominates media representations.
Livingstone & Lunt 1: *theguardian.com* is independent from IPSO and self-regulates. The Readers' Editor deals with all complaints and letters with the proximity of a person to the subject and likelihood of harm to an individual being some of the criteria applied in prioritising complaints that need to be addressed. However, with over 140 million combined readers, this is a difficult task.	**Jenkins 2:** *theguardian.com* readers participate in online communities such as Twitter and Facebook where, through sharing their comments and interests, they can develop or influence how the content should be understood.	**Baudrillard 2:** The comments section can transcend social distinctions but the reference to Government and image of the prisons' minister can be seen to identify the dominant group and those in power as white, male, middle-aged and middle-class. This challenges Baudrillard's ideas, as the dominant class, gender, politics and culture are clearly identified here.	**Gilroy 3:** While there is some reference to global culture, such as the Pakistan film industry, airstrikes in Yemen, and Argentinian abortion activists, the images selected of Banks and Johnson are personalised, which can be seen to reinforce the inherent superiority of white Western civilisation. Yet, in these circumstances, both Banks and Johnson are represented as corrupt, questioning the superiority of white civilisation and inviting the reader to ask about the values of the dominant social group.
	Shirky 4: Sharing stories and posting comments mean users create emotional connections, positive and negative, with others.		

Section A

Practice questions and sample answers

1 Analyse the use of media language in Sources A and B. Use Barthes' concept of semiology in your answer. [10]

ⓔ This question is asking you to analyse the media language conventions used on each of the unseen newspaper front pages (for these, refer to figures 2.1 and 2.4 on pages 31 and 41). It is also asking you to apply Barthes' ideas of semiotics in your analysis to show your understanding of how the technical conventions communicate meaning.

In your answer you could discuss:

- the genre conventions of each newspaper
- a range of examples of the technical elements used to construct the front page, such as typography, layout, mode of address, choice of camera shot
- for each example, the connotation(s) associated with the technical element and offer a suggestion as to why it has been used.

This question is worth 10 marks. Spend no longer than 17 minutes on your answer: 2 minutes to plan and 15 minutes to write your response.

Sample student answer

Both Sources A and B are tabloid newspapers, signified by their compact page size. However, while they are of the same genre, the front pages use media language conventions to connote differences in their news values, journalism and target audience. Applying Barthes' theory of semiology helps to identify meanings communicated on each front page. These are connoted in both papers through their use of layout, typography, mode of address and main image, communicating and naturalising ideology.

Source A, *The Guardian*, recently converted to a compact tabloid and so is organised across five columns. But many of the media language elements used connote serious journalism, hard news and a balanced style of reporting, which are conventions of the broadsheet genre. The front page is divided into two main sections with the masthead and cover lines taking up the top third of the page. This layout helps to clearly identify the name, *The Guardian*, which has connotations of protecting people. The simple blue and white colour palette of the masthead suggests the paper provides clear viewpoints and serious journalism. The lower two thirds of the page prioritise the lead story and the main image of Theresa May, signifying to the reader that the most important issue of the day is Brexit and the factions within the Conservative Party. The selection of this current affairs story will appeal to the paper's educated ABC1 audience. The ratio of text to copy denotes the text led approach of the broadsheet news genre and signifies the paper's centre-left agenda, again appealing to its largely Labour-supporting audience. The use of cover lines at the top left of the page and on the skyline both denote the World Cup, connoting that *The Guardian* is culturally, as well as politically, relevant. The mode of address, through the headline and sub-headings, is serious and formal, together with the choice of typography in a serif font, communicating to the reader that *The Guardian* still provides quality journalism. The main image is a medium close-up of May in natural lighting and wearing blue, signifying her leadership of the Conservative Party. She is smiling in the selected image, implying she is happy that Johnson has resigned. The use of this sign helps *The Guardian* to construct ideological 'myths' about May and the Conservative Party, naturalising these viewpoints for their target audience.

Source B, in contrast, uses media language conventions to signify its tabloid values. Divided up into two main sections, like Source A, the layout clearly identifies the paper's name, *The Sun*, which stands out in the bold red and white colour palette. The word 'Sun' connotes the paper is a vital part of everyday life. It also connotes the historical conventions of red top tabloids that rely on sensationalised journalism to appeal to mass audiences with the lower two thirds of the page prioritising the lead story. The use of technical elements here further signify the tabloid values connoting that *The Sun* reader is more interested in football than politics. The blurring of the distinction between politics and sport sensationalises both issues, signifying an emphasis on soft news. The inclusion of Kate, Duchess of Cambridge, on the cover line connotes that both *The Sun*, and its readers, support the royal family and traditional cultural values. The typography and use of sans serif font across the newspaper, except for a very small proportion of copy, is bold and the bulleted sub-headings clearly summarise the news story for the audience. This also sets up binary oppositions between Johnson and Hunt, acting as signs of *The Sun*'s support of Johnson. The mode of address in the sub-heading is informal and by stating '*The Sun*'s message', they can connote the paper's sense of its political power. The splash presents itself as a quote by Johnson, to personalise the story, with the word 'bloody' being particularly emotive; this is also achieved by using his first name, 'Boris', in contrast to Hunt's surname. This personalisation signifies Johnson's popularity with audiences. The paper's support for Boris, just like the English football team, over May and Hunt is further reinforced through the selection of images, with the main image of Johnson taking up the central third of the page in contrast to the cropped close up of May and tiny close up of Hunt. The combination of these signs connote *The Sun*'s nationalist, patriotic agenda and what Barthes would refer to as an ideological myth naturalising the idea that Britain is powerful culturally and could be victorious at the World Cup and over Europe.

Barthes' concept of semiology, and the study of signs to signify meaning through the use of media language elements in Source A and Source B, identifies the differences in the two papers. *The Sun* is a conventional red top tabloid, clearly signified by the layout, typography, mode of address and image selection, which combine to connote a nationalistic, patriotic agenda as natural. *The Guardian* uses dual convergence, incorporating media language conventions from both tabloid and broadsheet genres to signify it is a serious newspaper that provides balanced, progressive journalism despite its size. Simultaneously, this connotes a political bias to the centre-left as natural. Skilled use of these conventions enables both papers to connote meaning and communicate their political agendas, journalistic values and appeal to their loyal target audiences.

ⓔ

- This response succeeds in applying Barthes' theory of semiotics, the study of signs, to identify the connotations created by the use of media language conventions as signs.
- There is a strong analysis of the set products, with good use of terminology, in relation to media theory to identify how issues such as genre, political bias, journalist values and the target audience are addressed through a range of media language elements.
- Although the answer could have discussed Barthes' idea of using signs to create myths and naturalise ideology in more detail, overall this is a high-level answer.

2   How far has ownership influenced the representations used in Sources A and B? In your answer you must:
   - explain how ownership can influence news values
   - analyse the contrasting representations offered
   - make judgements and reach conclusions about how far ownership has influenced the representations. [15]

(e) This question is asking you to explain the extent to which you think owner-ship affects the representations used in the unseen sources (for these, refer to Sources A and B). The bullet points are telling you how to answer the question so you can use these, in the order you see them in the bulleted list, to structure your answer.

■ You will need to talk about the ownership of both sources.
■ You will need to give examples of representations in both sources. Explain how they are influenced by or what they tell you about ownership.

This is a 15-mark question. Spend no longer than 25 minutes on this answer: 5 minutes to plan and 20 minutes to write your response.

Sample student answer

The Guardian and *The Sun* newspapers have different types of ownership, reflecting different news values and therefore representations. *The Guardian* is owned by the Scott Trust, a private company founded in 1936 to ensure that no single owner could buy and control the paper. The intention of the Trust was to safeguard the paper from political and commercial interference and to protect the paper's news values of fair, investigative journalism that is independent of the financial element of the paper, owned by GMG Ltd. The Scott Trust appoints the editor to ensure that the gatekeeping process in the selection of stories and application of news values respects the liberal and progressive values of the Trust. *The Guardian*'s current editor, Katharine Viner, describes the paper's values as reflecting that we are all equal and we should be free and fair. This suggests ownership does influence news values.

The Sun is owned by Rupert Murdoch. It forms part of a large portfolio of newspapers including *The Times*, under the organisation News UK, a subsidiary of his parent company News Corporation. News Corporation is a global, cross-media converged conglomerate whose aim is to increase global profit and reduce risk, which he has achieved through the development of *The Sun* as a red top tabloid focusing on soft news. Through this proprietor model, Murdoch uses his organisation to reinforce his political and ideological values, which are likely to be reinforced through the gatekeeping processes and the representations used to shape the stories. *The Sun*'s current editor, Tony Gallagher, says *The Sun* 'makes an impact' and is 'brave, bold and bawdy', which is a very different approach to Katharine Viner's. These different types of ownership can therefore be seen to influence the representations constructed in Sources A and B through the news values applied.

The selection and combination of issues, events, social groups and individuals represented reflect the papers' ownership. Both papers feature the main story of Boris Johnson resigning but the representations constructed are contrasting. In Source A, *The Guardian* constructs a representation of May as momentarily in control with Johnson's resignation as not too negative. This is seen through the use of the medium shot of the main image juxtaposed with the headline. May in a blue suit represents the Conservative Party and the headline's mode of address is clear and serious, supporting *The Guardian*'s use of broadsheet news conventions despite its tabloid size. The headline anchors May's expression, suggesting she is pleased with the outcome. This also acts as a metaphor to reinforce *The Guardian*'s political values as centre-left and ideologically opposed to Johnson's hard Brexit stance. This suggests that ownership, but also the newspaper's use of media language and dual convergence, influences the representations constructed.

In contrast, Source B represents Johnson's resignation in a sensationalised way. The use of the main image and splash provide a representation of Johnson that personalises the issue. The medium long shot of Johnson in an England kit takes up the centre of the page and the splash anchors his expression to suggest his personal frustration about having to resign. Significantly, the combination of these elements, and the tightly cropped shots of May and Hunt, with the football reference, trivialises a representation of issues surrounding politics, Brexit and the Conservative MPs as a game made up of two sides. This ideologically tells the reader that *The Sun* supports a hardline Brexit deal and is in favour of Johnson's values. This indicates that ownership, as well as the newspaper's use of genre conventions, influences the representations seen here.

The use of positive and negative stereotypes of social groups is evident in the representations constructed, and those that are absent. *The Guardian* constructs a contrasting representation of gender. The main image of Theresa May takes up a large portion of the layout. Usual stereotypes of women in the media reinforce their role in the home, as mothers or dependent on men, so this is a positive representation that echoes *The Guardian*'s progressive values and own appointment of a female editor. However, the reference to Gareth Southgate reinforces stereotypical ideas about masculinity. The use of a big close up personalises Southgate, connecting masculinity with sport. Both May and Southgate are from the dominant social group, thus reflecting that representations in the news tend to favour majority groups regardless of gender and are influenced by the experiences of the journalists, the majority of whom are white and middle class. This contradicts the 'we are all equal' values suggested by the paper's editor, suggesting that the construction of representations are maybe more complex than simply the ownership of the paper.

The Sun can be seen to construct very stereotypical representations of gender on the front cover, that arguably is reinforcing the ideological dominance of white, middle-aged men. The image of Johnson, together with his football costume, can be seen to construct a representation of men being central to decision-making in politics. This contrasts with the image of Kate, Duchess of Cambridge, thereby arguably reinforcing stereotypes that women are mothers and nurturing, regardless of their social position. These stereotypes and, similar to *The Guardian*, the absence of other social groups, can be interpreted as reinforcing white, patriarchal assumptions about power within our society. Rupert Murdoch can also be seen in terms of this dominant group, and so the representations seen in his paper serve to further reinforce his social power and privilege.

Although the encoding of a preferred meaning through the representations offered on these front covers is constructed by the editors, who are appointed by the owners, they cannot determine their audiences' response. The ideological values communicated by the editors use of representations may reinforce the papers' agenda and political bias but readers who are not part of the dominant social group may take a negotiated or oppositional view because their social and cultural experiences are different, thus enabling them to question the representations constructed in the news.

To conclude, ownership hugely influences the representations constructed in Sources A and B through the use of news values applied in the selection of stories, the stereotypes used to shape them, the political values communicated and the generic conventions applied. However, newspapers also need to sell and so the appeal of the paper to audiences, and the editor's goal to encode a preferred reading, is also an important factor in influencing the representations used.

- The response is well-balanced in discussing the contrasting ownership of the two newspapers and the influence that this has on representations offered.
- It analyses some of the contrasting representations offered but focuses mostly on gender.

- It could have discussed the application of news values by the editor in the selection of stories.
- It makes a number of judgements and conclusions within the body of the answer to form an argument in response to the question. Overall, it is a high-level answer.

3 **Explain how the global cultural context in which online news is produced influences the content offered to audiences. Refer to the *MailOnline* and *theguardian.com* to support your answer.** [10]

(e) This question is asking you to demonstrate your knowledge and understanding of cultural developments and how they have influenced the production and consumption of online news.

- You will need to explain how the internet has encouraged globalisation and how the *MailOnline* and *theguardian.com* reach a global audience.
- You will need to provide examples of the content found on the *MailOnline* and *theguardian.com* websites to show how they appeal to global audiences.

This question is worth 10 marks. Spend no longer than 17 minutes on your answer: 2 minutes to plan and 15 minutes to write your response.

Sample student answer

The internet has encouraged globalisation, so in order to appeal to global audiences and increase reach, the production of online news by British news outlets must dilute the British cultural identity represented in the British printed press. Western cultural identities and values, rather than a specifically national identity, are represented in online news content as a way to appeal to a wider audience. One way in which this is achieved is through the relative universality of the English language. This helps news outlets such as the *MailOnline* and *theguardian.com* reach a global audience.

The *MailOnline* is the most visited English language news website in the world and is particularly successful in the United States. While the print edition reflects nationalistic values that reinforce a traditional British cultural identity, the *MailOnline* website offers a huge number of human interest and celebrity gossip stories that help to overcome cultural difference and attract a global readership. Many of the celebrities featured on the sidebar, such as personalities like Kim Kardashian, already have global identity across other online platforms, so this selection of news content helps cross cultural boundaries geographically and reinforces wider current tastes in global, celebrity culture. This helps news outlets to further attract their target audience.

The universality of the English language, and the ability to build on its reputation as a quality news provider, is a way in which *theguardian.com* has also managed to reach a global audience. This demonstrates how newspapers, a cultural form, have had to adapt from their print editions in a competitive online market in order to survive. *Theguardian.com* is an international outlet with American and Australian versions of its website, which produce content that is more culturally specific to audiences in those countries, but on all three sites there is cross-over of the same content under the topic of world and/or international news.

Global cultural movements such as consumerism are also encouraged through the range of content available on these online news platforms. The *MailOnline* offers an addictive stream of stories ranging from *Celebrity Big Brother*, Kim Kardashian and the royal family to humorous videos of jaguars attacking crocodiles, with online digital and moving image adverts. The amount of content offered is overwhelming. Similarly, *theguardian.com* provides content on its homepage that will appeal to the tastes of its target audience and is organised into clear sections such as headlines, opinion, sports, culture and so on. By providing content that will appeal to and be consumed by audiences, these news outlets have a greater chance of attracting advertisers, which helps to create revenue for their outlets, supports production, and in turn reinforces consumerism.

Technology is another way in which global cultural contexts, specifically developments with Web 2.0 and converged technologies, have influenced the cultural behaviour of contemporary media audiences and both the production and consumption of news content. Online news outlets target millennials, as they are attractive to advertisers. This social group are digital natives who want to interact with online communities and share their media consumption with others. Both the *MailOnline* and *theguardian.com* encourage audience participation with comment and share buttons and links to social media websites on every article. Their Facebook and Twitter pages are a further way to globally distribute news content and encourage audience participation. *theguardian.com* has over 7 million followers and the *MailOnline* a community of over 15 million likes, suggesting that news production is no longer limited nationally with a one-to-many approach but is a global, cultural product providing a many-to-many experience. Both the *MailOnline* and *theguardian.com* acknowledge citizen journalism, with a 'Tip us off' bar on *theguardian.com* encouraging the audience to approach the paper with stories confidentially. These participatory features also enable news outlets to monitor audience taste and behaviour with click streams using algorithms to create echo chambers whereby readers will always be presented with similar content. This reduces cultural diversity and access to a range of opinions, but identifies that within our contemporary global cultural context, news outlets are businesses and must adapt to the cultural changes presented as best they can to continue to appeal to audiences and survive.

ⓔ

- The response demonstrates knowledge and understanding of how cultural context influences production and processes. It addresses the question and equally discusses the *MailOnline* and *theguardian.com* as news outlets.
- It explains how the internet encourages globalisation and consumerism and the impact of this on cultural identities and cultural production.
- It provides a range of examples of the content found on the *MailOnline* and *theguardian.com* website, although it is weighted more to the *MailOnline*.
- This answer is at the bottom of the top-level range.

4   Evaluate the usefulness of one of the following in understanding media industries for newspapers such as the *Daily Mail* and *The Guardian*:

Either

- **Curran and Seaton's Power and Media Industries**

or

- **Hesmondhalgh's Culture Industries**   [10]

ⓔ This question is asking you to consider how useful an industries theory is in helping you understand issues within the newspaper industry. You will need to:

- choose which theorist you want to evaluate
- select and explain a number of points made by the theorist that are useful

- select and explain one or two points made by the theorist that are less useful
- support your idea with examples from the *Daily Mail* and *The Guardian*.

This question is worth 10 marks. Spend no longer than 17 minutes on your answer: 2 minutes to plan and 15 minutes to write your response.

Sample student answer

Curran and Seaton's ideas regarding power and the news industry are useful in developing an understanding of how the important patterns of ownership and control have led to the pursuit of profit and the narrowing of opinions represented in the British press.

Curran and Seaton argue that there is a long history of press barons owning newspapers to achieve status and political power. This is useful in understanding how the news industry functions to exert control either socially or politically, and is true of news outlets such as the *Daily Mail*. The *Daily Mail*'s ownership by Harmsworth, who is the sole shareholder in DMGT, repeats a historical pattern of ownership as the *Daily Mail* outlet has been in the Harmsworth family since it was founded in 1896. Harmsworth's business has diversified into a multinational outlet with an annual profit of over £200 million, showing how much status and power he has as an owner. Curran and Seaton's theory also helps identify how the control of multinational companies narrows the range of political opinions expressed by the British national press with a bias towards Conservatism. The *Daily Mail* is the second best-selling paper in the UK controlling over 20 per cent of the market. The influence of the *Daily Mail*'s conservative political agenda is reflected by 74 per cent of its readers voting Conservative in the 2017 election, indicating that the *Daily Mail* exerts considerable political power.

In addition, Curran and Seaton's study is useful in drawing attention to the effects of this type of ownership and control on the working practices of journalists and issues of reporting where profitability is emphasised over quality. This helps us understand DMGT as a capitalist organisation that prioritises commercial gain and power over quality, as seen with the *MailOnline* outlet. But this idea also helps us understand the importance of contrasting types of ownership. For example, *The Guardian*'s ownership by the Scott Trust model means commercial ownership of the newspaper is separate to the editorial side, so *The Guardian*'s values and liberal journalism aren't compromised by the need to sell the paper and make a profit. Curran and Seaton's theory therefore helps to reveal that journalistic practices can be very different within the industry, depending on the ownership model a newspaper has.

While Curran and Seaton's theories are useful, they prioritise the effects of ownership and control over the content of news products, which is equally important when developing an understanding of the UK news industry. Similarly, their viewpoints don't help develop an understanding of how audience choice or the use of media language conventions influences news production.

ⓔ

- The response successfully applies knowledge and understanding of the industries framework in relation to some issues linked to ownership.
- It evaluates the usefulness of Curran and Seaton's ideas, focusing clearly on three ideas and supporting them with relevant examples from the set products.
- The response could have provided more examples from *The Guardian* to balance those from the *Daily Mail*.
- The limitations of the theory could have been discussed in more detail with the very last point expanded, making this answer at the lower end of the top-level band.

■ Section B: Media language and representation

Introduction to media language and representation

Section B focuses on media language and representation. It requires you to consider how and why media language is used by media producers to construct various representations of events, issues, individuals and social groups in a number of different ways and through a range of different media forms.

What must you study?

The OCR specification states that Section B of Media Messages provides an opportunity to develop knowledge and understanding of media contexts, media language and representations through the study of set products for the following three media forms:

- magazines
- advertising and marketing
- music videos.

Section B is not an in-depth study. Therefore, you do not need to study the set products and media forms in as much depth as you are required to do for Section A: News and Online, Social and Participatory Media. Table 12.1 summarises what you do and don't need to study for this section.

Table 12.1 Summary of the OCR specification coverage for Section B: Media Language and Representation

Media forms	Magazines	Advertising and marketing	Music videos
Set media products	Two front covers of *The Big Issue*	Poster advertisements for male grooming, soft drink and charity adverts	Two music videos, one each from two specified lists
Media industries	✗	✗	✗
Media audiences	✗	✗	✗
Media language	✓	✓	✓
Media representations	✓	✓	✓
Media contexts	Political, social and cultural	Social and cultural	Social and cultural
Academic ideas	✗	✗	✗

As the table clarifies, the two theoretical frameworks that you must study for Section B are media language and representation. OCR defines these two terms as follows:

Media language
- How the media through their forms, codes, conventions and techniques communicate meanings.

Representations

■ How the media portray events, issues, individuals and social groups.

For Section B, it is useful to break these frameworks down further into the following elements for study:

Media language

■ Genre conventions of camera, editing, sound and mise-en-scene.
  □ How are these elements used together to construct the media form so that it looks the way it does?
  □ How are these elements organised or combined in a certain way to communicate meaning in the set product?
  □ How does the genre develop through the use of technical elements?
■ How does the content incorporate the viewpoints and ideology of the producer?
■ How can multiple meanings be communicated and interpreted by the producer and audience?

Representation

■ Which different groups, individuals and/or events are presented or shown in each set product?
■ What positive or negative stereotypes are evident and why?
■ What messages and values are communicated about different groups of people, individuals and/or events?
  □ What conclusions can we make about these representations?
  □ Which groups are misrepresented or under-represented?
■ How are representations constructed as real?

For each set product, OCR requires you to have studied media language and representation in response to a number of criteria. These can be found on pages 23–25 of the specification and will be referred to in relation to each set product in this section guide.

You will also need to study media language, representation and the set products in relation to three of the five media contexts. OCR specifies that the contexts you must study for section B are:

■ political*
■ social
■ cultural.

Table 12.2 provides a reminder of what each one means.

Table 12.2 What each media context means or could include

Context	What it means or could include
Political*	• The government, policy and public affairs of a country. • The way in which power is used or is achieved in a country or society.
Social	• Where people live together and interact with one another on a day-to-day basis. • The social structures by which we live our daily lives, such as religion, education, family, media communications, law and government. • How these social structures affect our behaviour, values and thinking.
Cultural	• The attitudes, values, beliefs, practices, customs and shared behaviour of people. • It includes all aspects of 'life': language, the products we make, the things we do and how we do them. • It also includes cultural products such as art, music, literature and media.

* Only for magazines

Knowledge check 71

Do you have to study academic ideas for Section B?

You will need to consider these contexts when studying your set products and be able to demonstrate how the set products have been influenced by or developed in response to each context.

How will you be assessed?

The exam paper for Component 1: Media Messages is worth 70 marks in total. Section B: Media Language and Representation is worth 25 marks. This is 35 per cent of the exam paper.

There will be two questions for this section.
- One question will be worth 10 marks.
- One question will be worth 15 marks.

They could be made up of:
- AO1 knowledge and understanding questions
- AO2 analysis questions.

You will only be asked about two of the three media forms on one exam paper:
- magazines
- advertising and marketing
- music videos.

There may be a number of unseen sources for this section.
- Analysis questions for magazines will have an unseen front cover of *The Big Issue* magazine.
- Analysis questions for advertising and marketing will be tested against one or more unseen adverts. These may be of:
  - □ men's grooming products
  - □ soft drinks
  - □ charity adverts.
- Music videos will not be unseen and will relate to those you have studied from either List A or List B, or both.

Advertising and marketing

Introduction to advertising and marketing

The specification requires that you study advertising and marketing in relation to the use of media language and media representations in three set products.

For this unit, you must study the following:

Table 12.3 Summary of the OCR specification coverage for Section B: Advertising and Marketing

Frameworks	• Media language • Media representations
Contexts	• Social • Cultural
Set products	• Soft drink advert: *Lucozade, 'I Believe'* • Men's grooming advert: *Old Spice, 'Smell Like a Man'* • Homeless charity advert: *Shelter, 'A Home for Everyone'*

Study tip

An analysis question (AO2.1) from this section involving magazines and advertising will be in relation to unseen sources. A knowledge and understanding question (AO1.1) will ask about the media form, usually with reference to the set product.

Knowledge check 72

How many exam questions will there be on the Section B: Media Language and Representation paper? How many marks are they worth in total?

In order to study these set products in relation to advertising and marketing, it is first useful to understand:

- What is advertising and marketing?
- What are the media language conventions of print adverts?
- What are the common genres?
- What are the common representations found in print adverts?

What is advertising and marketing?

Advertising is the process of making a product and/or service known to the market and the target audience. Essentially, it spreads the word about a brand or product.

Marketing is the process of preparing a product for the market place. Advertising is one of several components used in the marketing strategy to market a product or brand.

Adverts as a media form

Print advertising is a form of advertising that uses physically printed media and usually appears in print products such as newspapers and magazines, billboards or posters.

There are four key components to a print advert:

1 headline
2 visual design elements
3 body text or copy
4 call to action.

Advertising genres

Adverts are a media form that are usually categorised by the product or services that they are selling. Therefore they cover a range of different genres such as perfume adverts, sports adverts, lifestyle adverts, food adverts, service adverts and so on.

Your study of advertising and marketing requires you to look at set products from the following three genres:

- men's grooming product adverts
- soft drinks adverts
- charity adverts.

These different adverts will use some of the same conventions, but they may use them in a different way to appeal to their different audiences. Similarly, they may also use techniques to persuade differently. For example, charity adverts may rely on fear whereas soft drink adverts may use celebrity endorsements.

Media language conventions of print adverts

Media language, in terms of print adverts, refers to the technical elements used to construct a media product so that:

- it is identifiable as an advert
- it allows the producer to communicate specific messages about the product
- it appeals visually to the target audience who will want to purchase the product.

OCR specifies that in your learning of media language for advertising and marketing, you must study three adverts in relation to issues associated with media language as set out on pages 23–24 of the specification.

These can be categorised into the following areas to help organise the study of media language in relation to advertising and marketing:

- codes and conventions
- genre
- constructing and interpreting meaning.

Specific media language elements can be divided up into two distinct elements:

1 Technical conventions:
   - This refers to the actual technical construction of the advert, for example the colour palette or the shot type.
2 Techniques to persuade:
   - This refers to content, or the message created by the combination of technical elements, that persuade the audience to buy into the product.

Knowledge check 73

Which two distinct aspects of media language work alongside each other in a print advert?

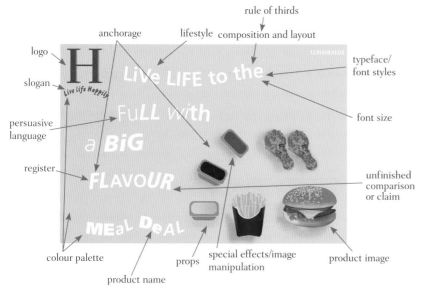

Figure 12.1 A food advert demonstrating the conventions used in print advertising

Table 12.4 identifies some of the most commonly used media language technical conventions of print advertising.

Table 12.4 Media language conventions commonly used in print advertising

Technical conventions	
Logo	Tells the audience which brand or company is selling the product.
Slogan	A short and catchy phrase associated with the product.
Product image	Shows the audience what the company or brand is selling. This is sometimes known as a pack shot.
Font size	The size of written text on the advert indicates a hierarchy of importance in what is read on the page.
Typeface/Font style	Different font styles evoke different meanings and attract different audiences. Serif and sans serif are the most common.
Shot types and angles	The camerawork, specifically shot distance and angles, used to capture the model and products in the shot.

Technical conventions	
Composition and layout	The way in which all elements in the advert are organised; how the text, images and product are positioned together on the page.
Rule of thirds	The page or advert is divided into three sections vertically and horizontally. The main part of the advert will usually take up two thirds or at least the central third of the page.
Colour palette	The use of colours in the advert's design to create a feeling in response to the product. Three colours that are complementary, from the same colour zones or contrast, will be used to create impact.
Special effects/Image manipulation	Effects that are achieved when editing the advert and are used to provide greater emphasis to the product or the message.
Props	Anything seen within the frame that is movable or portable. They provide realism, give additional meaning or can be the product itself.
Locations and settings	Location refers to the geographical place in which the advert is located. Setting is the actual production set and also the time period in which the advert is set. Some adverts might be set within a studio and so the location will be difficult to identify.
Costume and make up	What the models, actors or celebrities are wearing and how they appear. This helps to create a sense of realism, or mood or feeling. This may not apply to an advert that focuses only on the product itself.
Register/Mode of address	The way the advert 'talks' to the audience. The register may be informal or formal, fun or serious.
Anchorage	The juxtaposition of written text with an image. The placement of writing and image influences how we understand the image.
Intertextuality	Reference to another media product that provides additional meaning to the advert. This could include reference to a media celebrity.

Table 12.5 identifies some of the most commonly used media language techniques to persuade in print advertising.

Table 12.5 Media language techniques used in print advertising to persuade

Techniques to persuade	
Persuasive language	Wording that encourages the audience to purchase the product or service. This might include **rhetorical questions**.
Scientific or statistical claim	Scientific proof or experience, specific numbers or an impressive-sounding mystery ingredient.
Unfinished comparison or claim	The use of phrases that aren't finished so cannot be fully compared.
Humour	Play on words and exaggerated situations can all be used to create humour.
Beauty appeal	The use of beautiful places, people and things appeals to audiences' aspirations to become or have these things.
Lifestyle	The product is associated with a particular style of living or way of doing things.
Escape	The idea of getting away from it all or experiencing adventure.
Celebrity endorsement	Associates the product with a well-known person to reinforce consumer aspirations – we will buy the product because we admire/respect/want to be like the celebrity.
Fear	Some advertisers use fear to create worry that without this product things will not be as good as they could be.

These elements and techniques are used in a variety of ways across most adverts in order to sell the product.

Knowledge check 74

What is the rule of thirds?

Rhetorical question
A question asked for dramatic effect or to make a point.

Study tip

To practise identifying the use of media language in an unseen print advert, choose three adverts from the set genres and annotate them for media language elements. Note down which conventions are used by all three adverts and also what the key differences are.

How media language constructs meaning

Each media language technical element used in an advert can be referred to as a sign that helps the producer construct meaning in the advert in some way.

Semiotics is the study of **signs**. Semiotics identifies that every sign, known as a signifier, has a meaning known as the signified. Each signified has two levels of meaning:

Table 12.6 The difference between denotation and connotation

Denotation	Connotation
The literal meaning of each of the different signs you can see in the advert.	The additional meanings or implications of meaning created by each sign.
For example, a middle-aged white man in an expensive suit in an office with the product image of a bottle of aftershave in the bottom right-hand third of the poster.	For example, a successful businessman wears this aftershave, which helps to make him powerful. If you buy this aftershave, you too could be like him, be of similar status and own similar things.
Denotation in this sense is a DESCRIPTION of what you see in the advert.	Connotation in this sense is an ANALYSIS of what you see in the advert and what the combination of signs mean or tell you about the product.

Sign Anything that can convey meaning: an object, an image, a person, a word, and so on.

Knowledge check 75

What is the difference between denotation and connotation?

Representation in adverts

Representation in Media Studies means thinking about how an event, issue, particular social group or individual is presented to an audience through a media product.

Representation is unavoidably selective. The producer of an advert will decide how to promote the product to its target audience and in doing so will choose how to present the social groups and individuals that will be included. They will also make choices about which social groups and individuals not to include.

Producers, consciously or subconsciously, can also construct and reflect wider social attitudes to a range of issues and events, representations of which can be influenced by the following:

- Producers of adverts are usually part of the dominant social group.
- Representations constructed are likely to reinforce the producers' own experience and values.
- Adverts targeting wide audiences may be more likely to reinforce rather than challenge dominant ideology in an attempt to persuade audiences to buy unquestioningly rather than question the message behind the product.

As discussed in the print news section of this guide, CAGED provides a starting point for analysing print adverts in terms of:

- which groups tend to be represented positively, negatively or not at all
- what messages and values are communicated about different social groups and individuals as a result.

Many adverts arguably reinforce heterosexual values and so this is an important aspect of identity to include within any analysis. We could develop this mnemonic further to include sexuality so it now reads as CAGEDS.

Knowledge check 76

What does the mnemonic CAGEDS stand for? Why is it a useful way to analyse representation in adverts?

Processes of representation and constructing realism in print advertisements

OCR specifies the study of these aspects of representation for analysing print adverts:

- **Selection and combination of events, issues, social groups and individuals:** Refers to what and who we see in the advert and how these elements are combined to construct particular meaning.
- **Choices made about how to represent:** Refers to the decisions made about how to construct the representations we see. These choices depend on the values of the advertiser, the target audience and the product being sold.
- **The use of positive and negative stereotypes:** Refers to any stereotypes used to construct meaning about different events, issues, social groups and individuals in an advert. Question whether these reflect wider common stereotypes used in advertising or are something different to what we would expect.
- **Social groups who are under-or misrepresented:** The CAGEDS mnemonic can be used to identify which social groups are represented by the advert. Question how and why subordinate social groups are represented or absent.
- **Impact of industry contexts on choices producers can make:** Representation choices in adverts are usually driven by economic factors relating to production costs, the product being sold and the target audience.
- **How the media through re-presentation constructs versions of reality:** Refers to the way a print advert may use stereotypes as shortcuts to communicate the advert's message and reach the product's intended audience.
- **How representations make claims about realism:** Claims regarding realism in a print advert are made through the way the media language used influences the reader to accept its representations as real rather than simply a point of view.

Representations require interpretations. Although we are conditioned or influenced by social and cultural contexts to accept many of the representations we see in adverts, we also make judgements about them based on our own personal experiences, beliefs and values. This means that not all responses to an advert will be the same. Although the producer will aim to construct a preferred meaning to persuade the audience to buy into the product, audiences can respond to an advert in a number of ways:

1 Preferred or dominant: They agree with the advert's meaning and buy the product.
2 Negotiated: They accept the message from the advert but may not want to buy the product.
3 Oppositional: They reject the message from the advert and will not buy the product.

> **Knowledge check 77**
>
> What issues affect the choices made about how to represent issues, events, social groups and individuals in print magazines?

Soft drinks adverts: Lucozade

Please refer to this link in the study and analysis of the Lucozade set product advert:
https://www.facebook.com/LucozadeSport/photos/a.576437212371301.149800.576388689042820/720272364654451/?type=3&theater

Media language

The soft drink set product is the 'I Believe' campaign advert from 2013. This was created by Grey London and shot by Mitch Jenkins. The campaign was a £4 million mass-market campaign to educate consumers about the soft drink brand and how it could help to improve sports performance. It featured a range of sports personalities. This set product features footballer Gareth Bale, who played for Real Madrid and the Welsh national football team, as a key brand ambassador.

The campaign aimed to bring to life the product claim that 'it hydrates you better than water'. The brand's owners wanted the advert to reinforce how they were combining scientific expertise with product innovation to help athletes across the UK reach their sporting potential.

The use of advertising codes and conventions

Analysing the Lucozade set product will develop understanding and knowledge of the use of media language in relation to the OCR study points on page 128.

Before looking in more detail at the use of technical conventions in the advert, consider the following persuasive techniques that have been used to sell the product.

Table 12.7 Persuasive techniques used in the Lucozade advert

Persuasive techniques used	
Celebrity endorsement	The footballer Gareth Bale is used to endorse the product.
Unfinished claims	The statement 'In a different league' is an unfinished claim because the league it refers to is ambiguous. Another unfinished claim is at the bottom right of the advert where it states that the product is 'scientifically proven' to be in a different league to other drinks.
Statistical claim	Statistical claims are made in the top right of the advert regarding Bale's date of birth and height. The use of this factual data creates a sense of realism and 'truth' to the advert.
Lifestyle	The use of Gareth Bale associates the product with sport and fitness.

In terms of technical codes and conventions, the use of media language in the Lucozade advert is conventional.

Remember to refer to the link given on page 132 for the analysis of the Lucozade set product advert:

Table 12.8 Technical conventions used in the Lucozade advert

Technical conventions used (denoted)	
Logo	This is denoted twice to reinforce the branding: once on the product and also to the bottom left of the advert.
Product image	This is usually placed at the bottom right of the advert at the end of the eye line in order to make it easy to see. This is also known as a pack shot.
Font size	Range of sizes used to create an important hierarchy of information about the product.
Typeface/Font style	A sans serif font that is easy to read and, with the background, looks as if it is typed on a computer screen.
Shot types and angles	The medium close-up at eye level personalises Gareth Bale, whom the audience wouldn't usually be able to get so close to. The long shot of the product creates product recognition – the audience can see it fully so will know what to look for when purchasing.
Composition, layout and rule of thirds	The page is organised into two main sections. The left half carries the slogan and the right half Gareth Bale and the product.

Knowledge check 78

What is the aim of the Lucozade 'I Believe' campaign?

Technical conventions used (denoted)	
Colour palette	The blue, orange and white used with a black contrast reinforces the product packaging colours and helps the advert stand out.
Special effects/Image manipulation	The white border creates a computer screen effect. The bright blue of Bale's eyes and beads of sweat on his face are computer-generated.
Locations and settings	The advert is taken in a studio setting.
Costume and make up	Gareth Bale is wearing a sports kit, which helps identify him as a sportsman and the brand as being a sports drink.
Register/Mode of address	Scientific, factual and formal.
Anchorage	The placement of the slogan, Bale and the product image work together to reinforce the advert's overall message.
Intertextuality	The audience will be familiar with Gareth Bale from watching football matches on TV. There are also intertextual references to Bale's sponsorship deal with Adidas through his costume.

Constructing and interpreting meaning

In order to understand how meaning is constructed by the producer, and can be interpreted by the audience, it is necessary to consider how certain meanings and messages are connoted that help to sell the product. Some of the technical elements used, and their possible connotations, are identified in Table 12.9.

Table 12.9 Technical conventions used in the Lucozade advert and their connotations

Technical conventions	Connotation
Typeface/Font style	The unfinished claim 'In a different league' has the largest font size on the advert, indicating the importance of the text in creating meaning for the product. This connotes that Gareth Bale is in a different league and, by association, so is Lucozade Sport.
Shot types and angles	The medium close-up of Bale at eye level personalises him, helps create an emotional link and positions the audience, connoting that if they drink the brand they will be similar to Bale – an aspirational target for much of the audience.
Colour palette	The blue, orange, white and black colour palette is striking and creates a contrast between the font, the image of Bale and the product. The colour palette further aids recognition of the product packaging – the colour scheme signifies the product without having to refer to the pack shot.
Special effects	The Bale image is a studio shot but is manipulated by special effects to reinforce the concept of Bale being in a different league. The blue of his eye colour is heightened to complement the colour palette and connote the product. The beads of sweat created through CGI connote he is a sportsman and 'in a different league', reflecting the idea that this drink is for someone who participates in sporting activities.
Anchorage	The main slogan, the image of Bale and the product are aligned in a way to create meaning when read together. This placement anchors the meaning that not only is Bale in a different league, due to playing for Real Madrid and his sporting ability, but also connotes that Lucozade is in a different league to other drinks.

Knowledge check 79

What is the term used to refer to the product image on an advert?

Context

Cultural context: European supremacy, and the influence of cultural globalisation, is reflected by the use of Bale and the slogan.

Social context: The Lucozade advert reflects sports and fitness as social activities and the dominance of football as a male sport.

Representation

Processes of representation and realism

Table 12.10 considers the construction of the advert in relation to key elements of representation.

Table 12.10 Elements of representation used in the Lucozade advert

Element of representation	Lucozade, 'I Believe'
Selection and combination of issues, events, social groups and individuals	• Event: football • Issues: predominance of fitness and health within contemporary culture • Social groups: white male • Individuals: Gareth Bale The combination of these elements reinforces a stereotype that sport, and social activities, is dominated by successful white men.
Choices made about how to represent	The advert has made a choice to attract a male audience with a clearly gendered advert through the choice of celebrity and colour palette.
Positive and negative use of stereotypes (CAGEDS)	Positive stereotypes of white men can be seen to be reinforced, and thus, arguably repeating ideological values about patriarchy within society. This is not only supported by the selection of Bale as the celebrity endorsement but through the choice of colour palette that clearly genders both the product and sport as masculine.
Social groups who are under- or misrepresented (CAGEDS)	The sole use of Bale in the advert makes him a metaphor for successful sportspersons. By under-representing other social groups, the advert arguably serves to naturalise their lack of social power and presence.
Impact of industry contexts on choices producers can make	The choice of Bale as the celebrity endorsement is a key selling point selected by producers. Persuasive techniques to buy include scientific claims, while media language includes the image choice, colour palette, special effects, pack shot and choice of lexis. Interpretations of the advert's scientific claims led to it being banned, indicating that industry regulations can impact on the choice and success of a product.
How the media through representation constructs versions of reality	The use of special effects on Bale's face to create sweat heightens realism, helping to present Bale as an athlete and echo images that the audience are likely to see of Bale during football matches. It also reinforces the realism of the product's claim to hydrate during sport.
How representations make claims about realism	The use of data and statistics about Bale at the top right of the advert makes the advert feel factual and creates a sense of realism.

> **Study tip**
>
> Using the CAGEDS mnemonic, analyse the representation of social groups and stereotyping in a soft drink advert. How is media language used to construct stereotypes and what meanings do they offer? Record your notes in a table. Write a paragraph for each point you make about a social group.

Viewpoints and ideology

Lucozade's 'I Believe' campaign can be seen to reinforce patriarchal ideology. The use of a white man, reference to football and the predominance of the colour blue are arguably all stereotypically associated with masculinity. Bale as a celebrity endorsement can be seen to illustrate the privilege of white men within our society and positions the audience as fans of male sport.

This advert constructs representations that communicate to the male target audience the idea that if this product is purchased it will enable self-fulfilment.

> **Context**
>
> **Social context:** The ideology of managerialism is conveyed, in other words we should each be interested in keeping fit and managing our health with the help of Lucozade.
>
> **Social context:** The ideology of consumerism is conveyed, which includes aspirations and the desire to fit in.

Not only does the advert seem to draw on common patriarchal stereotypes, using them as short cuts to appeal to the target audience, but it also can be seen to reinforce ideological assumptions about lifestyle in relation to fitness and, importantly, consumerism and individualism.

Audience response and interpretation

The preferred reading of the Lucozade 'I Believe' campaign advert is that Lucozade is better than other drinks for hydration during sports. But there is an additional preferred reading that able-bodied men are interested in sport and more likely to be successful athletes than, for example, women or people with disabilities. This therefore implies that the audience response to and interpretation of the advert will depend on the demographic of the audience and their own experience of sport.

> **Study tip**
>
> Consider how each of the following social groups may respond to the preferred meaning in the Lucozade advert: an able-bodied man, a woman, a man with a physical disability. Identify what you think their interpretation of the advert would be. Use 'dominant', 'negotiated' and 'oppositional' as terms in your notes.

Context

Social context: People influenced by anti-capitalism, feminists and/or those influenced by campaigns against sugary drinks will respond differently to messages encoded in this advert.

Knowledge check 80

Which ideologies does the Lucozade 'I Believe' advert reinforce?

Men's grooming adverts: Old Spice

The 'Smell Like a Man' campaign advert from 2010 was considered a transformative mass-market campaign for the aftershave brand Old Spice. Prior to 2010, the Old Spice brand was associated with an older, more mature male audience.

The campaign features the American actor Isaiah Mustafa and was shot by Matthew Carroll for the Wieden and Kennedy advertising agency.

Media language

Analysing the Old Spice set product advert will develop understanding and knowledge of the use of media language in relation to the OCR study points. The annotated image in Figure 12.2 indicates which conventions are used and where they are on the advert.

The use of advertising codes and conventions

Before looking in a little more detail at the technical conventions used by the advert, it is evident that a number of persuasive techniques have been used to sell the product.

Table 12.11 Persuasive techniques used to sell the Old Spice advert

Persuasive techniques used	
Unfinished claim	The advert provides an unfinished claim, which it uses to create humour by saying 'This fact has not been fact checked'.
Humour	The exaggerated situation of the setting, the expression on the actor's face along with the unfinished claim help to create humour.
Escape	The idea of escape, also referenced in the TV advert with the phrase 'The man your man could smell like', provides a sense of escapism for the female audience. The setting of a tropical island also provides a sense of escape from everyday life.

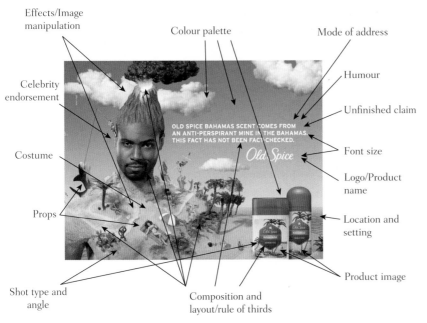

Effects/Image manipulation

Colour palette

Mode of address

Humour

Celebrity endorsement

Unfinished claim

Costume

Font size

Logo/Product name

Props

Location and setting

Product image

Shot type and angle

Composition and layout/rule of thirds

Figure 12.2 Old Spice advert showing conventions of print advertising used

In terms of technical codes and conventions, the use of media language in the Old Spice 'Smell Like a Man' print advert is conventional.

Table 12.12 Technical conventions used in Old Spice, 'Smell Like a Man'

Technical conventions used (denoted)	
Logo	Old Spice
Product image	The deodorant in two different forms.
Font size	Two different sizes of font; the largest font size is the name of the product, Old Spice. The slightly smaller font is the unfinished claim, which brings humour to the advert.
Typeface/Font style	Two font styles are used. The one used for 'Old Spice' is a cursive font, meaning it could be handwritten. The capitalised sans serif of the unfinished claim gives it impact and makes it stand out.
Shot types and angles	A mid shot is used of Mustafa so we can recognise him in the advert. A long shot of the products is used so they can be fully seen and to aid recognition when being purchased.
Composition, layout and rule of thirds	The advert uses almost every third of the space in terms of the composition and layout. The pack shot of the product image is conventionally in the bottom right of the shot as this is where the eye is drawn. Mustafa takes up the left-hand side and bottom third, creating an 'L' line to draw the reader's eye from the top of the page with his face to the bottom-right of the advert.
Colour palette	The colour choices reflect the Caribbean and Spice Islands theme. The blue and sand colours help to reinforce this while the white font and red product provide a contrast and so stand out.
Special effects/ Image manipulation	An erupting volcano has been visually manipulated onto the top of Mustafa's head. The props such as the shark, island, wind surfer and sunbathing woman have also been edited onto his body.

learn key terms

4-5 key terms (handwritten)

Technical conventions used (denoted)	
Props	Props such as the shark, sunbathing woman and trees all help to construct the idea that the setting is in the Caribbean and reinforce the campaign's theme of being able to be in the Caribbean with Old Spice.
Locations and settings	The studio set is made to appear as if the subject is on a tropical island. The assumption is that it's the Caribbean because the text refers to Old Spice as a Bahamas scent.
Costume and make-up	Mustafa's costume is the sand so that to the right-hand side of the advert it becomes indistinguishable from the setting.
Register/Mode of address	The mode of address is humorous. It retains the informal, jokey nature of the campaign's television adverts while also mocking the use of unfinished statements in adverts.
Anchorage	The alignment of the actor, text and product from left to right serves to anchor the three separate elements so that they make meaning in combination together.
Intertextuality	The unfinished statement is an intertextual reference to the campaign's television adverts. Mustafa's starring role in the *Shadowhunter* TV series may also make him appealing to audiences.

↳ reference (handwritten)

Constructing and interpreting meaning

In order to understand how meaning is constructed by the producer, and can be interpreted by the audience, it is necessary to consider how certain meanings and messages are connoted to help to sell the product. Some of the technical elements used, and their possible connotations, are identified in Table 12.13

Table 12.13 Technical conventions used in the Old Spice advert and their connotations

Technical conventions	Connotation
Typeface/ Font style	The cursive style of the product name Old Spice helps to personalise meaning, connoting that it is personal, friendly and real.
Shot types and angles	The mid shot of Isaiah Mustafa creates a personal connection and physical closeness that connotes that he is someone the audience would want to be near or with.
Colour palette	The colour palette evokes the colours of a tropical island, suggesting that if the audience wear or buy Old Spice they can escape their everyday lives and be transported to paradise!
Locations and settings	The reference to Old Spice as a scent from the Bahamas further reinforces the meaning of escapism and suggests the product's exotic appeal.
Register/ Mode of address	The humorous mode of address connotes that Old Spice, and anyone who wears it, is young and fun. It also connotes intelligence by being self-mocking, thus making it postmodern and culturally relevant.
Anchorage	The anchoring of image, text and product connotes that Old Spice is fun, humorous and exotic. If you buy or wear this product, you are also fun and humorous and could be as attractive, manly and funny as Isaiah Mustafa!

Representation

The representation study points, previously considered in Tables 12.9 and 12.10, can also be applied to the Old Spice 'Smell Like a Man' advert.

Activity

1 Analyse the elements of representation constructed in the Old Spice 'Smell Like a Man' advert. Create a table, like Table 12.10 to record your notes.

   In each row explain:
   - how the representation is constructed with reference to the use of media language, and
   - what message or meaning the representation communicates.

2 Consider the stereotypes used in the Old Spice 'Smell Like a Man' advert in more detail. Using the CAGEDS mnemonic, analyse and make notes on the representation of social groups in the advert.
   - What media language conventions are used to construct these stereotypes?
   - What meanings do they offer?

   Use your notes to write a paragraph about each group. Organise each paragraph in the following order
   - Start with a statement about how the social group is represented.
   - Follow with an explanation of which media language element is used to construct the representation.
   - Finally, analyse what this might reveal about stereotypes of that social group within society.

Study tip

Consider how three different social groups of your choice may respond to the preferred meaning in the Old Spice advert. Use the terms 'dominant', 'negotiated' and 'oppositional' to describe how you think each group would respond to the advert, giving some reasons for their differing responses.

Viewpoints and ideology

Old Spice's 'Smell Like a Man' campaign can be seen to reinforce patriarchal ideology. The use of Isaiah Mustafa to promote the product, slogan and the actual product itself all reinforce masculinity and the ideological dominance of men within our society.

The advert, as a media form whose purpose is to sell a product, constructs representations that communicate to men, and women, the idea that if this product is purchased it will enable self-fulfilment and men can become better men. The product invites its target audience, including women who buy the product for men, to accept this ideological viewpoint.

Therefore, not only does the advert draw on common patriarchal stereotypes, using them as shortcuts to appeal to the target audience, but it also reinforces ideological assumptions about lifestyle in relation to our appearance to others and, importantly, consumerism and individualism. The representation of masculinity also arguably reinforces ethnic stereotypes about hyper-sexualized black men in the media.

Audience response and interpretation

The preferred reading of the Old Spice 'Smell Like a Man' campaign advert could be that Old Spice can make you manly and a better version of yourself. It could also be argued that for the intended female target audience who are expected to buy the product, Old Spice could make their partner more attractive, with the endorsement of Mustafa to illustrate this. But the audience response to and interpretation of the advert will depend on the demographic and experience of the audience.

Knowledge check 83

Which ideologies does the Old Spice 'Smell Like a Man' advert reinforce?

CAGED
- class
- age
- gender
- Ethnicity
- Disability

Charity adverts: Shelter

Figure 12.3 Shelter's 'A Home for Everyone' poster

Media language

Shelter is a charity that alleviates the distress caused by bad housing and homelessness. Shelter aim to ensure there's a safe, secure and affordable home for everyone.

Unlike the Lucozade and Old Spice set products, Shelter's 'A Home for Everyone' campaign is a non-commercial product that uses media language elements and constructs representations to encourage donations to the charity rather than a product purchase. Shelter's 'A Home for Everyone' campaign should therefore be studied as a contrast to the other two set products.

The use of advertising codes and conventions

Analysing the Shelter set product advert will develop understanding and knowledge of the use of media language in relation to the OCR study points.

It is evident that a number of persuasive techniques have been used in the advert to persuade people to donate.

Table 12.14 Persuasive techniques used in the Shelter advert

Persuasive techniques used	
Persuasive language	The use of persuasive statements position the audience to read the advert, and its message, from a particular point of view.
Rhetorical questions	The three rhetorical questions in red placed in front of each face demand a response that the audience can't answer. This helps position the audience to sympathise.
Fear	The use of three individuals, each with a different anxiety about their housing, creates a fear that this can happen to anyone and could happen to the reader.

Context

Social context: The advert echoes social anxieties about economic and family issues that lead to people losing their home, which contrasts well with people who value trivial matters such as buying the latest hair product.

Activity

Identify the media language conventions used by the Shelter 'A Home for Everyone' campaign.

1 Trace the Shelter advert (Figure 12.2). Using the examples in Table 12.4 and Figure 12.2, annotate the tracing to identify the technical conventions used on the advert.

2 Select five of the technical conventions used in the Shelter advert and describe what each one denotes. You could create a table, like Table 12.4, to record your notes.

Constructing and interpreting meaning

In order to understand how meaning is constructed by the producer, and can be interpreted by the audience, it is necessary to consider how certain meanings and messages are connoted that help to sell the product. Some of the technical elements used, and their possible connotations, are identified in Table 12.15.

Table 12.15 Technical conventions used in the Shelter advert and their connotations

Technical conventions	Connotation
Typeface/Font style	The sans serif font connotes the urgency of the situation and the immediate impact for the individual. This creates a sense of fear for each figure, making the audience more likely to want to help.
Shot types and angles	The close-up and direct address of each character looking directly into the camera, and therefore to the audience, personalises the characters and heightens the emotion that can be seen in their faces. This helps connote their plight and difficulty, subsequently creating sympathy in the audience for the cause of the charity.
Colour palette	The stark colour palette of red, black and natural tones creates a simplicity that allows the red font of the statements to stand out. This connotes the urgency and danger of the situation that each character finds themselves in and conveys this to the audience so they feel they should donate.
Register/Mode of address	The mode of address is serious and the use of lexis connotes the sense of hopelessness faced by the characters. The rhetorical questions such as 'where will we live?' signify the fear of homelessness and create empathy among the audience, encouraging them to donate.
Anchorage	The placement of each statement on top of a character signifies that different situations can cause homelessness for different people. The positioning of the statements above the lips connotes that by supporting Shelter, the audience will be giving people affected by homelessness a voice.

Study tip

In your studies, you should identify how each media language convention used in the Shelter advert constructs meaning. Identify which conventions are not used in Table 12.15. For each one, note down the meaning it connotes and how it may persuade the audience to donate to the charity.

Knowledge check 84

Which three advertising techniques does the Shelter advert use to attract the audience?

Context

Cultural context: The concept of consumerism and the need to consume images when reading an advert are relied upon to shock audiences.

Content guidance

Developing the advertising genre

Although Shelter's 'A Home for Everyone' campaign offers a contrast to the other two set products in this unit, it is a good example of charity advert genre conventions. Charity adverts use the following techniques to create sympathy or 'shock' their audience:

- facts and statistics
- characters who appear desperate or needy
- direct address of the character looking directly into the camera at the audience
- creation of empathy for the characters by requiring the audience to consider how they would feel if they were in the same situation
- shock and fear, often with the use of disturbing images or language, to make the audience feel they must contribute to the charitable cause.

These tactics make audiences feel guilty and that they must help those less fortunate.

In this sense, Shelter's 'A Home for Everyone' campaign can be considered conventional because it uses these tactics to attract donations to its charitable cause.

Representation

Processes of representation and realism

The representation study points, previously considered in Table 12.10, can also be applied to the Shelter 'A Home for Everyone' advert.

> **Activity**
>
> 1 Analyse the elements of representation constructed in the Shelter 'A Home for Everyone' advert. Create a table like Table 12.10.
>
>   For each row explain:
>   - how the representation is constructed with reference to the use of media language
>   - what message or meaning the representation communicates.
>
> 2 Consider the stereotypes used in the Shelter 'A Home for Everyone' advert in more detail. Using the CAGEDS mnemonic, analyse and make notes on the representation of social groups in the advert.
>   - What media language conventions are used to construct these stereotypes?
>   - What meanings do they offer?
>
>   Use your notes to write a paragraph about each group. Organise each paragraph in the following order:
>   - Start with a statement about how the social group is represented.
>   - Follow with an explanation of which media language element is used to construct the representation.
>   - Finally, analyse what this might reveal about stereotypes of that social group within society.

misrepresentations / underrepresentation

Viewpoints and ideology → *grasp the understanding.*

Shelter's 'A Home for Everyone' campaign can be seen to communicate a number of ideological values, some of them contrasting.

The advert, as analysis suggests, reinforces a viewpoint that social inequality is unjust and that those in positions of social power or wealth have a duty to help those who are not. In this context, the advert supports a social, liberal view with the idea that we have a social duty to help one another.

Additionally, the advert reinforces the ideological values of individualism by suggesting that every individual has the right to self-fulfilment and a better life, including those who have less than others.

To some extent, this value is reinforced through the ideology of consumerism by using the advert form, which relies on the consumption of messages and values to create empathy and persuade the audience to donate to the charity.

Audience response and interpretation

The preferred reading of the Shelter 'A Home for Everyone' advert could be that homelessness can happen to anyone for a number of different reasons. There is also an additional preferred meaning that suggests we should feel empathy and responsibility for helping others who are less fortunate than ourselves. But the audience response to and interpretation of the advert will depend on the demographic and experience of the audience. In particular, it will depend on their views towards charity and how they respond to the representations constructed.

> **Study tip**
>
> Select three different social groups; one could be a middle-class woman. Identify how each may respond to the preferred meaning in the Shelter advert. Use the terms 'dominant', 'negotiated' and 'oppositional' to describe how each group audience member would respond to the advert with some reasons for their differing responses.

Context

Cultural context: The advert reflects ideologies of social care linked to the welfare state and the context of the positive cultural evaluation of charity originally coming from religion.

Knowledge check 85

Which ideologies does the Shelter 'A Home for Everyone' advert reflect?

Magazines

Introduction to magazines

The specification requires that you study magazines and *The Big Issue* in relation to media language and media representations.

For this unit, you must study the following:

Table 13.1 Summary of the OCR specification coverage for Section B: Magazines

Frameworks	• Media language • Media representations
Contexts	• Social • Cultural • Political
Set products	• Two front covers of *The Big Issue* magazine. • They must be from September 2017 or later. • They must demonstrate alternative representations to the mainstream. • They must be of national significance.

In order to demonstrate how *The Big Issue* is an alternative to mainstream magazine forms, it is useful to first consider what mainstream magazines are before studying *The Big Issue* as the set product.

Magazines as a media form

A magazine is a periodical publication containing a collection of articles that are targeted at entertaining and informing a particular audience.

As a print form, magazines share some of their characteristics with newspapers but there are significant differences between the two media forms. Magazines are:

- usually printed on higher quality paper
- usually stapled or bound
- published less frequently than newspapers – weekly, monthly, quarterly or biannually
- usually organised by theme or topic.

The importance of front covers

The front cover of a magazine is of vital importance because it is the first part of the publication that the reader will see. Therefore, it must do the following:

1 indicate who the magazine is intended for, appealing to the attention of the target audience

2 indicate the type of magazine it is (customer, consumer, business or a sub-genre of one of these)

3 help the magazine stand out from its competitors by conveying a clear sense of brand.

Magazine conventions

Magazines have a number of technical conventions that identify them as magazines and help them appeal to their target audience. Figure 13.1 shows a conventional magazine front cover and illustrates some of the key conventions that usually appear on the front cover of a magazine.

Knowledge check 86

Which contexts must you study for magazines and *The Big Issue*?

Knowledge check 87

Why are magazine front covers important?

Figure 13.1 Front cover of a magazine showing key magazine conventions

Table 13.2 Description of magazine conventions

Magazine convention	Description of convention
Masthead	This is usually at the top of the page and is the placement for the name of the magazine. It is instantly recognisable to the audience as a brand image.
Tag line	A tag line is a catchy phrase that represents the brand.
Slogan	A slogan is a catchy phrase that represents the product and helps it to stand out against rival products.
Date line	The line for the date of the magazine.
Feature article	The main feature or story, usually in the largest font size and possibly in a different colour to stand out.
Central image	The main image on the magazine, it is usually connected to the feature article and appeals to the audience.
Cover lines	Short, catchy phrases referencing content inside the magazine and helping persuade the reader to buy.
Colour palette	Usually made of no more than three colours that contrast but complement one another. Each edition may use different colours to reflect a theme for that issue.
Barcode	The placement of the barcode used to purchase the product.
Price line	The placement of the price.
Composition and layout	The way in which all the elements on the cover are organised; how text, images and shapes are positioned on the page. The rule of thirds is used when composing the page, with the central image usually in the middle third of the page. This ensures that it takes up the main part of the page and is the most eye-catching feature. The most important text will be across the top, the top left and the centre, as this is where our eye is drawn to first.

Study tip

You will need to demonstrate how *The Big Issue* differs from mainstream magazines. First, you must understand what mainstream magazine conventions are. Pick three best-selling consumer magazines and analyse the use of media language conventions on the front covers. Make a note of the most commonly used conventions across all three covers.

Magazine convention	Description of convention
Typography	The style and size of font used indicates its relevance. Different font styles can evoke different meanings; serif and sans serif are both commonly used to evoke different meanings. No more than three sizes or styles of typography will be used.
Mode of address and language	The way the magazine 'talks' to the audience will depend on the genre of magazine and who the target audience is. Lexis is usually straightforward so readers can make quick decisions about whether to buy the magazine.
Shot types and angles	The central image is usually a long or mid shot. The angle may depend on the subject in the image and the message the magazine wants to communicate.

There are additional conventions that are commonly used on magazine front covers, although not in Figure 13.1.

Table 13.3 Description of other magazine conventions

Magazine convention	Description of convention
Strapline	Bands or lines that go at the top and/or bottom of the page, usually filled with text.
Puff	A shape, usually in a contrasting colour, that attracts the reader's eye.
Logo	Some magazines may also have a recognisable image that runs across every issue.

important for contrast of representation (handwritten)

The Big Issue

needs to be known (handwritten)

The Big Issue magazine was launched in 1991 with the aim of transforming the lives of London's homeless through its mantra: 'A hand up not a hand out'.

The Big Issue, while a magazine, is sometimes referred to as a street paper. It supports the homeless and those seeking to escape poverty. Vendors buy the magazine for £1.25 and sell it to the public for £2.50. *The Big Issue* has helped almost 100,000 people since it began.

The Big Issue reader is likely to:

understand the mission statement (handwritten)

- be university educated
- be interested in politics, popular and high culture
- have a limited disposable income
- want to help make a difference to the society we live in.

The front covers, and content, of *The Big Issue* must therefore attract this reader. The use of media language and the representations it constructs must also appeal to the reader in order to ensure that street vendors can sell each issue and make money.

Media language

Media language, in terms of magazines, refers to the technical elements used to construct a media product so that:

Knowledge check 88

What does composition and layout refer to?

Study tip

If you are asked to analyse the use of media language on an unseen front cover of *The Big Issue*, you must make reference to the codes and conventions used on the front cover, the way the front cover develops the genre or sub-genre and how these conventions construct and connote specific meanings.

- it is identifiable as a magazine, along with its sub-genre within this form
- it allows the producer to communicate specific points of view on the front cover about the magazine's contents
- it appeals visually to the target audience enough to ensure they purchase the magazine.

The use of media language for magazines follows print conventions. These include:

- camera work – shots and angles
- mise-en-scene – location, lighting, make-up and costume
- layout and typography
- mode of address and language
- other editing features required to construct the page.

OCR specifies that in your learning of media language and *The Big Issue*, you must study two front covers in relation to issues associated with media language as set out on pages 23–24 of the specification.

These can be categorised into three areas:

1 codes and conventions

2 genre

3 constructing and interpreting meaning.

The Big Issue is a **niche** magazine that is outside the commercial mainstream. It is a contrasting example of how elements of media language can be used to construct alternative representations that appeal to a particular audience.

This section will consider the use of media language on the following two front covers:

- Issue 1305, 30 April 2018, 'The Greatest Show on Earth' (www.bigissue.com/ magazines/the-greatest-shows-on-earth-your-complete-guide-to-the-summer/)
- Issue 1315, 9 July 2018, 'Flake News'.

The use of magazine codes and conventions

Masthead
Price line
Date line
Tag line
Central image
Feature article
Cover lines
Puff
Colour palette

Figure 13.2 *The Big Issue's* 'Flake news' cover

Table 13.4 summarises which conventions both front covers have in common.

Although the two front covers are very different in the way they look and the themes they feature, they display a number of similarities in terms of the media language conventions they use.

Knowledge check 89

What functions as a logo across *The Big Issue* magazines?

Table 13.4 Description of magazine conventions used on *The Big Issue* covers

Magazine convention	Description of convention
Masthead	The mastheads have a different placement and different colour on each magazine but look the same, and both use the black and white contrast.
Strapline	Straplines are absent, although the placement of the cover lines on 'Flake News' is similar to a strapline, drawing the eye to these words.
Tag line	'A hand up not a hand out'. This is conventional to both covers but placed differently. This stands for the ethos of *The Big Issue* as a charity rather than just the magazine itself.
Slogan	Uses a tag line instead of a slogan.
Date line	The date line is evident on both covers but in different places.
Feature article	Both covers have one feature article and this takes up most of the cover.
Central image	An illustrated central image is used on both covers. This can reduce operating costs.
Cover lines	The main cover line is the feature article. 'Flake News' offers three, but their wording is minimal and it is ambiguous whether they are actually cover lines or statements similar to those Donald Trump might tweet.
Puff	Both front covers feature puffs in unconventional shapes that reinforce meaning for the covers and add to the central image: • 'The Greatest Show on Earth' puff is in the shape of a circus tent to reinforce the issue's theme of festivals. • The 'Flake News' puff is sun-shaped to reinforce the summer theme.
Colour palette	Each cover uses different colour palettes but they are conventional in using three main colours. This creates cohesive front covers that are visually appealing.
Barcode	There is no barcode. *The Big Issue* is sold on streets so a barcode is unnecessary.
Price line	The price features at the top left-hand side of the magazine, where the eye looks first. As the price of the magazine is a hand-up for the street vendor, its placement and larger font size than the date line is significant.
Logo	The masthead works as a logo on the magazine and across the charity itself.
Composition and layout	Both front covers use a composition that offers symmetry in the layout to enhance the main image. The use of image and the placement in the middle third or across most of the cover helps focus the reader's eye on the central image and feature article.
Typography	The masthead uses sans serif font and is the same across both covers. However, each cover uses a different typeface to help reinforce the issue's theme: • 'The Greatest Show on Earth' uses a serif font, which is traditional so reinforces the cultural tradition of festivals in Britain. • 'Flake News' uses a sans serif font, which helps reflect the Trump theme by being direct and simple to read.
Mode of address and language	The use of language on both front covers makes references to cultural expressions: • 'Flake News' is referring to the cultural tradition of the 99 Flake ice cream while satirising Donald Trump's over-quoted use of 'fake news'. • 'The Greatest Show on Earth' is referring to the circus with the words 'Roll Up Roll up', and also to the films *The Greatest Show on Earth* and *The Greatest Showman*.
Shot types and angles	Although illustrated, the images can still be referred to in terms of their shot type and angle: • 'Flake News' uses a medium close-up of Trump so we can see his melting face, which is humorous. • 'The Greatest Show on Earth' uses a slight low angle with the majority of the characters in mid shot. This suggests that they are considered of cultural importance and the mid shots allow the reader to identify them.

Developing the magazine genre

Through this analysis, it is evident that while it looks very different to mainstream magazine genres, *The Big Issue* still uses the key conventional elements of print media language in its construction.

However, it uses them in slightly different ways. This helps to identify the magazine as different from other niche and mainstream magazines, which is a selling point. It also helps to develop the genre in interesting ways.

Table 13.5 Magazine conventions used differently in *The Big Issue*

Typical conventions used in *The Big Issue*	Typical conventions not used	Conventions used, but differently to mainstream magazines
Masthead Tag line Date line Feature article Central image Puff Colour palette Composition and layout Typography Mode of address and language Camera shot types and angles Cover lines	Barcode Slogan	**Central image** – use of illustrations rather than a photograph **Composition and layout** – changes with every front cover rather than having a standard layout that is recognisable as part of the magazine's brand **Mode of address and language** – often these will incorporate intertextual references to other media products or cultural traditions **Puffs** – the shapes used help to reinforce the theme of the issue and create coherence with the main image **Cover lines** – these aren't always used and when they are they are usually integrated into the main image in some way

Constructing meaning

When looking at media language, it is also necessary to consider how *The Big Issue*:

- uses **intertextuality** in different ways
- constructs multiple meanings through the codes and conventions used.

The 'Flake News' front cover creates meaning and makes intertextual references through the central image, feature article and puffs.

Table 13.6 Intertextual references and their meanings on the 'Flake News' front cover

Convention	Intertextual references	Multiple meanings
Central image	The denoted image is of an ice-cream in an ice-cream cone. Two intertextual references are made through this image: 1 Donald Trump's face within the ice cream is a reference to Trump, politics and his imminent visit to the UK. 2 The flake and sprinkles make reference to a 99 Flake, which is a British cultural tradition associated with the summer.	The use of the intertextual references constructed by the central image provides multiple meanings. The producer can construct a political point of view about Trump's visit to the UK. The 99 Flake and British weather is a cultural reference to British traditions and communicates the potential impact Trump could have on British culture.

Intertextuality The referencing of another media text or cultural product. In making this reference, the meaning is further shaped and developed.

Context

Cultural context: British cultural identities and the influence of American culture are reflected on the front cover.

Convention	Intertextual references	Multiple meanings
Feature article – theme and language used	The use of language in the feature article sell line is a play on words. Trump's phrase 'fake news' is combined with the description of the ice cream with a flake to read 'Flake News'. The language makes the same two intertextual references as the central image, further reinforcing the intertextuality.	The use of language for the feature article helps anchor and reinforce meaning to the image. The play on words provides a humorous but politically serious message about Trump and his attitude towards the media. It invites the reader not to take him seriously as the combination of the image and text is funny.
Puffs	The golden puff is the shape and colour of the sun, continuing the metaphor of a summer heatwave. The image inside the puff is an intertextual reference to the theatre play *Hamilton*, about the American founding father.	The use of the puff and reference to *Hamilton* juxtaposes a melting Trump with a triumphant and shining Hamilton, positioned as the sun. This helps the producer mock Trump's position as the president of the USA in comparison to America's serious founding father.

Representation → how things appear

Representation refers to the re-presentation of an issue, event, social group or person from the particular point of view of the person who constructs the representation.

As previously discussed, common representations in the magazine industry tend to support the dominant social group, as they are usually the media owners and producers. This means that media representations often serve to reinforce the social status quo, so that those considered to be in minority or subordinate groups remain stuck in these social roles.

The Big Issue is a charity that, through the magazine, aims to help those who are marginalised in society and subsequently misrepresented or under-represented in the mainstream media. It also aims to provide a platform for social issues that are of national and global importance.

However, the magazine's owners and target audience can be seen to fall into the dominant group in that they are white, male, middle-aged and middle-class. This suggests that *The Big Issue* is likely to offer complex representations that possibly both challenge and support those seen in mainstream magazines.

OCR specifies that in the study of representation and *The Big Issue*, you must consider two front covers in relation to specific issues associated with representation. These can be categorised into the following three areas:

1 processes of representation and realism
2 viewpoints and ideology
3 audience response and interpretation.

Processes of representation and realism

Through the use of media language elements, the producers of *The Big Issue* are able to satirise political and cultural figures, issues and events. OCR specifies the study of the following aspects of representation in the analysis of representation on a front cover:

Context

Political context: The use of the phrase 'Flake News' reflects Trump's political dismissal of journalism and news that may be critical of him and his policies.

Political context: Trump's values are far removed from the political values of the founding fathers that were motivated by social welfare and creating a better life

Study tip

To develop your skills in identifying how *The Big Issue* front covers use media language elements to construct intertextual meanings, select another front cover. What references to other media products can be seen through the central image, feature article and puffs? Analyse the meaning created, use a table similar to Table 13.5 to note down your observations.

Knowledge check 90

Why does *The Big Issue* use intertextual references?

These representation study points can be applied to a front cover of *The Big Issue*. The Table 13.7 considers the construction of representations on Issue 1315, 9 July 2018, 'Flake News'.

Table 13.7 The analysis of processes of representation and realism in *The Big Issue* – 'Flake News' front cover.

Element of representation	The Big Issue, 'Flake News' front cover
Selection and combination of issues, events, social groups and individuals	*This refers to what and who we see on the front cover and how combining different events, issues, social groups and/or individuals constructs particular meanings.* The selection and combination of the featured issues, events, social groups and individuals suggest they are all interconnected and this helps the magazine make a link between Trump, mental health, and British and American culture. • Issues: mental health; Trump's political ability; the impact of US culture and politics on the UK • Events: Trump's UK visit; the British heatwave; *Hamilton* play • Social groups: dominant group • Individuals: Donald Trump.
Choices made about how to represent	*This refers to the decisions producers make regarding how to construct the representations we see. These choices depend on the values of the owner/editor of the magazine, the target audience, the theme and topic of the issue.* The magazine's use of political satire and Trump's harsh views regarding journalism and social issues suggest *The Big Issue* has chosen to represent Trump in a way that will reflect the magazine's values and appeal to the social and political interests of its audience.
The positive and negative use of stereotypes	*This refers to any stereotypes used to construct meaning about different events, issues, social groups and individuals on a front cover. You should question whether these reflect wider common stereotypes used on magazine covers or are different to what we would expect.* Trump, as white, male, middle-class, middle-aged and conservative is a member of the dominant group, and would usually be represented positively in the media. In order to reinforce their values, the producers of this image have constructed a negative stereotype of Trump as a leading political figure, which invites the reader to laugh at him.
Social groups who are under- or misrepresented	*The CAGEDS mnemonic can be used to identify which social groups are represented on a front cover. You should question how and why subordinate social groups are represented or absent.* By focusing the front cover on Trump it appears that only the dominant group is represented. However, the use of the 99 Flake ice cream as a visual representation of Britain and the use of the puff to reference *Hamilton* represents American history and politics. In this way, the British and American people are represented as being affected by Trump and the dominant group.

Knowledge check 91

What factors affect the choices made about how to represent issues, events, social groups and individuals on the front covers of *The Big Issue*?

Context

Social context: The selection on the front cover reflects social anxieties in the UK regarding Trump's competence as president, his visit to the UK and his influence over British policy and therefore society.

Social context: The use of Trump as the central image reflects his impact on social issues such as immigration, social welfare and economic trade policies, which all impact Western society.

Social context: The front cover reflects that Trump has considerable influence over our political situation, globally and nationally.

Cultural context: Cultural capital and knowledge of Trump's phrase 'fake news' and of British cultural references in relation to ice cream is required for the pun to work.

Content guidance

Element of representation	The Big Issue, 'Flake News' front cover
Impact of industry contexts on choices producers can make	*Representation choices on front covers are usually driven by economic factors, which relate to production costs, the vendors' need to sell the magazine, and the target audience.* The reliance on illustration to cut production costs has a positive impact on the representation of Trump for this cover. It offers a humorous and creative representation that wouldn't be seen in mainstream magazines.
How the media through representation construct versions of reality	*By providing an alternative point of view to mainstream magazines and media, The Big Issue offers a version of reality that isn't usually seen in the media and possibly reflects a more 'real' experience, and the diversity of the British public, rather than just one dominant group.* The use of Trump's melting face presents a representation of Trump as under pressure and not looking forward to his imminent visit to the UK. In constructing this version or 'reality' of Trump, the producers are able to satirise him and invite readers to question Trump's motives, social and political values and the impact of his visit on Britain.
How representations make claims about realism	The Big Issue *relies on illustration and text to construct representations, so the claims regarding realism are made in the way the media language influences the reader to accept that what they are reading is real rather than a point of view.* Through the play on the words 'flake news', the producers are able to construct a representation of Trump that claims he is an unfit president. His representation as an ice cream caricatures him and constructs a message that he cannot be taken seriously in reality.

Study tip

To practise your skills in identifying representations, select a different front cover of *The Big Issue*. Using each of the elements provided in Table 13.7, analyse the representations constructed by your chosen front cover. When completed, write a paragraph for each point.

Viewpoints and ideology

The Big Issue as a brand is considered to be a business that functions to produce money, which is socially invested to create employment and ease poverty for people rather than providing profit for those who own it.

It therefore represents a viewpoint that runs counter to the mainstream and can be seen to question dominant ideology and the dominant group.

The political bias of the magazine isn't direct, as this could affect sales of the magazine for the vendor, but the magazine has a clear social agenda with features covering:

- social welfare
- current affairs
- politics
- culture
- the environment
- finance
- health
- food
- sport.

The Big Issue agenda can be seen to be counter to right-wing politics, which do not value progressive social welfare policies but instead value individual and financial profit from business above access to social provision and equality for all social groups.

Therefore, although the owners of *The Big Issue* are members of the dominant group in that they are predominantly white, male, middle-class and middle-aged, ideologically their alternative viewpoint is bound with creating opportunities to support social welfare and values. This is achieved in the following ways:

- Through the use of satire, the representation of events, issues, social groups and individuals can be critiqued without there being an overtly political message.
- The interesting and creative use of media language helps communicate the magazine's ideological values that we should care about all social groups and the society we live in, not just those with political, social and cultural power.

This helps to position the audience from the point of view of the producer, inviting the reader to question the meanings constructed on the front cover and in turn question established mainstream ideological values.

Audience interpretation of meaning

Through the use of media language elements, the producers of *The Big Issue* are able to satirise political and cultural figures, issues and events.

The media language conventions used, and the meanings constructed by the producer as a result, are intended to communicate a preferred meaning to the reader. However, this relies on a number of assumptions about *The Big Issue*'s target audience:

1 The reader will decode the meaning encoded by the producer in the preferred way.
   □ The reader may not decode the same preferred reading that the producer has intended.
2 The reader has the cultural capital and experience to understand the intertextual references made by the front covers in order to interpret the different meanings.
   □ The use of intertextual references on the front cover relies on the audience to have experience or knowledge, or be interested in the intertextual references made in the magazine.
3 The reader shares the same ideological values as the producer of the representation.
   □ The audience has to actively seek to buy the magazine from street vendors and in doing so is contributing to the social welfare and development of the vendors.
4 The reader enjoys satire and is interested in political, social and cultural figures, issues and events.
   □ The target audience of *The Big Issue* is left wing, with the main occupations being in the civil service, charities or government, suggesting that these readers will see the satire constructed through the use of media language conventions on the front covers as relevant to their values and daily social experiences.
   □ The use of satire will appeal to their social and political convictions and also to their educational level.

Study tip

To develop your understanding of the way in which audiences interpret meaning from the use of media language and constructed representations, pick a different *Big Issue* front cover. Identify three things that would appeal to the target audience, and for each example say why and what meaning it conveys.

Knowledge check 92

How does *The Big Issue* offer an alternative viewpoint to dominant ideology on its front covers?

Knowledge check 93

What four assumptions are made about *The Big Issue* readers and the ways they may interpret meaning from the front cover?

Music videos

Introduction to music videos

Music videos must be studied in relation to media language and representations, including a consideration of the social and cultural contexts that influence how media language is used to construct representations in music videos.

You should study the differences in the use of two music videos; one from List A and one from List B.

List A	List B
Corinne Bailey Rae, 'Stop Where You Are'	Fatboy Slim, 'Ya Mama'
Massive Attack, 'Unfinished Sympathy'	Radiohead, 'Burn the Witch'
Emeli Sandé, 'Heaven'	David Guetta, 'Titanium'

You will be required to explore the differences in the use of media language and the representations constructed between the two music videos chosen.

What are music videos?

A music video can be defined as a filmed and edited performance of a recorded song.

The main purpose of a music video is to promote the single, the album the single is from and the artist to as wide an audience as possible. To do this, a music video has to:

1   sell the song in a way that helps the audience to remember it from the video

2   provide the viewer with a better understanding of the song so they engage with it both visually and audibly

3   entertain the viewer by highlighting the talents of the artist – dancing, singing, performing and their physical appearance.

Music videos have become an integral part of the music industry, playing a vital role in the success of the artist.

Music videos as a media form

The 1970s saw the popularisation of the music video, with Queen's 'Bohemian Rhapsody' (1975) and The Buggles' 'Video Killed the Radio Star' (1979) considered to be two of the first commerical music videos. They provided a performance and set a visual story and tone for the songs. The launch of MTV in 1981 created a wider market for the form and by 1983 the release of Michael Jackson's 'Thriller' music video illustrated considerable developments in music videos over a few years, largely due to developments in technology and visually exciting ways of storytelling that blurred the conventions of music video with film.

As a media form, music videos have continued to evolve and can be described as postmodern. They can be very experimental and stylised, utilising camera and editing techniques and a visual structure different to conventional broadcast moving image texts such as TV drama or news.

As a postmodern form, music videos rely on intertextual references that require some cultural capital from their audience. They can also be **self-reflexive**, can repeat conventions and can offer a number of narrative elements or disconnected moments within the music video.

> **Knowledge check 94**
>
> How many music videos are you required to study from List A and List B?

> **Self-reflexive** When a product makes a reference to its own artificiality and the way it has been made.

Given the usually stylised, evolving and often experimental nature of music videos, many are unconventional so it is difficult to prescribe a list of what the set conventions of the form are.

Music video genres

Music video genres tend to be categorised in terms of the musical genre the video is for; for example, indie rock, pop or country music videos. Each genre will follow slightly different conventions, to help visually identify it. Indie rock often relies on performance and studio shots of the band, while pop music will often have a choreographed dance element and/or bright colours.

Another way of categorising music videos is in terms of the way they look and how we see the artist.

1 **Performance:** This is when we hear the song and see the artist performing in a number of locations or settings. The video will cut between the locations at different points in the song but we always see the artist singing. Locations, settings, camera angles and edits are key to this type of video.

2 **Storyline:** The lyrics and/or feeling of the song are used to help create a story. The artist may or may not feature in the music video. These are sometimes known as narrative music videos and may look like a short film with the song in the background.

3 **Experimental:** These can be storyline and/or performance music videos but may not be related to the lyrics or feature the artist. They may not make sense but they create a mood, tone or comment that drives the video. This type of music video is also known as **conceptual**.

Conceptual A thought or idea that might not be based on reality or may use elements such as symbolism to communicate meaning.

Music videos can be very innovative and blur conventions to become hybrid genres, which helps to develop the form. For example, an indie rock music video may be a mix of a performance video in the choruses but cut to a storyline during the verses of the song to amplify the lyrics. This blurring of genres helps music videos to promote their artists in new and interesting ways to appeal to their audiences.

Audiences for music videos

As promotional tools, music videos sell the artist so must visually appeal and communciate with the audience. This is achieved through:

- the way they look
  - □ visually stylish, engaging, experimental but repetitive.
- the stories they tell
  - □ stories help songs visually come alive
  - □ they provide escape or offer solutions.
- the proximity they provide to the artist and their performance
  - □ the audience feels closer to the artist
  - □ a relationship between the artist and fans can develop.

These appealing elements are all created through the use of media language and representation.

Knowledge check 95

Which three genres can music videos be seen to fit into?

Codes and conventions of music videos

The media language conventions of music videos can be broken down into the techncial elements of camera, editing, mise-en-scene and sound. These can vary depending on the genre and type of music video chosen. Table 14.1 describes some of the usual conventions of music videos across genres and categories.

Table 14.1 Common conventions of music videos

Technical element	Common conventions
Camera	• Mid shots and close-ups to personalise the artist so the audience feels proximity. • Establishing shots, crane shots and wide angles to identify location. • A range of angles to keep the music video engaging. • Continuous camera movement rather than static shots to track and follow the artist.
Editing	• Edits and cutting follow the tempo of the song and will cut on the beat. • Cutting across master shots in different locations. • Predominance of jump cuts and match cuts. • Slow motion to reflect changes in tempo in the song. • Colour grading to reflect the tone or genre of the song. • Special effects to make the video visually interesting and appealing. • Graphics and sub-titles can be used to introduce the artist and/or illustrate lyrics in the song.

Mise-en-scene	• Locations and settings
	  – Variety of locations, usually two or three, to create realism, set a tone and tell the visual story.
	  – Studios.
	• Costume and make-up
	  – Create a brand image and identity for the artist.
	  – May reflect the genre of the song.
	  – Can be used to reinforce a wider colour scheme and tone of the music video.
	• Props
	  – Can be used to illustrate the lyrics.
	  – Create realism.
	• Lighting and colour palette
	  – Studio-lit with high key or low key lighting or the effect of natural lighting if shot on location.
	  – A colour theme running through the video, such as black and white or primary colours.
	• Performance
	  – Performance of the artist.
	  – Choreographed dancing or playing of instruments.
	  – Performance of characters.

Sound

The use of sound in music videos is fundamental, as a music video is the visual sychronisation of sound with image. However, the analysis of sound as a convention in music videos is less straightforward than in other moving image forms, such as film. Sound in music videos is often an element of the editing technique, which is when the sound and image are sychronised in terms of sound effects, cutting to the beat of the song and lip-synching. The discussion of sound in this section will cover sound in relation to editing.

However, sound can also be analsyed in music videos in terms of:
- the genre
- the range or type of instruments heard or used

Study tip

To identify common music video conventions, analyse at least four music videos of different genres. Watch each one and make notes on the use of camera, editing and mise-en-scene. List the similarities they share regardless of the genre. Use these conventions to compare with your chosen videos.

Study tip

In order to analyse the use of sound in music videos in detail, analyse your chosen set products in relation to music video sound conventions. For each product, compare the editing techniques used to show cutting to the beat, changes in tempo and what we might see when specific lyrics are heard.

- the identification of specific lyrics that may be amplified by the visuals
- the emotions and atmosphere created by the song.

Developing technologies and music videos

The proliferation of technological convergence has impacted how music videos are produced and consumed and their development as a form.

The scope in production provided by new technologies allows music video directors to become increasingly experimental. Additionally, converged technologies mean music videos can be produced, distributed and consumed on a smartphone through YouTube, Instagram or Snapchat. These factors have led to evolution in the music video form with:

- visual albums
- 24-hour albums
- interactive music videos that the viewer develops
- virtual reality music videos
- vertical video filmed and/or edited in portrait mode for Snapchat and Instragram
- 360 degree music videos.

Representation in music videos

Music videos offer a range of representations depending on the genre of music, the lyrics of the song and the type of music video. As promotional tools, a music video represents the artist in a favourable way that will appeal to the target audience. However, it may also reflect wider social stereotypes with regard to different social groups.

A number of different ideologies in relation to representation can be considered in an analysis of music video. These include globalisation, individualism, consumerism, patriarchy, multiculturalism and feminist ideologies. However, as identified in other sections of this guide, it is useful to start an analysis of representation by considering the representation firstly of the artist and then of the key markers of social identity in relation to different social groups using the CAGEDS mnemonic. This helps identifiy how different social groups, and those who are usually under- or misrepresented in the media, are stereotyped positively or negatively in music videos. For example, common representations of gender in music videos tend to objectify and sexualise women, regardless of the genre or gender of the artist, reflecting negative stereotypes of women more generally.

List A music videos

The three music videos are performance videos, they all feature a female artist and construct similar representations, subsequently raising awareness of social issues, around urbanity and 'street life'.

Corinne Bailey Rae, 'Stop Where You Are': media language

'Stop Where You Are' was released in 2016 from the album *The Heart Speaks in Whispers* and is categorised as a contemporary RnB song. It is a conventional performance video featuring the artist in a number of different settings at the same

Study tip

To identify common representations in music videos, analyse at least four music videos of different genres. Using the CAGEDS mnemonic, make notes on the representations constructed for each social group. List the similarities they share in their use of positive and negative stereotypes regardless of genre. Compare the conventional representations in your list with those in your set product videos.

location. The story or meaning is created through the use of characters and in particular the use of mise-en-scene to amplify the meanings of the lyrics.

Genre conventions

'Stop Where You Are' uses a number of technical conventions we would expect to see in a music video.

Table 14.2 Technical conventions used in 'Stop Where You Are'

Media language element	Conventions used
Camera	• Extreme long shots, long shots, mid shots and close-ups on the artist and different characters. • Two shots and group shots of the different characters and the artist together. • Predominance of low angles on the artist, the buildings and the environment. High angles for some of the characters. • Tilt ups, pans to left and right, tracking. • Framing – narrow framing with depth of field and use of pull focus. • Lens flares.
Editing	• A visual structure reflects the verse-chorus structure of the song: the verses introduce the different social groups and the choruses see Bailey Rae connecting with them. • Long takes with cuts on the beat of the song to reflect the pace and tempo of the song. • Use of slow motion throughout to reflect the pace of the song and create a stylistic feature. • Colour grading to create muted tones of greys and neutrals.
Mise-en-scene	• Location – an urban, city location. • Setting – different areas within and around a building within the location. • Costume and make-up – Bailey Rae in a red dress and high heels; the social groups are identified through the use of street wear, hoodies, suits, tattoos. • Props – dog, coffee cup, briefcase. • Lighting – naturalistic lighting with lens flares to emphasise the daylight and sun. Use of shadows. • Colour palette – black, white, greys, neutrals and red. • Performance – Bailey Rae walking, singing to camera and at times dancing; extras performing as characters.

'Stop Where You Are' doesn't challenge or subvert music video genre conventions. It is socially and historically relative in that it is conventional of the form, so fits in to what we would expect a music video to look like, providing a perspective into the attitudes towards certain social groups and 'street life'.

In being conventional, the message of the song can be communicated clearly and the artist's image is the central focus, both of which are essential for the music video to promote if it is to be successful.

Intertextuality

Intertextual references aren't explicit in this music video but 'Stop Where You Are' can be seen to make intertextual references in two ways:

■ The use of urban locations, muted colour palette and social groups who can be seen to be marginalised are evocative of the British Social Realist film genre.

■ The use of social stereotypes for the characters depicted in the video references wider common stereotypes seen across media texts, which helps the video further communicate ideas about prejudice and discrimination.

Study tip

Watch 'Stop Where You Are'. Note down at least two more conventions used in the music video for each technical area of camera, editing and mise-en-scene. Create a list or table to record your observations.

How media language incorporates viewpoints and ideologies

The use of media language conventions helps construct an image for the artsit and communicate meaning for the song. This helps to incorpoate the artist's viewpoint about social inequality. The use of conventions work as signs to help communicate or connote specific viewpoints or ideologies.

Table 14.3 Conventions used in 'Stop Where You Are' and their connotations

Media language convention	Connotations
Camera	• The use of close-ups on the artist creates proximity and an emotional connection between the artist and viewer in contrast to the use of extreme low angles of the building and environment. This connotes that she is warm and friendly in an environment that can feel unfriendly and overwhelming.
Editing	• The use of colour grading to create muted tones of black, white, grey and neutral colours reflects the urbanity of the colours we usually see in cities, heightening the contrast of the environment with the red dress. This editing effect connotes that life in cities can be cold, hard and contrasting for the different groups of people who live there.
Mise-en-scene	• The settings, in different areas within and around the grey, concrete building, feel cold and impersonal, helping to connote a feeling of isolation for the characters we see, so the audience can empathise with them and accept Bailey Rae's message that we should stop and think about life. • The use of costumes, make-up and props create recognisable stereotypes of the different social groups. For example, the use of tattoos and the pit bull dog connotes that the male youth is unfriendly, unapproachable and possibly violent. • The performance of the artist helps to promote her to the audience but also as someone who is socially aware and wants to break down social barriers, connoted through her interaction with the different characters and raising her hands to illustrate the lyric 'Stop Where You Are' when she sings it in the chorus. The characters perform in a way that subverts stereotypes connoted through their costume. This communicates the viewpoint that we shouldn't judge people and have the power to address social discrimination if we can stop and think about our behaviour.

Context

Cultural context: The colour grading evokes the feel of British Social Realist films that focus on social issues and inequality.

Social context: The setting in an urban environment reflects the social contrasts and inequalities found in large cities and the social anxieties these can create.

Cultural context: The cultural diversity and multiculturalism of contemporary Britain is celebrated through the performance element of the music video.

Study tip

To practise identifying how different media language elements communicate viewpoints and ideologies in 'Stop Where You Are', select three examples of media language that have not been discussed in Table 14.3. For each one, note down the meaning connoted by the convention. Compile a list of the viewpoints offered and summarise the meaning of the video in one sentence.

Corinne Bailey Rae, 'Stop Where You Are': representation

Corinne Bailey Rae states on her website (www.corinnebaileyrae.com/news/85/) that the song 'Stop Where You Are' is about being present, stopping and celebrating what is happening at that very moment.

Representing events, issues, individuals and social groups

The representations constructed and the choices made about how to represent events, issues, social groups and individuals in the music video are influenced by the meaning and message of the song.

- **Events:** The artist performs in an inner-city setting.
- **Issues:** Social prejudice, discrimination, urbanisation, individualsim, multiculturalsim.
- **Social groups:** Middle-class/working-class/unemployed; adults/youth; men/women; white British/British ethnic minorities; able-bodied.
- **Individauls:** Corinne Bailey Rae.

The artist is the only individual who takes a central role in the video. This ensures she is the focus and promotes her to the audience.

The selection of different social issues and groups constructs a representation that comments on social and cultural issues that affect these social groups. This selection, through the use of media langue elements, therefore helps to communciate the values of the song.

The representation of positive and negative stereotypes

'Stop Where You Are' constructs a number of positive and negative stereotypes. In doing so, the music video constructs binary oppositions of each group to reflect the artist's message in the song. The use of media language elements, such as the mise-en-scene, constructs realism so the audience can easily identify and understand the messages and values communicated through the stereotypes used.

Representations of the artist

Positive representations of the artist are essential if the music video is to promote the artist and appeal to the audience. In 'Stop Where You Are', a positive representation of Bailey Rae as a British, middle-class woman of ethnic minority is constructed.

The artist's musical and performance skills, alongside a story that highlights the artist as addressing prejudice, is achieved by placing her in an urban environment encountering characters who are stereotypically on the edge of society or who are considered delinquent. Although the artist is represented as feminine and unthreatening, the use of low angles, the red dress and her performance helps to make her, and the message, stand out as powerful. This is a positive representation.

One way in which the representation of positive and negative stereotypes of social groups can be analysed in 'Stop Where You Are' is by using the CAGEDS mnemonic.

Study tip

Watch 'Stop Where You Are'. List four ways in which the artist is constructed through positive stereotypes. For each one, identify a media language element used to create the representation. Note what the message of the stereotype tells us about the artist and how it might appeal to the target audience.

Context

Social context: Issues around gender equality and feminism are reflected to comment on the patriarchal society we live in.

Table 14.4 Representation of positive and negative stereotypes in 'Stop Where You Are'

Social group	Representation/Use of positive and negative stereotypes
Class	A binary opposition between middle classes and the unemployed is constructed through the use of the businessmen and the homeless woman. The representation is constructed through the costume and props, with the businessmen wearing suits and carrying briefcases and the homeless woman sitting on the floor. Initially the representation of both groups is negative with a businessman ignoring the woman and the woman shouting at him. But this is then contrasted with positive representations of the two groups; the businessman brings the homeless woman a coffee, they talk and laugh. This representation constructs the idea that despite their difference in class and status, they are both equal.
Age	Youth are represented through a number of different stereotypes in the music video, with the use of costume, make-up and performance to initially construct shortcuts of youth as aggressive, threatening, in gangs or as isolated and lonely. In constrast, the artist as an adult is positively stereotyped and integrates between the different groups, encouraging a different representation. For example, she reaches out to the lonely girl, we see her laughing with the tattooed white boy and his pit bull; she dances with the young black men in hoodies. The video aims to turn the negative stereotypes into positive ones. implying that what youth wear or how they behave doesn't define them individually.
Gender	Gender is represented positively and negatively. The artist is represented as caring and nurturing – a common stereotype – but in contrast also as vibrant and socially aware with the power to change preconceptions about different social groups. Young men and women are represented as misunderstood or delinquent – a common stereotype – but this is an equal representation and suggests that both male and female youth are discriminated against not because of their gender but due to their age.
Ethnicity	Whilst British cultural identity is clearly represented through the use of location, setting, costume and props, the music video offers a diversity in the representations of ethnicity that is reflective of contemporary British multiculturalism and, through the subverting of stereotypes, positions audiences to respond positively to these representations.
Disability	The artist and characters are able-bodied; their performance and movement is central to constructing messages in the music video. This reinforces common stereotypes about able-bodied people and, by the absence of disability, reflects common social stereotypes of people with disabilities having less social power and being less visible.

Context

Cultural context: Youth sub-cultures are defined through their clothing, appearance and behaviour, which are usually stereotyped to be oppositional to mainstream adult culture.

Social context: The values of individualism are reflected through the stereotyping of marginalised groups. By subverting often negative representations of these groups, the value that everyone deserves a chance to flourish and reach their potential is expressed.

Knowledge check 96

What message is communicated by offering two contrasting representations of youth?

Claims about realism

These representations are constructed as real through the use of mise-en-scene, in particular location, setting and costume. These media language elements repeat identities that are recognisable across wider media and, in terms of location and clothing, feel true to everyday life. Through the repetition of these familiar elements, the message and values associated with stereotypes can make claims to being real. 'Stop Where You Are' cleverly uses these wider stereotypes and, by subverting them, creates a new 'truth' or reality which helps to position the audience and reinforce the message that discrimination is wrong.

Viewpoints and ideology

'Stop Where You Are' can be seen to communicate a number of ideological values through the use of media language as specific signs or codes. The message of the song and video reflects social issues and aims to raise awareness of the impact of discrimination within the world we live in. The video reflects a viewpoint that social inequality is unjust, and supports a social, liberal view with the idea that we have a social duty to respect one another.

Feminism is also communicated through the music video; as a media form, music videos usually construct negative sexualised representations of women that objectify them for the **male gaze**, even if the artist is female. 'Stop Where You Are', while presenting the artist as feminine and kind hearted, focuses the representation on her powerful social message and we see her comment on social issues that affect our social and cultural lives. This questions patriarchy and the social privilege of men.

'Stop Where You Are' also reinforces some values of individualism by suggesting that every individual has the right to self-fulfilment and a better life. The contrasting representations of youth reflect this.

The ideologies of capitalism and consumerism are also reinforced. The music video form is a promotional product intended to sell the artist as a commodity in order to make profit. Its success relies on the consumption of messages and values, to create empathy and position the audience to accept the artist and the meaning behind the song.

Audience response and interpretation

The preferred reading of 'Stop Where You Are' could be for the viewer to stop in the moment and reflect on the world around them. There is also an additional preferred meaning that suggests we should feel empathy for social groups who experience discrimination and are responsible for stopping prejudices and creating a more equal, friendly world. But the audience response to and interpretation of the video will depend on the demographic and experience of the audience. In particular, it will depend on their views of the artist, the social groups they are part of and how they respond to the preferred meanings constructed.

Massive Attack, 'Unfinished Sympathy': media language

'Unfinished Sympathy' was released in 1991 from the album *Blue Lines* and is categorised as trip hop. The video for 'Unfinished Sympathy' is a performance video featuring the artist walking along a street in a Los Angeles neighbourhood, oblivious to the people and her surroundings as she sings.

Notably, the entire video was filmed in one shot, using a shot-maker arm and a steadicam. This subverts conventional camera work and editing that usually cuts across different master shots on the beat. The use of mise-en-scene constructs an image of American street life and related social issues.

'Unfinished Sympathy' has been described as setting a benchmark and similar to a short film rather than just a pop video promotion (adapted from Sean O'Hagan, *theguardian.com*, 28 October 2012). It has influenced a number of music videos since, such as The Verve's 'Bittersweet Symphony'.

Study tip

To identify how audiences may respond to the preferred meaning in 'Stop Where You Are', select three social groups represented in the video. Using the terms 'dominant', 'negotiated' and 'oppositional', describe how an audience member from each group would respond to the video's preferred meaning, giving some reasons for their differing responses.

Male gaze This refers to the way women are represented in the media. It suggests that women are typically · represented from the point of view of the male cameraman/ director in order to appeal to and satisfy a heterosexual male audience. This is one way to explain why representations of women in the media are objectified and over-sexualised.

Knowledge check 97

Which ideologies does 'Stop Where You Are' reflect?

Knowledge check 98

What benchmark did Massive Attack set for performance music videos?

Massive Attack, 'Unfinished Sympathy': representations

Although the lyrics of the song refer to love, the music video amplifies the meaning through representations of street life and social issues. 'Unfinished Sympathy' provides both positive and negative stereotypes, reflecting certain viewpoints and ideologies in relation to the preferred meaning the producer has constructed.

Emeli Sandé, 'Heaven': media language

'Heaven' was released in 2011 from the album *Our Version of Events* and is categorised as RnB/soul. The video for 'Heaven' is a performance video featuring the artist in various street locations in London.

'Heaven' is conventional in that it uses a range of common media language conventions for camera and editing in its construction. The use of mise-en-scene presents an image of British urban life and related social issues. There is also imagery of heaven through repeated shots of the sky and religious iconography to illustrate the lyrics of the song and create synchronisation between image and sound.

Emeli Sandé, 'Heaven' – Representations

Sandé states that 'Heaven' is about what it means to be good for the current generation when social and cultural life is so fast there are many negative influences to try and overcome.

For more analysis on music videos, please see Tables 14.8 and 14.9 on pages 170-172.

List B music videos

These videos do not feature their artists and instead 'celebrate the power of narrative and signification and a postmodern emphasis on intertextuality' (2017 OCR A Level Media studies specification: www.ocr.org.uk/Images/316672-specification-accredited-a-level-gce-media-studies-h409.pdf).

The three videos are storyline or narrative videos. They use very different representations and contrast clearly in visual style from the videos in List A.

David Guetta, 'Titanium': media language

'Titanium' was released in 2011 from the album *Nothing but the Beat* and is categorised as a house/urban dance genre song. The video for 'Titanium' is an unconventional music video. It is a narrative video that doesn't feature the artist at all and instead constructs what looks like a short film to visually accompany the song. The meaning behind the song's lyrics is amplified through the use of the main character and in particular the use of mise-en-scene and intertextual references to heighten meaning and appeal to the target audience.

Genre conventions

As an unconventional narrative music video, 'Titanium' uses a range of technical conventions that position it outside convention but at the same time help the audience recognise it as a music video. The most obvious is the synchronisation of sound and image, and cutting to the beat to develop the narrative structure of the video. Some of the media language elements used by 'Titanium' are listed in Table 14.5.

Knowledge check 99

How are the lyrics of the song 'Heaven' illustrated through the use of mise-en-scene?

Table 14.5 Media language conventions used in 'Titanium'

Media language element	Conventions used
Camera	• Close-ups, mid shots, long shots and exteme long shots of the characters • Two shots • High angles, low angles and worm's eye views • Frequent use of tracking • Whip pan point of view shot
Editing	• Narrative structure that has a beginning, middle and end • Predominance of slow motion used in the verses • Editing pace reflects the tempo of the song but cuts on the beat • Jump cuts used during the bike riding scene • Colour grading to create a retro 1980s feel • Special effects used for the teddy bears, keys and supernatural force field
Mise-en-scene	• Location: Midwest suburban America • Setting: the 1980s; high school, house, living room, bedroom, kitchen, roads, woods • Costume and make-up: everyday clothing; leisurewear, uniforms • Props: lockers, poster of Guetta, telephone, bike, TV, Superargo poster, teddy bears, planetary mobile, keys, backpack • Lighting: high key in school, low key in house; use of bright lighting to refer to supernatural moments • Colour palette: muted, earthy tones of browns, greens and yellows to create a retro feel • Performance: the main character is the protagonist or anti-hero who comes against the teacher, policeman and FBI; use of the two female joggers to reflect the setting and create humour

'Titanium' can be seen to be socially and historically relative in that it references 1980s American suburbia. References to the supernatural and American high school culture also help to evoke a sense of Americana that is popular in many contemporary media texts.

Additonally, prior to 'Titanium', Guetta's music videos were all performance videos featuring Guetta on the decks in his role as DJ with the vocalist performing. 'Titanium' marks a departure in the way Guetta is promoted through the form. Through a narrative music video, 'Titanium' creates an engaging video that comments on a number of social issues and groups, amplifies the lyrics and positions Guetta as culturally sophisticated.

Intertextuality

Intertextual references are an important feature in 'Titanium'. They:

1 allow the director to play with genre conventions and ways of presenting a brand identity for the artist

2 create additional meaning within the music video to amplify the lyrics

3 create audience engagement and satisfaction in recognising the texts.

Study tip

Watch 'Titanium'. Note down at least two more conventions used in the music video for each technical area of camera, editing and mise-en-scene. Create a list or table to record your observations.

Context

Cultural context: American popular culture of the 1980s, and the issues, social groups and individuals that existed at this time, are reflected in the video's storyline.

Cultural context: Postmodernism, as a cultural movement, encourages stylised and innovative developments of media forms that are different to mainstream representations.

The intertextual refrences in 'Titanium' help communicate the theme of science fiction, the supernatural and American popular culture. They also mark or author the song as Guetta's:

- **ET (1982)**: Iconic Spielberg film about extraterrestrial life. The bicycle chase, surburban 1980s America and the scenes with the FBI in the woods in 'Titanium' all make reference to ET.
- **Super 8 (2011)**: Ryan Lee, the actor in the music video, starred in Super 8 and the film has a similar supernatural theme. Spielberg is also the producer.
- **Terminator 2 (1991)**: The character T-1000 is made of liquid metal, resistant to physical injury and damage, and possesses superhuman strength, similar to the representation constructed of the boy in 'Titanium' and conveyed in the song's lyrics.
- **Superargo (1969)**: There is a poster of *Superargo and the Faceless Giants* in the boy's house. This was a science fiction superhero film from 1969.
- **David Guetta**: There is a poster with Guetta's face on the school wall in the corridor the boy walks through.

How media language incorporates viewpoints and ideologies

The use of media language conventions help construct an image for the artist and communicate meaning for the song. They work as signs to help communicate or connote specific viewpoints or ideologies about a range of issues or themes in the video, for example ideas regarding inner strength, youth or authority. A number of binary oppositions are also constructed through the use of media language:

- youth vs adult
- teacher vs pupil
- authority vs inferiority
- right vs wrong
- supernatural vs natural.

Some of the media language conventions used in the music video are analysed in Table 14.6 to illustrate how they may connote certain viewpoints in the music video.

Table 14.6 Media language conventions used in 'Titanium' and their connotations

Media language convention	Connotations
Camera	<ul><li>The use of close-ups of the character in the opening shots connotes that the music video will be about this character. The close-ups help to make a connection between the character and audience before a cut to an extreme long shot is used to reveal his location in the high school.</li><li>Frequent use of tracking helps to position the audience with the main character. This creates an allegiance between the character and audience, connoting that he is good and we should identify with his experience in the video.</li><li>This is also refleced in the point of view whip pan of the character in the kitchen, connoting the tension that the character must be feeling and positioning us with him rather than with the police.</li></ul>

Context

Cultural context: The use of intertextual references requires a cultural capital and knowledge of cultural products that emphasises the meaning of the video and provides pleasure for the audience.

Knowledge check 100

What themes do the intertextual references communicate in 'Titanium'?

Study tip

Note which words are key media language technical terms in Table 14.6 , for example, 'close ups'.

Media language convention	Connotations
Editing	• The shots are edited to create a narrative structure that is unconventional of a music video and feels like a film that has a beginning, middle and end. This editing technique provides a different experience for the viewer but also engages them, signifying the experience of the character within the story and connoting the meaning in the lyrics. • There is one jump cut used during the bike riding scene which creates a contrast with the earlier slow-motion shots of the first verse. It allows the music video to feel conventional because the cutting on the beat matches the increased tempo of the song. It also creates focus on the boy on the bike, connoting the importance of his freedom but also the urgency and fear he feels. • The special effects used for the teddy bears, keys and supernatural force field at the end of the video connote the super-human powers the boy is portrayed to have and help to amplify the lyrics.
Mise-en-scene	• The props are significant in providing meaning in the video where the characters can't be heard speaking. This helps develop the narrative and illustrate the lyrics of the song. For example, the lockers signify the setting, the poster of Guetta creates an intertextual reference and is the only point where we see the artist; the telephone connotes the teacher's reporting of the boy and the bike is a means of escape. • The characters selected, and their interaction with one another, connote the social divisons seen within suburban America in the 1980s and present day. Along with other aspects of the mise-en-scene, such as costume and use of camera work, they create binary oppositions that connote further meaning about who and what is seen to be acceptable within our society. However the dominant performance of the boy connotes that his perspective is the one we should adopt, so the performance of characters subverts accepted ideals about adults and authority.

Context

Social context: Authoritarianism as a way to address and enforce social order is reflected in the video through the use of the school, teacher, police and FBI.

Study tip

To practise writing about the way in which media language conventions construct meaning, write a paragraph for each of the media language examples provided in Table 14.6. Begin by stating the media language element, such as camera, use an example of the element, such as shot types, and discuss the meaning connoted.

David Guetta, 'Titanium': representation

There are a number of possible meanings represented in 'Titanium'. It can be seen to provide an empowering message of inner strength for those who feel vulnerable, isolated or like outsiders. The video also offers an alternative representation of youth, adults and authority than those mostly presented by mainstream media products.

Representation of events, issues, individuals and social groups

The representations constructed and the choices made about how to represent events, issues, social groups and individuals in the music video are influenced by the meaning and message of the song.

- **Events:** A supernatural occurance at a local high school.
- **Issues:** 1980s America, youth and authority, socially acceptable behaviour, isolation, inner strength, the supernatural and science fiction.
- **Social groups:** Age, gender, class and status, regional identity, ethnicity, authority groups.
- **Individuals:** The main character, the teacher, the policeman.

The selection of a range of different social issues and groups constructs a variety of representations within the narrative of the video. This selection, through the use of media language elements, helps to communciate the themes and values of the song.

Representation of positive and negative stereotypes

'Titanium' constructs a number of positive and negative stereotypes.

Representations of the artist

The representation of Guetta is implicit but can be seen through intertextual references and **value transference**. The juxtapostion of the boy to the left of the frame with the poster of Guetta's face to the right at 0.34 mins sets up a connection between the artist and main character. The poster not only works as a cameo or stamp to identify that this is Guetta's song, but the positioning between the characters indicates that the boy, and his actions, are representative of Guetta.

One way in which the representation of positive and negative stereotypes of social groups can be analysed in 'Titanium' is by using the CAGED mnemonic.

Table 14.7 Representation of positive and negative stereotypes in 'Titanium'

Social group	Representation/Use of positive and negative stereotypes
Class	Representations of class can be seen in terms of social status, power and occupation. The police, teacher and FBI are all seen to have superior social roles in contrast to the boy, signified through their costumes, props, shot types and the audience's prior understanding of stereotypes of authority as powerful and good. 'Titanium' constructs a negative representation of these groups to imply they misunderstand and feel threatened by the boy, who in contrast is represented more positively. The subversion of common stereotypes about social status reflects wider social anxieties about youth held by adults and questions the accuracy of these misconceptions.
Age	Youth vs adult as a binary opposition is represented through subverted stereotypes in 'Titanium'. Although adults are seen in positions of authority and the youth as a delinquent to be feared – common stereotypes within the media – the use of media language invites us to question this. The shots types position the audience with the boy, inviting us to experience his point of view so he is the focus of representation in contrast to the adult. The teddy bears reinforce that he is still a child but the narrative structure represents his ability to outsmart the adults who misunderstand him with his superhuman powers. This constructs youth as resilient, strong and independent, which is not a common stereotype for youth.
Gender	'Titanium' features a mostly male cast reflecting common stereotypes of gender roles, with men playing the role of police officers and FBI agents and women as teachers, thus reflecting patriarchal ideologies.

Context

Cultural context: The dominance of a white supremacist culture is reflected in 'Titanium'.

Value transference
The values of the artist or the music video are transferred to the audience by the way the artist, social issues, events, groups and individuals are represented through the selective use of media language.

Context

Social context: The concept that occupation and social status provide social power is reflected in 'Titanium'.

Social context: The social anxieties and fear of delinquency and youth culture are reflected in 'Titanium' through the theme of youth vs authority.

Knowledge check 101

How is David Guetta represented in 'Titanium'?

Social group	Representation/Use of positive and negative stereotypes
Ethnicity	White American suburban culture is the dominant ethnic group represented in 'Titanium'. This could be reflective of the location the music video is set in and also of the intertextual cultural references the video pays homage to. The two overweight women jogging mocks the American lifestyle and the video constructs a negative representation of American culture as insular and aggressive, regardless of minority ethnic groups within this wider culture; the inclusion of an African American FBI agent with a bulletproof vest and gun is also represented in this way. This arguably presents a view of American culture as hostile and exclusive.
Disability	The characters are all able-bodied and their performance and movement is central to constructing messages in the music video. This can be seen to reinforce common stereotypes about the able-bodied and, by absence, arguably reflects common social stereotypes of people with disabilities as having less social power and visibility.

Claims about realism

The media language elements of characters, location, props and costume repeat identities that are recognisable across wider media and via the intertextual references they make. The characters, locations and clothing feel true to everyday life or versions we have already seen. Through the repetition of these familiar elements, the messages and values associated with stereotypes can make claims to be real. 'Titanium' uses common stereotypes of adult and youth but, by subverting them, creates a new 'truth' or reality which helps to position the audience and reinforce the message of the song and video.

Viewpoints and ideology

'Titanium' communicates a number of ideological values. The song and video reflects social issues and anxieties in contemporary American culture about deviant youth and authority. For example, 'Titanium' was pulled from radio stations in the USA after the Sandy Hook shooting in 2012, due to the gun-related lyrics in the song and the use of a high school as one of the settings in the music video.

'Titanium' can be seen to convey the values of patriarchy with the predominance of male characters and representation of men in stereotypically masculine roles reflecting male privilege. 'Titanium' also reflects individualism by suggesting that every individual has the right to self-fulfilment and a better life; this is signified by the adults, who feel the boy is a threat to their self-fulfilment, and by the boy, who is hoping to find a better life.

Ideologies of capitalism and consumerism are also reflected in the video. Music videos are promotional products intended to sell the artist as a commodity to make profit – the reference to Guetta despite his physical absence in the video is a reminder of this. The video's success relies on the consumption of messages and values to create empathy and position the audience to accept the artist and meaning behind the song.

Audience response and interpretation

The preferred reading of 'Titanium' could be that even if we find ourselves subject to discrimination or as outsiders, we can have the inner strength to cope with these situations. The video uses the character of a boy and themes of adults, youth,

Study tip

Analyse how location, setting and themes are represented in 'Titanium'. What positive and negative stereotypes do they offer? What meanings do they reinforce or add to in the music video?

authority and the supernatural to encode this reading. But the audience response to and interpretation of the music video will depend on the demographic and experience of the audience. In particular, it will depend on their views of the artist, the social groups they are part of, their understanding of the intertextual references and how they respond to the preferred meanings constructed.

> **Study tip**
>
> To identify how audiences may respond to the preferred meaning in 'Titanium', consider how a teenager, a teacher and a police officer would interpret the preferred meaning. Using the terms' dominant', 'negotiated' and 'oppositional', describe how an audience member from each group would respond, with some reasons for your answers.

Knowledge check 102

Which ideologies does 'Titanium' represent?

Fatboy Slim, 'Ya Mama': media language

'Ya Mama' was released in 2001 from the album *Halfway Between the Gutter and the Stars* and is categorised as electronic dance music. The video for 'Ya Mama' is a narrative video that uses the concept of a tape of the song, which makes listeners move uncontrollably in chaotic dance movements. The audience follows three characters who take the tape to the local market in the hope of making money with it. This amplifies the lyrics of 'push the tempo/pull the tempo' and also references the song's genre.

The music video was filmed by the creative collective Traktor, who have also produced videos for other electronic dance songs.

'Ya Mama' makes a number of intertextual references throughout the video and mixes references to other cultural products and identities through **bricolage**, to further add meaning to the video.

Bricolage When a media product is created from a range of diverse references or other products.

Fatboy Slim, 'Ya Mama': representations

The lyrics of the song, and the concept of the music video, construct representations that reflect dancing and the culture of dance music. However, through the visual narrative chosen to amplify the lyrics of the song, the representation of social issues, groups and individuals are constructed through the use of stereotypes to further reflect specific ideologies and viewpoints.

Radiohead, 'Burn the Witch': media language

'Burn the Witch' was released in 2016 from the album *A Moon Shaped Pool* and is categorised as an alternative/indie genre song. The video for 'Burn the Witch' is a narrative video that uses stop motion to tell the story of an idyllic village community who take in and attempt to sacrifice an outsider. The story amplifies the lyrics and, importantly, communicates a specific social commentary through the way it is constructed.

The music video is in the style of the the Trumptonshire Trilogy, a series of British children's TV programmes in the 1960s. The video also makes further intertextual references, which it combines into the one story, to communicate and reflect the social and political issues that are touched on in the lyrics.

Knowledge check 103

What concept does 'Ya Mama' follow through its narrative?

Radiohead, 'Burn the Witch': representations

'Burn the Witch' represents events, issues and social groups to provide a social commentary on the climate of fear created by right-wing politicians in response to immigration. Through the song and the video, Radiohead aim to raise awareness of Europe's refugee crisis and social attitudes and anxieties surrounding this.

For more analysis on music videos, see Tables 14.8 and 14.9 on pages 170-172.

Knowledge check 104

What does 'Burn the Witch' provide a social commentary on?

Analysis of media language in music videos: Lists A and B

Refer back to the media language content guidance in Tables 14.1, 14.2, 14.3, 14.5 and 14.6 to guide your analysis for the five media language activities below.

Table 14.8 Activities to analyse codes, conventions and meanings in the set product music videos

Analysing codes, conventions and meanings constructed in the set product music videos (You will need access to the music videos and will be required take notes as you watch the videos for these activities.)		
The activities here **can be applied to each music video** from List A and List B.	**Activity 1** **Analysis of media language conventions**	**Activity 2** **Analysis of meanings constructed by the media language elements**
	• Identify the media language conventions used by the music video. • Use the examples in Tables 14.1, 14.2, 14.3, 14.5 and 14.6 to help you. • Make a note of the camera, editing and mise-en-scene conventions used in the video. • Organise your notes into the different technical elements using a grid or a mind map. • Compare the conventions used in the video to those in Table 14.1 and identify whether the music video is conventional or not.	• Analyse the meanings constructed by the conventions of media language used in the music video. • Using the examples in Tables 14.3 and 14.6 to help, select six of the technical elements used in the video: two each from camera, editing and mise-en-scene. • For each technical element you have selected, analyse the meaning connoted by its use in the video. • Organise your notes using a grid or a mind map. • When you have finished, identify what you think are the key meanings in the video and which two technical elements are most useful in creating this meaning.
Researching the intertextual references used in the set product music videos (You will need access to the internet and the music videos for this activity. The individual activities for each video below will help you focus your internet search and the notes you take. For each intertextual reference you find, note down how these add to the videos overall meaning and look.)		
The activities here are **unique to each music video** from List A and List B.	**List A**	Massive Attack, 'Unfinished Sympathy'	Which intertextual references and media forms does 'Unfinished Sympathy' include? Look for: • references to the band members featured in the video – who are they and when do you see them? • reference made by the song's title • other songs and music sampled by this song.
		Emeli Sandé, 'Heaven'	Which intertextual references and media forms does 'Heaven' include or allude to?

| | List B | Fatboy Slim, 'Ya Mama' | Which intertextual references and media forms does 'Ya Mama' include? Look for:
• references to American cartoons
• samples of other songs and music
• other music videos of the same genre
• cultural products such as commercial Hollywood films. |
| | | Radiohead, 'Burn the Witch' | Which intertextual references and media forms does 'Burn the Witch' include? Look for:
• references to British children's TV from the 1960s
• references to a British horror film from the 1970s
• cultural references to medieval times and pagan traditions
• reference to a Radiohead marketing technique known as 'The Dawn Chorus' when releasing new material. |

Analysis of representations in music videos: Lists A and B

Refer back to the representation content guidance on pages 160–170 and Tables 14.4 and 14.7 as a guide to help your analysis.

Table 14.9 Activities to analyse representations in the set product music videos

Analysing representations constructed in the set product music videos (You will need access to the music videos and will be required take notes as you watch the videos for these activities.)			
The activities here **can be applied to each music video** from List A and List B.	**Activity 1** **Choices in representing events, issues, individuals and social groups**	**Activity 2** **Representations of positive and negative stereotypes**	**Activity 3** **Claims about realism**

	• Which events are referred to in the video (if any)?
	• What social, cultural or personal issues are represented in the video?
	• Which social groups can you identify?
	• Which social groups are absent?
	• Which individuals are selected for representation?
	• What is the overall message or connotation of the video in relation to the events, issues, individuals and social groups represented?
		• Which stereotypes are used to represent:
		  – the artist
		  – different social groups using the CAGEDS mnemonic (and also looking at regional identity)
		  – the location and setting of the music video?
		• Are the stereotypes used positive or negative?
		• Do they support or challenge common stereotypes in other media products and/or the media in general?
		• What is the overall message or connotation as a result of the use of stereotypes in the video?
			• Which media language technical elements (features of camera, editing, mise-en-scene and sound) make the following features in the video feel 'real':
			  – the artist
			  – locations and settings
			  – social groups?
			• What is the overall message or connotation as a result of the use of realism in the video?

Analysing representations constructed in the set product music videos (You will need access to the music videos and will be required take notes as you watch the videos for these activities.)				
The activities here are **unique to each music video** from List A and List B.		*Music video*	**Activity 4** **Viewpoints and ideologies** Identify at least one example from the music video that illustrates the following viewpoint, contexts and/or ideologies:	**Activity 5** **Audience response and interpretation** What is the preferred meaning of the video? What is the main message? How might a viewer from the following groups respond to the video and the preferred meaning?
	List A	Massive Attack, 'Unfinished Sympathy'	• Individualism • Globalisation • Consumerism • Feminism • Capitalism • Poverty • Multiculturalism	• A woman • An American • A British teenager
		Emeli Sandé, 'Heaven'	• Poverty • Feminism • Capitalism • Individualism • Hedonism • Consumerism	• A homeless man • A young girl • A businessman or woman
	List B	Fatboy Slim, 'Ya Mama'	• Globalisation • Feminism • Individualism • Capitalism • Consumerism • Ethnicity	• A woman • An indie rock fan • Someone from the Grenadines
		Radiohead, 'Burn the Witch'	• Xenophobia • Populism • Nationalism • Authoritarianism • Individualism • Consumerism • Globalisation	• A refugee • A right-wing politician

■ Section B

Practice questions and sample answers

1 Explain why music videos use intertextuality. Refer to one of the music videos
you have studied to support your answer   [10]

ⓔ This question is asking you to give reasons why music videos make references to
other media or cultural products. In your answer you could discuss intertextuality as:

- a postmodern feature and a convention of the music video form
- a way to fulfill the purpose of music videos in promoting the artist's identity
- a technique to make the video appealing for the target audience
- a way to amplify the meaning in the music video and storytelling of the song.

This question is worth 10 marks. Spend no longer than 17 minutes on your answer –
two minutes to plan and 15 minutes to write your response.

Sample student answer

Intertextuality can be defined as the referencing of another media text or cultural product to shape and
develop meaning. Music videos are postmodern, frequently using intertextual references to create visually
interesting videos that appeal to their audiences and help sell the song.

David Guetta's 'Titanium' is a narrative video that doesn't feature the artist at all and instead looks like a
short film. The meaning behind the song's lyrics is amplified through the use of intertextual references to
media products such as *ET*, *Super 8*, *Terminator 2*, *Superargo* and David Guetta himself. The use of these
references is an important feature in the video, allowing the director to create additional meaning to
amplify the lyrics and engage the audience, who will find satisfaction in recognising the references. They
also help the director play with genre conventions and ways of presenting a brand identity for the artist.

'Titanium' creates a narrative that references 1980s American suburbia and culture. This is achieved
through a number of intertextual filmic references that refer to suburban 1980s America, the science fiction
genre themes of youth versus authority and the supernatural. The film *ET* is referenced during the bike
chase where the boy is riding quickly through the streets during the chorus and the at the end of the video
in the wooded location. This reference helps the audience identify the location and time period as it looks
similar to the era and locations used in *ET*. It also communicates that the boy is in opposition to authority
and similarly to *ET*, we find out he has supernatural powers. This gives additional meaning to the lyrics as
we learn that, as in *ET*, although he might frighten people, he is good, thus reinforcing the lyrics of the song
and themes of youth versus authority and inner strength.

The film *Super 8* is also directly referenced in the music video through the actor Ryan Lee. Lee's role in
Super 8, also about the supernatural, helps audiences who have seen the film understand the themes in
'Titanium', amplifying the lyrics. This promotes the video to fans of *Super 8* who may not be aware of David
Guetta, thus further promoting the artist to a wider audience. Both *ET* and *Super 8* are directed or produced
by Steven Spielberg. This is a further intertextual reference made by the video, which pays homage to the
style, characters, locations and genres of Spielberg's iconic films. These references not only amplify the
meaning of the song but position the audience to identify each reference, so the song and video will appeal to
as wide an audience as possible: those who will be familiar with the older filmic references and a younger

audience who appreciate the retro feel of the video. Younger audiences may also make connections between 'Titanium' and more recent media products such as *Stranger Things* that reference the same location, era and themes.

The poster of *Superargo and the Faceless Giants* in the boy's living room relates to the science fiction genre and superheroes, communicating the boy's interest in science fiction and as the hero in the video. The song title 'Titanium', along with the boy's superhuman ability, can also be understood as a reference to *Terminator 2*. The character T-1000 is made of liquid metal, like titanium, that is resistant to physical injury and damage, and possesses superhuman strength, just like the boy at the end of the video who is able to shield himself from the authorities' bullets.

The use of intertextual references in 'Titanium' marks a departure from Guetta's brand identity, with his previous videos favouring the performance genre and his identity as a DJ. Intertextual references to these cultural products, and the social issues and groups they invoke, positions Guetta as culturally sophisticated. His representation in the video is implicit but can be seen through intertextual references made to him through the mise-en-scene. For example, the poster of Guetta's face on the wall in the high school corridor points to him as the video's author. The juxtaposition of the boy and Guetta's faces in the same shot creates a connection between the two, inviting the audience to understand the boy and his actions as Guetta's, thus creating value transference. This will appeal to the audience who will enjoy spotting the reference to Guetta and will help them connect with the video, indicating that intertextual references are also used to create satisfaction and promote the artist for the audience.

To conclude, intertextual references are used by music videos as a technique to allow directors to create additional meaning, to amplify the lyrics and engage the audience. Intertextual references also enable the director to play with the formal conventions of music videos using interesting ways of presenting a brand identity for the artist so the purpose of a music video, to sell the song and artist, can be achieved.

ⓔ

- The answer clearly defines intertextuality and is structured with a relevant argument to explain why music videos use intertextuality.
- The answer clearly refers to a chosen video from List B to respond to the question.
- Most of the intertextual examples used in the video are discussed.
- A range of media terms and appropriate terminology is used.

A top-level answer.

2 **Explain why magazines outside the commercial mainstream construct alternative representations. Refer to *The Big Issue* magazine in your answer.** **[10]**

ⓔ This question is asking you to demonstrate your knowledge and understanding of *The Big Issue* magazine as a publication that is outside the mainstream magazine industry. In this answer you could discuss:

- how *The Big Issue* is a business that is focused not on profit for the owner but on providing opportunities for the vendors who sell it, so must appeal to a particular niche audience
- the media language conventions used by *The Big Issue* and how they are different from mainstream magazines

- the representations they construct of events, issues, social groups and individuals and how these may be different to mainstream magazines
- the positive and negative use of stereotypes and how these may be different to mainstream magazines
- how the producer's viewpoint and ideology is communicated to the audience.

Give examples from at least one front cover you have studied in your answer. This question is worth 10 marks. Spend no longer than 17 minutes on your answer – two minutes to plan and 15 minutes to write your response.

Sample answer

The Big Issue magazine was launched in 1991 and can be described as an alternative magazine that sits outside the commercial mainstream magazine market. The magazine aims to transform the lives of London's homeless. Vendors buy the magazine for £1.25 and sell it to the public for £2.50, enabling *The Big Issue* to provide 'a help up, not a hand out'. There are several reasons why *The Big Issue* constructs alternative representations but, as a niche magazine with a very specific audience, it can be argued that the representations constructed are to appeal to the audience so their vendors can sell as many magazines as possible each week.

While *The Big Issue* looks different to commercial mainstream examples, a study of *The Big Issue* front covers for the issues 'Flake News' (July 2018) and 'The Greatest Show on Earth' (April 2018) identifies that *The Big Issue* uses most of the key conventional elements of print media language in its construction, with the exception of a barcode, due to the way it is sold on the street, and a slogan, as the tagline works across every issue. However, many of the conventions it uses construct alternative representations. For example, the central images tend to be illustrations and the composition and layout changes with every issue, keeping the brand interesting on a weekly basis. The mode of address and language often incorporates a play on words and intertextual references to other media products or cultural traditions that require a cultural intelligence to understand. Puffs are used as part of the illustration or main image, creating coherence and reinforcing meaning. Additionally the cover lines tend to be integrated into the main image in a creative way. The use of media language to construct representations therefore provides an alternative approach so that the media language elements themselves work together to build and further enhance the meanings constructed, creating an engaging, satisfying experience for the reader.

Intertextual references are used by *The Big Issue* to construct alternative representations that are different to mainstream magazines. For example, on the 'Flake News' issue, although the front cover looks like a simple illustration of Donald Trump's face melting within an ice cream, the intertextual references communicate meaning and ideological values without losing sales for the vendor. The juxtaposition of the central image of Trump's face within a 99 Flake ice cream refers to the influence of American culture on British cultural identities, his imminent visit and the British summer heatwave. The language used in the cover line for the feature article 'Flake News' plays on the image but also Trump's saying 'fake news', suggesting this issue provides a politically serious message, positioning the reader to take a similarly cynical view as the magazine towards Trump's presidency and visit to the UK.

The representation of issues, events, social groups and individuals also shows how the representations constructed by *The Big Issue* are different to commercial mainstream magazines. For example, on the 'Flake News' front cover, the representation of Trump's visit to the UK, the British heatwave and the Hamilton play are combined with the representation of issues such as Trump's political ability, mental health awareness and the impact of American politics on British policy and culture. These aspects are all achieved through the single main image, cover line, puff and three sell lines. This contrasts significantly to mainstream magazines such as TV listings and *Woman's Weekly* consumer magazines, which usually feature a common pattern in each issue of TV celebrities or models with the masthead and cover lines selling the magazine. 'Flake News' and 'The Greatest Show on Earth' construct representations of a range of different events, issues, social groups and individuals, suggesting that the magazine constructs not only alternative representations to the mainstream but also diverse and varied representations that will be different each week, continuing to attract their audience and helping the vendor sell the magazine.

The Big Issue's use of positive and negative stereotypes is another way in which it constructs alternative representations. The 'Flake News' issue focuses on Donald Trump, a white, middle-aged, middle-class, Christian, able-bodied, Western man. As such, he can be seen to display characteristics that define him as part of the dominant group. Usually, the dominant group is represented through positive stereotypes in the media to reflect the social power they hold. However, to reinforce the social and cultural issues of the magazine, along with their political viewpoint, Trump is represented negatively despite being a leading political figure; his face melting into the ice cream illustrates this. The use of the ice cream and the puff advertising *Hamilton* also represent the British and American people and culture as being affected by Trump's presidency and the dominant group. In this way the magazine becomes a voice for the everyday person, reflecting the values of its vendors and audience.

As a brand, *The Big Issue* functions to produce money, which is socially invested to create employment and ease poverty. It therefore represents a viewpoint that runs counter to capitalist culture and the commercial magazine industry. While the political bias of the magazine is not direct, as this could affect sales for their vendors, the magazine has a clear social agenda and values social welfare and equality for all social groups rather than the consumption of commodities to benefit the owner and individual reader. YouGov.co.uk identifies the typical *Big Issue* reader as left wing university educated, middle-aged and interested in popular culture. They also tend to work in occupations with a social focus such as public service or the charity sector. This means that they are likely to hold similar values to the magazine as a result. *The Big Issue* constructs representations that use satire so political messages can be communicated without being overtly critical. Also, their interesting and creative use of media language communicates values that suggest we should care about the society we live in and the people in it. This can be seen in the cover lines in the 'Flake News' issue, which tells us how to survive in a heatwave, avoid meltdown and deal with anxiety.

To conclude, *The Big Issue* magazine, as a magazine outside the commercial mainstream, constructs alternative representations to those found in mainstream magazines through creative use of media language conventions, the combined representation of political, social and culturally relevant events and issues, the subversion of common stereotypes of the dominant group and providing a voice for the mis- or under- represented. As a magazine it is concerned with the social welfare of its vendors rather than profit for the owner, values that are shared by their niche, target audience. The construction of alternative representations therefore allows *The Big Issue* to communicate a specific viewpoint, appeal to the audience and give their vendors a hand up out of poverty.

- This is a lengthy response for 10 marks but the answer directly addresses the question.
- The answer includes an argument and is well-structured
- The answer covers a number of different points to help explain why *The Big Issue* constructs alternative representations.
- Specific examples from the set products are used to support the answer.
- A range of media terms and appropriate terminology is used.

This would be a top-level answer.

3 Analyse how the representations constructed in Source C reflect the social context in which they are produced. In your answer you must:
- analyse the representations constructed through the use of positive and negative stereotypes
- make judgements and reach a conclusion about the influence of social contexts on representations. **[15]**

Source C: Advertisement for Dove deodorant available at https://www.facebook.com/ DoveMenCarePh/photos/a.392836960755057/533310593374359/?type=3&theater

ⓔ This question is asking you to apply your knowledge and understanding of social contexts to show how they are reflected in the representations constructed in the unseen advert. In your answer you could:

- consider how the representation of events, issues, social groups and individuals reflect society at the time the advert was produced
- examine the positive and negative stereotypes used and how this reflects social groups and diversity
- explore the different meanings communicated by the representations in the advert and how they reflect social ideologies
- make a conclusion about the influence of the social context on the product.

This is a 15-mark question. Spend no longer than 25 minutes on this answer – five minutes to plan and 20 minutes to write your response.

Sample answer

Source C is an advert for a men's grooming product. It denotes a man in an apron opening and looking into an oven. Men's grooming adverts often feature muscular white men outdoors or objectified images of women to sell the product. The representations constructed in the Source C advert, especially to do with gender and gender roles, can be seen to reflect the social context in which it was produced.

The representation of a man cooking in the kitchen could be seen to be unconventional because, traditionally, cooking is often presented as a feminine role. We can tell the man is cooking rather than fixing the oven, a more stereotypically masculine behaviour, because he is wearing an apron over his clothes. The traditional stereotype is for a woman to be wearing this costume but the use of a shirt and watch make the wearing of the apron appear masculine. This representation reflects changes to social attitudes and behaviour within the contemporary household, which is no longer made up of a housewife who stays at home and cooks the dinner for her husband, who is the breadwinner and goes out to work. The concept of patriarchy as a social structure, in which men are socially privileged and dominate in social or public positions, is challenged here and suggests that ideas about masculinity, and what it means to be a man, are evolving and social movements such as feminism, which argues men and women should be equal within society, has influenced the representation constructed.

However, although the main image suggests gender roles are subverted, the advert could be argued to be reinforcing traditional gender stereotypes. For example, the colour palette is grey and blue, which are gendered colours associated with masculinity, so their use here clearly signals the product, and the target audience, as masculine. Additionally, the phrase 'operate complex machinery' refers to the oven as if it were an engine or machine rather than a cooking appliance, implying the male cook is a mechanic. His rolled up sleeves also connote that he is ready for work which is in-line with the traditional stereotype of a man working. The use of the words 'tough' and 'real' further portray this conventional representation of masculinity. The representations in the advert therefore reflect social distinctions between men and women and their roles in and out of the home, indicating that adverts socialise us into understanding behaviour such as masculinity and, by contrast, femininity.

Representations are selective and these contrasting representations help the product reach as wide a target audience as possible. While some men are happy to cook at home, others may see this as less masculine so the advert, through the choice of image, colour palette and language, can address a wider social demographic to sell the product. The advert, and selection of the representations constructed, could be interpreted as reflecting capitalist ideologies and the social values of consumerism. The model is well dressed and the oven looks expensive, suggesting that middle-class values are important, such as purchasing products to enable one to look and feel good. The aim of the advert is to sell the product to create a profit. The pack shot takes up almost half of the final third of the layout which creates product recognition. In doing this, it encourages the audience to consume the product that it promises will make them 'tough' and 'real' thus maintaining masculinity even when helping out at home. This tells us that we should care about our appearance and personal hygiene regardless of who we are and what we do, while also persuading us to buy the product.

Source C offers a positive stereotype in that the representation of a man cooking subverts traditional social thinking about gender and reflects a more contemporary social landscape. The representations constructed highlight that society is diverse and made up of different people who may have different attitudes to the same issue. The advert suggests that we shouldn't be defined by our social characteristics such as gender, ethnicity, social class or ability but instead we should buy products that will help us achieve our individual potential. But audiences are complex and the audience's interpretation of the representations constructed will depend on their social demographic and personal experience as a man or woman. Individuals or social groups who are anti-capitalists, feminists or traditionalists, for example, will respond to the messages encoded by the advert's representations differently, reflecting their own social values.

ⓔ This answer:

- addresses the question, covers a number of different points that are relevant to social contexts, reaches some conclusions and makes some judgements
- uses specific examples from the previously unseen source to support it
- uses a range of media terms and appropriate terminology.

This would be a high-level answer.

4 Explain how the representations in the adverts you have studied reinforce stereotypes. Refer to the Lucozade 'I believe' advert in your answer. **[10]**

ℯ This question is asking you to identify the ways in which the Lucozade 'I believe' advert that you have studied for advertising reflects wider social stereotypes. You will need to:

- discuss the advert
- identify which events, issues, social groups and individuals are represented with some explanation of the positive and negative stereotypes used
- explain how different media language elements construct and reinforce stereotypes
- give specific examples
- identify the viewpoints and ideology expressed as a result of the representations constructed.

This question is worth 10 marks. Spend no longer than 17 minutes on your answer – two minutes to plan and 15 minutes to write your response.

Remember that the Lucozade advert referred to here can be found at
https://www.facebook.com/LucozadeSport/photos/a.576437212371301.149800.57638868904
2820/720272364654451/?type=3&theater

Sample answer

Representation is the act of presenting an event, individual, social group or issue in a certain way or from a particular point of view. Representation is selective and will always depend on the perspective and intention of the producer, reflecting their ideas and values. Representations in advertising can be seen to reflect the bias of the dominant social group as white, male and middle class. This not only reflects the experience of those within the advertising industry, who are predominantly from this social group, but also those who own the media. Stereotyping is used to communicate socially constructed messages about different issues, events, individuals and social groups and work as shortcuts to express meaning to the audience. Adverts that have wide audiences, like the Lucozade 'I Believe' advert, are more likely to reinforce rather than challenge dominant stereotypes to persuade audiences to buy the product unquestioningly rather than questioning the representations, and therefore the wider social or ideological messages, behind the product. The advert can be seen to reinforce common stereotypes to do with ethnicity, gender and social values such as consumerism, individualism and self-managerialism.

The advert can be seen to be representing white men in a positive way. The sole use of Bale in the advert, heightened by the use of layout so that he takes up half of the advert, makes him a prominent image and a metaphor for success. His appeal to the audience is reinforced by the use of the medium close up which allows audience proximity to him so he is non-threatening. The combination of media language here helps to provide a positive representation of Bale as a white man and can be seen to be reinforcing the view that white men within our society are the dominant group.

Additionally, the predominance of the colour blue genders both the product and sport as an activity. The colour palette relies on blue as the dominant colour to the extent that Bale's eye colour has been manipulated so they match the blue background. This not only reinforces men as the dominant gender but also traditional gender roles within our society, such as men rather than women being better and more successful at sport. The sole use of Bale in the advert could be interpreted as suggesting that Lucozade is a product for men, thus repeating ideological values regarding patriarchy and male privilege in our society.

The inferred positive reinforcement of the common stereotype that successful, able-bodied white men dominate sport also supports the ideologies of consumerism and individualism. The use of Bale and the unfinished statement 'in a different league' directly anchors meaning to the drink, with Bale's ability as a footballer and his move from the Premier League to Spain's La Liga, an intertextual reference, as a metaphor to the drink as better than other sports drinks. It also can be seen to imply that, as he is the dominant figure on the advert, the social group represented by Bale is 'in a different league' and superior to other social groups. The idea that if we consume certain products, such as Lucozade, we will have the opportunity to fulfil our potential and become as good as we can possibly be, like Bale, is suggested in the advert. The concept of self-managerialism, looking after oneself and keeping fit as a way to improve oneself, is also seen through the use of special effects. Beads of sweat on his face suggest Bale has just finished playing a game of football, connoting that he is also successful because he is active.

Therefore, the absence of a range of social groups and the anchoring of Bale's image with the unfinished claim to the left and the pack shot of the product to the right, appears to serve to naturalise the power and social presence Bale holds as a representative of white men within our society. It also naturalises ideologies of consumerism and individualism. The conventional use of data and statistics at the top right of the advert, making the advert feel factual, creates a sense of realism so that the reader is more likely to accept the connotations constructed by the stereotypes used in the advert and the ideologies that seem to be communicated as a result.

To conclude, adverts use and reinforce common social stereotypes to construct representations that will help sell the products to their target audience. The stereotypes that are seem to be used by the Lucozade 'I Believe' advert work as short cuts to reinforce positive representations of the dominant social group, whilst under-representing other social groups by their absence. The repetition of these positive stereotypes, in combination with the selective use of media language conventions and techniques, naturalises their use, thereby, arguably continuing to reinforce the ideological values of capitalism, patriarchy, consumerism and individualism within our society, whilst also maintaining the social status quo.

e This response is quite lengthy for a 10 mark answer but it directly answers the question and:

- discusses the set product
- explains the representation of issues, events, individuals and social groups represented in the advert
- identifies and explains some of the positive and negative stereotypes used
- considers how the absence of social groups offers negative representations
- selects and analyses some specific uses of media language conventions to explain how representations are constructed
- discusses the meanings constructed and makes reference to some viewpoints and ideologies communicated as a result of the stereotypes used.

The response also uses a range of appropriate terminology and makes a clear conclusion as to why adverts may reinforce common stereotypes. Overall, a high-level response.

Academic ideas Critical ideas or theories written by academic researchers in a particular field or area of expertise. They help to develop understanding and knowledge about the specific topic they are written about.

Ad-like Also known as approach, ad-liking is liking or clicking onto a digital advert on a website.

Anchors The use of an image next to text, either a caption or heading, anchors the image with meaning so that it positions the reader to think it means a particular thing.

Bias Preference or prejudice for or against someone or something.

Binary Having two parts or halves.

Brand A product made by a particular owner with a specific name.

Bricolage When a media product is created from a range of diverse references or other products.

Capitalist A person or company who uses their wealth to invest in a service or industry with the sole intention of creating profit.

Click stream The precise tracking of what users 'click on' and how long they spend on each online article.

Consumerism Encourages the acquisition of goods and services in ever increasing amounts. Economic policies emphasise consumption and are linked to the idea of individualism with consumption as the free choice of the consumer. It cuts across social groups such as religion, age, gender and ethnicity in focusing on the interests of the consumer.

Contexts Refers to circumstances that can shape or influence something.

Converged devices The integration of two or more different technologies into a single device, for example a desktop computer, mobile phone and social media sites.

Cultural capital The accumulation of knowledge in relation to culture, social and political issues, behaviour, dress, and taste. It is usually acquired through educational development. It is connected to, and can help change, someone's socio-economic status.

Digitally convergent This term refers to the combining of more than one product into one device as a result of technology. It also means that a range of media content and services can be accessed on one device, such as being able to watch a film, view a tweet and read an email on the same smartphone.

Disequilibrium When a sense of balance and order is disrupted. In narrative film and TV drama, this would require the protagonist to find a resolution to bring the balance back to equilibrium.

Dominant group A a sociological term used to refer to a social group that controls the value systems in any given society. They may not be the largest social group in terms of size but the group is made up of the social identities that hold social, political and economic power, privileges and social status. It is generally considered that the dominant social groups within our society - using the key markers of class, gender, age and ethnicity - are white, middle aged, middle class men as this group dominate our social, economic and political value systems.

Dual convergence Tabloids and broadsheets borrow conventions from each genre in the use of media language and values so they increasingly resemble one another.

Echo chamber A situation where a person only encounters beliefs and values that are consistent with their own. This allows existing values to be reinforced and amplified rather than the consideration of new or alternative ideas.

Editor The person who is in charge of and decides the final content of the newspaper.

Equilibrium A sense of balance and order.

Fourth Estate A term meaning that newspapers and journalists play a role in safeguarding the public from decisions made by the wealthy or politicians which could influence political and/or national policy and outcomes.

Free press A news industry that isn't restricted or censored by government in its political views or wider values and beliefs.

Front door traffic If 'traffic' is the term given to the number of people who view a website and engage in the content, then 'front door traffic' refers to encouraging readers to come directly to the newspaper's website rather than accessing its content via other sources. Such direct visits help attract advertisers for the news brand.

Gatekeeper A person responsible for filtering or selecting stories based on assumptions of their importance or appeal.

Global Worldwide.

Globalisation A process by which the world is becoming increasingly interconnected due to increased trade and cultural exchange. This has seen greater trade and freer movement of capital, goods and services, with the most successful companies being multinationals.

Gross value added The economic term given to the measurement of the value of products or services produced by a company.

Hegemony The predominance of one social group over another. The idea of ideological hegemony is proposed in the work of Gramsci, a neo-Marxist who looked at the way in which ideology was used to reinforce the social power, through economic and political systems, of the elite ruling class over the subject or working classes.

Homogenous Singular, similar and undistinguishable. In the news industry this means that most newspapers offer a similar view of the news they report, which reinforces a singular view about our culture and the world.

Content guidance

Hybrid When two conventions or characteristics are combined into one to create a new product.

Hyperbole Exaggerated statements and claims that are over the top in their expression.

Ideological State Apparatus This is a concept developed by the French cultural Marxist, Althusser. It refers to the social structures that are owned and used by the dominant group to reinforce and communicate dominant ideology so that they can retain social, political and economic power. He argues that these structures work together to indoctrinate the subordinate groups into the belief systems and production practices of the ruling dominant class to further maintain their dominant social position and keep the subordinate groups subordinate.

In-depth study This requires you to study the unit across all areas of the theoretical framework, contexts and academic ideas.

Individualism A social theory that emphasises the worth of the individual over the social group. It is associated with capitalist ideals of free enterprise, the pursuit of profit and the right to self-realisation (fulfilment of a person's potential) and freedom.

Intertextuality The referencing of another media text or cultural product. In making this reference, the meaning is further shaped and developed.

Journalism The profession of writing for a newspaper, news website, news broadcast or magazine.

Male gaze This refers to the way women are represented in the media. It suggests that women are typically represented from the point of view of the male cameraman/director in order to appeal to and satisfy a heterosexual male audience. This is one way to explain why representations of women in the media are objectified and over-sexualised.

Market (In media) A group of consumers who are interested in a product.

Media forms Newspapers, television, websites and radio are all different media forms that can communicate and broadcast news. Each media form is unique in the way it looks and how it communicates to its audience.

Mid-market tabloid A newspaper that offers a mix of both soft and hard news content in its coverage of news to appeal to its target audience.

Millennials Anyone who turned 18 in the early twenty-first century, so they fall into the 18–35 age group.

Newspaper outlets Also known as media outlets, these media organisations provide news stories and features for the public through various distribution channels.

News values Guidelines used to identify which news is considered to be most valuable, newsworthy and appealing for audiences.

Niche Subject-specific or specialised, targeted at small audiences who have a particular interest.

Ofcom Ofcom is the regulator for the communications services that we use and rely on each day. This covers regulation of broadband, Wifi, home phone and mobile services, as well as TV, On Demand and radio. www.ofcom.org.uk

Oligarchy A small group of people who have control.

Ombudsman An official appointed to investigate public complaints against a company, organisation or public authority.

Philanthropy Generous donations of money to a good cause in order to promote the welfare of others.

Platform A material or digital form, service or method of delivering media to an audience.

Plurality More than one. In the news industry context plurality refers either to the number of companies that own and produce media or to the range of ideas and viewpoints expressed in news reporting. It is the opposite of homogeneity.

Political agenda The topics or issues that reflect the policy of, or are supported by, a particular political group.

Portfolio The name given to a range of investments owned by a person or organisation.

Postmodern Of an era that occurred as a response to, and alongside, Modernism in the second half of the twentieth century. A cultural movement reflected in the arts, architecture and film, it is characterised by conventions and features that set it apart from modern ideology and products.

Progressives People who are forward-thinking and advocate social reform.

Proliferation The rapid increase and development in something, such as digital technology.

Proprietor An individual who is the sole legal owner of a business.

Prosumption The act of consuming and producing content. From the term 'prosumer', referring to a consumer involved in designing, customising, editing and sharing products for their own needs.

Protective coverage The withholding of information or not reporting a story on the grounds that it would be harmful to powerful people or the public, or impede a criminal or legal investigation from taking place.

Revenue Money received from the sale of a product or advertising.

Rhetoric Writing in a persuasive way to manipulate the reader into agreeing with a point of view.

Rhetorical question A question asked for dramatic effect or to make a point.

Sans serif A font without a stroke, it appears modern and bold.

Self-reflexive When a product makes a reference to its own artificiality and the way it has been made.

Serif A font with a stroke at the end of each letter traditionally used in broadsheets or literature to aid reading of large passages of text.

Set products The name given to the media products the exam board have stipulated must be studied for the unit.

Sign Anything that can convey meaning: an object, an image, a person, a word, and so on.

Simulations Imitations or copies of something.

Socially constructed When a social process creates and shapes a product, idea or service as a result of human interaction. It involves people and social agencies who help to shape and reinforce or accept the product as reflecting reality.

Statistical data Information that is collected, analysed and presented in number form.

Structure The way in which things are organised. In TV drama it could be the structure of the narrative or for new stories the order the events of the story are written in. Social structure refers to institutions like family, religion, education and media that are important in organising our daily lives.

Subsidiary A small company owned and controlled by a larger, parent company.

Synergy When two elements, for example companies, work together for mutual benefit.

Technical codes Camerawork, editing and mise-en-scene choices that require technical equipment and skill to produce, such as the use of a camera or editing software.

Unseen sources This refers to stimulus visual material that will be included in the exam paper that you will be expected to refer to in at least one of your answers but will not have seen before the exam.

Value transference The values of the artist or the music video are transferred to the audience by the way the artist, social issues, events, groups and individuals are represented through the selective use of media language.

Web 2.0 The second phase of the internet that enables dynamic web pages, sharing of files and social media.

Whistle blower A person who informs on immoral or illegal activity conducted by an organisation or individual.

Acknowledgements

The Publishers would like to thank the following for permission to reproduce copyright material.

Text credits

p.12–13 © Media Reform Coalition, "Who Owns the UK Media" (2019), www.mediareform. org.uk. Reprinted with permission; **p.21** © Daily Mail and General Trust, reproduced under fair use; **p.23** © Daily Mail and General Trust, reproduced under fair use; **pp.26-27** © Guardian News and Media Limited, reproduced under fair use.

Photo credits

p.31 © The Sun / News Licensing; **p.36** © Daily Mail via Solo Syndication; **p.41** © The Guardian Newspaper; **p.48** © Daily Express/Express Syndication; **p.51** © Daily Mail via Solo Syndication; **p.53** © The Guardian Newspaper; **p.81** © Daily Mail via Solo Syndication; **p.84** © The Guardian Newspaper; **p.88** © Daily Express/Express Syndication; **p.90** © Daily Express/Express Syndication; **p.137** © Hugh Kretschmer via Wieden+Kennedy; **p.140** © Shelter; **p.145** © Kaspars Grinvalds/stock.adobe.com; **p.147** © The Big Issue.

Every effort has been made to trace all copyright holders, but if any have been inadvertently overlooked, the Publishers will be pleased to make the necessary arrangements at the first opportunity.

Although every effort has been made to ensure that website addresses are correct at time of going to press, Hodder Education cannot be held responsible for the content of any website mentioned in this book. It is sometimes possible to find a relocated web page by typing in the address of the home page for a website in the URL window of your browser.